The Visual Experience

P9-BUI-772

The Visual Experience

Jack Hobbs & Richard Salome

Davis Publications, Inc.
Worcester, Massachusetts

Paul Cézanne, *Still Life with Apples and Peaches,* (detail), ca. 1905. Oil on canvas, 32″ x 39 ⅝″ (81 x 101 cm). National Gallery of Art, Washington, DC (Gift of Eugene and Agnes Meyer).

Jack Hobbs

Jack Hobbs has been a professor of art at Illinois State University for twenty-four years. He also served as Art Supervisor for nine years at Crystal Lake Public Schools in Illinois. He completed his Ph.D. at the University of Iowa. Dr. Hobbs is also the author of several college texts including *Art in Context*. He has been active as an exhibiting artist and has been featured in such shows as the *National Exhibition of Prints* and *The Art in the Embassies Program* held in Washington, DC.

Richard A. Salome

Richard A. Salome is Professor Emeritus at Illinois State University where he instructed undergraduate and graduate art education courses for twenty-five years. He also taught at the University of Minnesota and at Stanford University where he received his Ed.D. Dr. Salome has also developed and taught art programs for secondary students. He served as coeditor and senior editor of the NAEA's publication *Studies in Art Education* and served on its Commission on Research in Art Education.

©1995 Davis Publications, Inc.
Worcester, Massachusetts, U.S.A.

All rights reserved. No part of this publication may be reproduced or transmitted in any form or by any means, electronic or mechanical, including photocopying, recording, or any storage and retrieval system now known or to be invented, except by a reviewer who wishes to quote brief passages in connection with a review written for inclusion in a magazine, newspaper or broadcast.

Printed in U.S.A.
Library of Congress Catalog Card Number: 93–74640
ISBN: 87192–291–6
10 9 8 7 6 5 4

Acknowledgments

We wish to extend our appreciation to the graduate and undergraduate students at Illinois State University who contributed their time, talent and expertise to this project: to Barbara Caldwell who contributed numerous multicultural suggestions as well as photographs; to Linda Willis-Fisher who contributed to the teacher's manual; and to the members of Dr. Salome's classes who permitted us to use their artwork. We wish to acknowledge those whose counsel we sought while compiling the text: Kent Anderson, David Baker, Laura Chapman, Robert Daugherty, Michael Hagenbuck, Connie Newton and Ronald Silverman.

Managing Editor: Wyatt Wade
Associate Editor: Claire Mowbray Golding
Production Editor: Nancy Burnett
Production: Steve Vogelsang
Copyeditor: Janet Stone
Editorial Assistance: Holly Hanson, Amee Bergin, Denise Nephew

Design: Douglass Scott, WGBH Design
Design Advisor: Karen Durlach
Electronic Page Makeup: Carol Hoyle Ballard
Illustrator: Susan Christy-Pallo

Front Cover: Robert Hudson, *Drawing #26,* 1975. Mixed media on paper, 30 ½" x 25 ½" (77 x 65 cm). From the collection of Jan Perry Mayer, Denver, Colorado.

Back Cover: Lawrence Beck, *Punk Walrus Spirit (Poonk Aiverk Inua),* 1987. Mixed media, 10" x 17" x 16" (25 x 43 x 41 cm). Photograph: Garry Sutto.

Preface

Have you ever wondered about the world of art? Have you ever been stimulated, or turned off, by an artwork? Have you ever liked an artwork, but didn't know why? Did you know that artworks come in all sizes and shapes? Some works are as big as buildings. Some are small enough to fit in the palm of your hand. Some are as new as today. Some are thousands of years old. If you follow the news, you know that some are very expensive. A painting by van Gogh, for example, recently sold for nearly $53,000 a square inch!

Art is much more than just sensational facts and figures, however. If you stop to think about it, art — at least certain kinds of art — is part of your daily life. Consider, for example, the effects of graphic or applied art on your life. Magazine illustrations stimulate you to like everything from clothes to compact discs; movies provide you with fashionable role models that are hard to resist; television lures you to crave everything from pizzas to sunglasses; music video informs you about what is "in" in all kinds of things — music, celebrities, clothes, hairstyles, and much more.

Many people are very critical of commercial imagery. They believe that much of it is so poor in visual quality that it lowers public taste. They disapprove of its content, believing that it sends the wrong message about what is truly important in life. The authors feel that there is both good and bad in commercial imagery. But the point is: *images are powerful.* They can and do influence people's attitudes and desires.

Art images are also powerful, yet they do not try to persuade you to buy products or convince you to be fashionable. They do say things about life, however. Some artworks celebrate modern society, others criticize it; some works arouse our anxieties about life in general, others reassure us. Still other works delight us

Kazuaki Tanahashi, *Heki*, 1965. Ink on paper, 36″ x 28″ (92 x 71 cm). East-West Center, Honolulu.

by their high standards of originality and visual quality. Did you know that the styles of advertisements and commercials often follow the styles of art?

The pages of this book will introduce you to all kinds of art and ways to look at it, analyze it, judge it, and even make it. After using this book, you will definitely know more about art. But we sincerely hope that you *never* stop wondering about it.

How to use this book . . .

The Visual Experience is made up of many different elements. We hope these elements will help you understand what art is, how it is made, and how it can make your life richer. The next few pages point out important features in the book, and show how to get the most out of your study of the visual world.

The **table of contents** is your map of the entire book. It helps guide you through the textbook. Where was that chapter on color and value? Was Chapter 14 or 17 about careers in art?

The **part titles** are the book's major divisions. Each part is like a small book itself.

Chapters make up each of the parts. Each chapter covers a different aspect of the study of art.

The **glossary** tells you what important art terms mean. All the boldface terms in the text are defined here, plus many other terms as well. If you can't remember what *chiaroscuro* is (and don't know how to pronounce it!) or how *radial balance* differs from *symmetrical balance,* take a look in the glossary.

The **index** is like a very detailed table of contents, only it's in alphabetical order. You can go straight to the idea you want, find the page number, and turn to the right page.

The **captions** are the short bits of text beneath or beside the illustrations in the book. A caption might tell you who created a work of art, when it was created, what it is made of, and who owns it. Pay close attention to the measurements given for artworks — they'll help you imagine whether the art takes up a whole room, or just a sheet of notebook paper. The caption may also mention special things to notice about a work of art or ask you questions about it. Each caption has a number. The number will help you find the images referred to in the text.

The **text** is what we call the words the authors have written in each chapter. The text is like a voice, explaining, defining, asking you questions, helping you think. The voice points out things you might not notice in artwork, in the world around you, in your own thoughts. It might make you laugh, too.

The **artworks** shown in the book are photographs of actual works of art. They are as large as possible, because they are the most important part of the book, and because we want you to see what the artist wants to show. Most artists create because they have something to say. Their art can speak to you in any language. It might tell you things it doesn't tell anybody else.

How to use this book . . .

You can probably work on the **Experiences** (in the light yellow boxes) without anyone else's help, but they'll mean a lot more to you if you "experience" them with your teacher and the rest of the class. Some ask you to create artwork, others let you experiment with materials or techniques. Some just give guidelines for a report or have you analyze a work of art. Most of them include pictures of artworks done by students your age.

Where's Borobudor, anyway? And were there really more Roman Catholics than Calvinists in Europe in the 1500s? **Maps** will tell you. Each one has an inset globe to help you find out where in the world you are, and an enlarged area to help you see the region being discussed.

If you lose your place in the book, it's easy to find it again. Look in the lower lefthand or righthand corner of almost any page. There you'll find the **folio** (page number) and **running foot** (chapter number and title) for that page.

Try it Yourself (in the green boxes) suggests things you can do that will help you understand some of the ideas in the text. You won't be tested on these activities — they're there to get you going, get your mind working on something other than reading. You can "Try it Yourself" without any special materials, besides your mind, a piece of paper and a pencil.

Did you get so involved in the artwork that you forgot the main points of the chapter? Take a look at the **Summary**, which always appears at the end of the chapter. It will help you review the important ideas.

Diagrams and illustrations make complicated ideas clearer. They're used to simplify the information in a work of art, focus your attention on a particular feature, or explain a concept visually.

Which artist created a spoon so large it spans a river in Minnesota? Who found rural Iowa so appealing that he made it the subject of most of his paintings? Find out when you **"Meet the Artist."** These short biographies let you in on what shaped the lives of some of the artists featured in *The Visual Experience.*

Contents

Part I Introduction

Part II What to Look For

Part III How Is It Organized?

Part IV What Is It Made Of?

Part V What Is It Saying?

Part VI In the Final Analysis

Part I
Introduction

Robert S. Duncanson, *Blue Hole, Flood Waters, Little Miami River* (detail), 1851. Oil on canvas, 29¼″ x 42¼″ (74 x 107 cm). Cincinnati Art Museum, Gift of Norbert Heermann and Arthur Helbig.

Chapter 1
Seeing, Wondering, Enjoying

What does the word *art* mean to you? Does it remind you of paintings and sculptures—objects that are often called *works of art* or *artworks*? (In a minute or two, you will have a chance to test your knowledge about these kinds of objects.) Does it make you think of an art gallery or art museum where these objects are displayed? Or does art make you think of a classroom full of paints and other supplies where you and your classmates make artworks and talk about them?

If the word *art* made you think about those kinds of objects and places, you were correct. But art is more than that. It is also people. It is **artists** who make art and **viewers** who visit galleries and museums. It is *teachers* who talk about art and *students* like you who study it. All of these people are taking part in *seeing*, *wondering*, and *enjoying*.

Art obviously involves seeing. But effective seeing of art is a special skill. If you know how to see art, art can fill you with wonder—with a sense of curiosity, amazement, or even astonishment. And, finally, art can provide enjoyment, not just because the experience of seeing art is pleasant, but because it is meaningful and worthwhile.

A good place to begin this book is with the artwork itself. What is an artwork? What sets it apart from other objects? You probably already have some ideas about this subject.

Try it Yourself

List some examples of artworks that you have seen or know of. (If you do not know the title of a work, simply describe it in three or four words, for example, "a painting of yellow flowers," "a wood carving of a head," and so forth.) Compare your list with that of a friend or classmate.

Aesthetic Experience 1.1

Variety in the World of Art

Before you turn the page, take two minutes to list the medium (what it is made of) and subject matter of as many artworks as you can. Try a second list after reading the chapter, and compare them.

1-0 This is a painting about being an artist—a painting about paintings. The artist tells his own life story through works he painted at various times in his career. Early in his life, he painted with his young daughter at his side (can you see her?); an older self may be seen at the bottom left, holding a portrait. What does a painting like this tell you about art's importance? How many different ways to remember a time, a place or a person can you see here? How important is his art to this artist? Pierre Subleyras, *The Artist's Studio*, Fine Arts Academy, Vienna.

The Variety of Art

Test your ability to recognize an artwork by taking the quiz on this page. You will not be graded on this. You can score it yourself for your own information.

Art Quiz

There are ten photographs on this page. Look at each one. Decide whether or not it is a work of art by answering "yes" or "no." The answers for this quiz are given on the next page.

1

2

3

4

5

6

7

8

9

10

All the answers to the art quiz were "yes." (To score yourself, use the following scale: ten yes's = 100%, nine = 90%, eight = 80%, and so forth.)

In the following list, each of the works is identified by the kind of artwork it is, the name of the artist or the culture in which it was made, and its date.

1. Acrylic painting by Roy Lichtenstein, 1963.

2. Oil painting by Robert S. Duncanson, 1851.

3. Construction by Ron Anderson, 1984.

4. Ceramic sculpture by Marilyn Levine, 1985.

5. Buckskin shirt by an American Indian, early nineteenth century.

6. Environmental piece by Christo, 1969.

7. Performance piece by Joseph Beuys, 1974.

8. Painting on a cave wall by members of the Ice Age culture in western France, around 15,000–10,000 BC.

9. Lithograph by Joseph Albers, 1967.

10. Construction by Robert Rauschenberg, 1959.

Were you surprised that all of the answers were yes? If you answered no to some, you may have thought that artworks were mostly just pictures and statues. You probably did not think that they came in so many different forms and materials.

Probably you and everyone in your class answered yes to artwork 2, the painting of a landscape (fig. 1–1). It is very **traditional**. It has a familiar and recognizable form, style, and subject matter.

Most of you probably answered yes to artwork 8, the cave painting (fig. 1–2), even though this kind of art cannot be seen in a museum. Cave paintings were painted directly onto cave walls. However, reproductions of them are found in many art books. This ancient art was discovered about a century ago and then brought to our attention by art historians.

Probably fewer of you said yes to artwork 5, the Broulé Sioux Indian shirt (fig. 1–3). The shirt is not a painting or a sculpture. Yet objects like this—especially if they are from an old culture or a tribal culture—are found in many museums. In addition to items of clothing, masks, banners, water jugs, spoons, tools, and even weapons from older cultures are often looked upon as art.

1–1 Robert S. Duncanson, *Blue Hole, Flood Waters, Little Miami River*, 1851. Oil on canvas, 29 ¼″ x 42 ¼″ (74 x 107 cm). Cincinnati Art Museum.

1–2 Painted in a cave near Lascaux, France around 17,000 years ago, these images of animals are the oldest paintings known to us. Although we have theories about this art and the people who made it, it is still a mystery. Chapter 18 will discuss some of those theories and the mystery. Cave painting, Lascaux, ca. 15,000 BC. Dordogne, France.

1–3 This is neither a painting nor a sculpture. Is it art? Shirt, Broulé Sioux, early nineteenth century. Buckskin with quillwork, beads and hair locks, 58″ (147 cm) arm spread. Courtesy of The National Museum of the American Indian/Smithsonian Institution.

1-4 Might people in 3990 AD be interested in "junk" like this? Do you think they would put any of it in a museum?

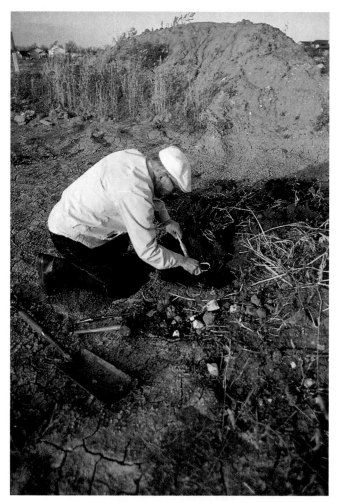

1-5 Archaeologists excavate to discover relics in places called "digs."

One hundred years ago you probably would not have found such objects in an art museum. At that time, people in this country and Europe had a very narrow idea of art. Only paintings, sculptures, and the styles of certain kinds of public buildings, called *architecture*, could be called art. Furthermore, in order to be considered an artwork, a painting, sculpture, or building had to be from the *Western civilization*. It had to be based on styles that developed in Europe and spread to the Americas.

Now the idea of art has become much broader. It can include many different kinds of objects. Objects can come from anywhere in the world, from any type of society, and from any time in history. In fact, almost any object has a good chance of being considered art if it is from a different culture or is very old or both.

Can you imagine some people from a society two thousand years from now digging in the rubble (fig. 1–4) and discovering objects from our present society? Suppose they found your radio. Would it be considered a work of art? Of course the answer depends on the abilities and interests of those future people. They might not recognize the object as a two-thousand-year-old radio. Even if they did, they might not find it interesting enough to save, much less call a work of art.

Try it Yourself

Look around you. Imagine that some of the objects you see will be discovered many years from now. Make a list of the things you think will survive and be valued. Discuss your list with your classmates. Imagine how these objects will look to someone who has never seen them before.

Objects from the past are often called *relics*. Scientists who explore ancient cities and villages to discover, identify, and catalog relics are called *archaeologists* (ark'kee ol'o jist).

Museum directors and art historians are especially interested in many of the things that archaeologists find (fig. 1–5). These people collect and study art of other times and places. They provide us with a great variety of things to see, wonder about, and enjoy.

Let us go back to the test to look at artworks 1, 3, 4, 6, 7, 9, and 10. These works are called ***contemporary***

1-7 Is this art or a comic? Roy Lichtenstein, *Whaam!*, 1963. Acrylic on canvas, 68″ x 160″ (173 x 406 cm). Tate Gallery, London/Art Resource, NY.

because they were done in our own day and age. You probably identified artwork 9 (fig. 1–6) as an example of ***abstract*** art. Abstract art does not resemble things in real life. Artwork 2 (fig. 1–7) is not abstract and is not made from unusual materials. Because of its style, you may have thought it was a comic strip. Were you fooled by artwork 4, the ceramic sculpture (fig. 1–8)? Ceramic (se ram'ik) refers to fired clay, a material that has been used for thousands of years for making pottery. Until quite recently ceramic artists made only useful objects such as plates, bowls, jars, and vases. Now, many artists feel free to make anything out of

1–6 Josef Albers, *Homage to the Square: Glow,* 1966. Acrylic on fiberboard, 48″ x 48″ (122 x 122 cm). Hirshhorn Museum and Sculpture Garden, Smithsonian Institution, Gift of Joseph H. Hirshhorn, 1972.

1–8 Marilyn Levine, *H. R. H. Briefcase,* 1985. Clay and mixed media, handbuilt (slab constructed), 16″ x 17 ½″ x 6 ¾″ (41 x 45 x 17 cm). O. K. Harris Works of Art.

1-9 Ron Anderson, Photograph of *"Killing of a '69 XR–7"* by Bob Albright, from the August 12, 1984, issue of *The Daily Oklahoman.* ©1984, Oklahoma Publishing Company.

clay, even including fake briefcases. Artworks 3, 6, 7, and 10 may have misled you. Possibly you found it difficult to think of used cars on scaffolds (fig. 1–9), wrapped coastlines (fig. 1–10), stuffed goats (fig. 1–11), and performances (fig. 1–12) as art.

Years ago, people had a difficult time accepting even abstract paintings as art. Yet the abstract art by artists of the early twentieth century were paintings on canvas. The art could be framed and hung on a wall. Many of today's artists, however, do not feel limited by such restrictions. They are apt to make art out of almost any material and shape it into almost any form. They may even perform their art, as Joseph Beuys does. Not only that, new technologies have allowed some artists to experiment with neon lights, photography, film, video, and computers, to mention just a few materials. Some of this new art uses techniques that

1-10 Christo, *Wrapped Coast, One Million Square Feet, Little Bay, Australia*, 1969. Erosion control fabric and 35 miles of rope. Photograph: Harry Shunk. ©Christo, 1969.

1–11 An assemblage by Robert Rauschenberg that can be hung on a wall. How would you feel about hanging an artwork like this in your room? Robert Rauschenberg, *Monogram*, 1959. Construction, 48″ x 72″ x 72″ (122 x 183 x 183 cm). Statens konstmuseer, Stockholm.

were not available even thirty years ago. Perhaps you are already filled with some wonder at the variety of art. This new freedom and technology, however, has raised some questions about the definition of art. These questions will be explored in the next chapter.

Summary

Usually, the word *art* makes people think of artworks, museums, and galleries. Art, however, is also people: artists, viewers, art historians, archaeologists, teachers, and students.

You have read just one chapter in this book. Yet you have already learned that today's art comes in an endless variety of forms. In the past, art objects included only paintings, sculpture, and public buildings found in Europe and the United States. Today the idea of what art is and can be has broadened. Common everyday objects from the past and from other cultures are now considered art.

One of the purposes of this book is to introduce you to some of the rich variety of today's art—a world of objects, places, and people for you to see, wonder about, and enjoy.

1–12 The artist, Joseph Beuys, was actually involved in this "performance art" for three days. Joseph Beuys, *Coyote—I Like America and America Likes Me*, 1974. ©1993 ARS, New York/VG Bild-Kunst, Bonn.

Chapter 2
When Is It Art?

In Chapter 1 we saw many things called art—from a stuffed goat to a ceramic briefcase. Today's art can be almost anything. It can even be a wrapped coast or an Indian shirt. However, the exciting variety of art in our time raises questions: Can anything be art? Are all stuffed goats and Indian shirts art?

These questions are part of the larger question, What is art? Long ago, this question was easy to answer. If something was a painting, a sculpture, or an architectural monument, it was art. But today, this question is difficult to answer. So many objects have been called art. If you saw an Indian shirt or stuffed goat in a store window, would you know whether or not it was art?

Think of some other ordinary things that may or may not be called art. For example, there are millions of photographs in the world. Some of them are art. They are shown in art galleries and discussed in art magazines. But many more are not art. Photographs in newspapers and magazines of events, people in the news, and products are not called art (fig. 2–1). They are called news photos or advertisements. Other photographs, called snapshots, are the kind you take at family gatherings or put in an album. If you saw a photograph in a store window, would you know whether or not it was art?

Perhaps a better question to ask is: *When* is it art? Under what **conditions** do things like used cars, stuffed goats, Indian shirts, and photographs become art? What is needed for something, *anything*, to be called an artwork?

Philosophy of Art

Asking serious, hard questions and then trying to answer them is called *philosophy*. Asking good questions is often more important than finding the answers. Philosophical questions often have many answers. Some cannot be answered at all, but can make people think in more creative ways.

2–1 Photographs like this are printed in newspapers every day. They are not usually thought of as works of art. Other photographs hang in art museums, and are called works of art. What is the difference?

2–2 Photograph: Barbara Caldwell.

Try it Yourself

Are you a philosopher (fig. 2–2)? Do you have questions about astronomy, prehistoric life, geography, animals, or just life in general? List some questions that you wish you knew the answers to. List questions that you think are important about art. What does art mean to you?

The **philosophy of art** involves asking and answering all kinds of questions about art. Philosophers of art are interested in discovering more than just what art is. They want to know how art can be evaluated, how people respond to it, and how art relates to personal and social values.

Artworks as a Class of Objects: What Do They Have in Common?

A philosopher may try to answer questions about art by grouping them into a *class* of objects. That way, he or she can begin by asking what all these objects, as a class, have in common. Look back at the objects we saw in Chapter 1. They do not seem to have anything in common. Art can be made out of anything from cars to stuffed animals. Furthermore, some artworks, like Joseph Beuys's performance piece, are not even objects in the usual sense of the word. Clearly, the materials and form of an artwork are not what artworks have in common.

Good design may be an important trait to consider besides material and form. Good design can be defined as a logical and **harmonious** relationship among all the parts of an artwork. The opposite of good design is *chaos.*

Good design seems to be very important in evaluating art. Young people who are studying to become artists are taught the *principles of design.* Artists use these principles to make their art better. Knowing these principles can help you to appreciate art more. (The principles of design are covered in Chapter 10.)

Now, look again at some of the objects in Chapter 1. Do they all have good design? Is the relationship among the animals in the cave painting (fig. 2–3) logical and harmonious? The animals are placed haphazardly. Some animals are smaller than others for no reason. Some are not even finished. Furthermore, what is logical or harmonious about the combination of a tire and a stuffed goat (fig. 2–4)? Does a ceramic briefcase (fig. 2–5a) have a better design than a real briefcase (fig. 2–5b)?

2–3

2–4 Is the relationship between the goat and the tire logical and harmonious? Is this construction a work of art? Are the animals in the cave painting arranged haphazardly? Is the painting a work of art?

2–5a

2–5b Does a ceramic briefcase have a better design than a leather one? Is the leather briefcase a work of art? 2–5a Marilyn Levine, *H. R. H. Briefcase,* 1985. Clay and mixed media, handbuilt (slab constructed), 16″ x 17 ½″ x 6 ¾″ (41 x 45 x 17 cm). O. K. Harris Works of Art. 2–5b EC 28 Lawyer's Briefcase. Courtesy Hartmann Luggage Co.

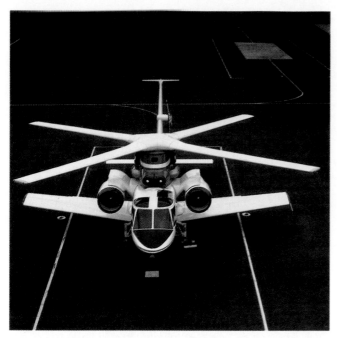

2–6 Can you identify some ways a Sikorsky X Wing plane demonstrates high standards of unity and balance? Is it a work of art? Photo courtesy United Technologies.

2–7 Compare the design of this snowflake to that of the *Mystic Circle* (fig. 2–8). Is the snowflake a work of art? Photomicrograph of a snowflake. ©Roger J. Cheng.

The example of the fake briefcase points out an important fact. Many things that are not artworks have good design. For example, we admire the design of products from real briefcases to Japanese cameras to military planes (fig. 2–6). In nature, we admire the design of trees, flowers, crystals, rocks, and snowflakes (fig. 2–7). The list seems endless. Many objects that are not art—whether manufactured or natural—have logical and harmonious relationships among their parts.

Even though good design may be important for many works of art, it is not found in all works of art. Many philosophers of art now say that there are probably no special traits that *all* artworks have in common. Therefore, you could not decide if an object was an artwork on the basis of its materials, form, or design.

The Aesthetic Experience

Suppose a philosopher of art has admitted that artworks as a group of objects have nothing in common. He or she may try to decide if an object is art by looking at the experience it gives a person. As a general rule, the purpose of an artwork is to provide viewers with an **aesthetic** (es the´tick) **experience**. Philosophers have struggled to define this concept for centuries. Most tend to agree that an aesthetic experience has to do with enjoying something for its own sake. Artworks are made to be seen and enjoyed for their own sake. They do not have to be useful. Some artworks, like pottery, jewelry, and weaving, are meant to be used *and* to provide aesthetic experiences. The Broulé Sioux Indian shirt, which was made to be worn as well as admired for its beauty, is a good example of this kind of art.

However, looking at an artwork is not the only way to have an aesthetic experience. For example, have you ever enjoyed watching a sunset (fig. 2–9), cheered at a parade, smelled roses, or blown seeds off a dandelion ball? When you do things like this, you are not trying to impress friends, earn money, or get a good grade. Instead, you do them for their own sake. In other words, you do them because you like the colors of an evening sky, the smell of roses, or the sight of dandelion seeds floating lazily on a gentle breeze.

You may also like to watch sports, especially when a team from your high school is involved (fig. 2–10). Suppose you did not care about the score and you watched the game for its own sake. Just by enjoying the movements of the players and the drama of competition (regardless of who won), you would have an aesthetic experience.

2–9 One of these scenes is quiet and contemplative; the other (fig. 2–10) is noisy and festive. Which do you prefer? Could you have an aesthetic experience in response to either? Skjold Photographs.

2–8 *Mystic Circle*, Sri Yantra, late eighteenth century, Rajasthan. Burnaby Gallery, British Columbia.

2–10 Which is more important—the drama of the action or the final score?

2–12 This Indian shirt was probably determined to be a work of art by the board of directors of a museum. Shirt, Broulé Sioux, early nineteenth century. Buckskin with quillwork, beads and hair locks, 58″ (147 cm) arm spread. Courtesy of The National Museum of the American Indian, Smithsonian Institution.

2–11 Would seeing a Beuys performance be an aesthetic experience for you? Why? Joseph Beuys, *Coyote—I Like America and America Likes Me*, 1974. ©1993 ARS, New York/VG Bild-Kunst, Bonn.

Try it Yourself

Think of some events you have been to, such as fairs, parades, festivals, and concerts. Also recall some things you have done with family or friends: celebrations, picnics, hiking, nature walks. Have you taken any trips recently? Have you been to the beach?

Which memories are the most vivid? Did you enjoy any of these events purely for their own sake? Make a list of the events that gave you an aesthetic experience. Describe one or two of them to a friend or classmate.

As you have discovered, many things besides looking at art can provide aesthetic experiences. Therefore, you will not be able to tell if something is an artwork just because it gives you an aesthetic experience.

On the other hand, would it be possible to tell if something is *not* an artwork because it does not give you an aesthetic experience? No. In reality, artworks do not always succeed in providing aesthetic experiences for everyone. Sometimes it is the *attitude* or *mood* of the person who sees the artwork that matters, not the quality of the artwork. We all have our personal feelings. Suppose you saw Joseph Beuys's performance piece, *I Like America and America Likes Me* (fig. 2–11), and were bored by it. This would not mean that others would not enjoy it. Indeed, on a different day, you might enjoy it yourself. The point is this: you cannot rely on your personal likes and dislikes on any given day to judge whether something is a work of art.

Intentions and Art

Today, many philosophers of art say that *human intention* is a necessary factor in determining whether or not something is art. People who make paintings, for example, "intend" them to be art. When Robert Rauschenberg attached an old tire to a stuffed goat, mounted them to a canvas, and smeared them with paint, he *intended* the whole thing to be a work of art. The museum director *intended* the Broulé Sioux Indian shirt (fig. 2–12) to be a work of art when he or she put it in the Museum of the American Indian even though the Broulé Sioux themselves may not have intended it to be art. If you saw a piece of driftwood on the beach (fig. 2–13), you probably would not call it art. But if you saw it mounted on a wall in someone's home, you probably would. The person who mounted the driftwood intended it to be seen as art.

The principle of human intention seems to be the answer to our question, When is it art? Perhaps this principle explains all of the examples presented in Chapter 1.

But does it answer all the questions? *Who* is to do the intending: just artists and museum directors? Can anyone—you, for example—intend something, *anything*, to be art? Suppose you wrapped your house with bed sheets. Would other people consider it a work of art—or a mess (fig. 2–14)? Would your neighbors appreciate it? Would your art teacher praise you for it? Suppose, like Joseph Beuys, you wrapped yourself in felt and walked around a room with a coyote. Would anyone take you seriously?

2–13 Under what conditions would this piece of driftwood be a work of art? Photograph: Barbara Caldwell.

2–14 What do you think your dad would say if you wrapped your garage in "plastic-wrap"? Would he consider it a work of art? Christo, *Wrapped Coast, One Million Square Feet, Little Bay, Australia*, 1969. Erosion control fabric and 35 miles of rope. Photograph: Harry Shunk. ©Christo, 1969.

2–15 Objects like these, whether old or modern, are easily recognizable as art. Why are they so easy to recognize? These examples, along with those that are less traditional, including the Broulé Sioux shirt, the stuffed goat, the wrapped coast, and even the Beuys performance, belong to a world of things called *fine art*. Can all of these be found in museums or galleries? Where can we find pictures of these things? Robert S. Duncanson, *Blue Hole, Flood Waters, Little Miami River*, 1851. Oil on canvas, 29 ¼″ x 42 ¼″ (74 x 107 cm). Cincinnati Art Museum.

The Art World

Some art is ancient like the cave paintings. Some is traditional like Duncanson's (fig. 2–15). Some is modern like Albers' (fig. 2–16). Regardless of their styles, we have no trouble telling that these objects are art. It is other kinds of art that often raise questions. Useful objects from old or tribal cultures, like the Broulé Sioux Indian shirt, are not always easy to recognize as art. Experimental forms, like the ceramic briefcase, used car, wrapped coast, stuffed goat, and performance piece also raise questions.

In the final analysis, *there is no perfect method for determining when things like these are art*. Human intention is necessary. Good design and the aesthetic experience are important. But ultimately, determining when something is art seems to be a matter of judgment.

Who makes the judgments in these matters? It is people like artists, dealers, collectors, art critics, museum directors, and art teachers. All of them make up what is known as the *art world*—just as players, coaches, managers, umpires, and team owners make up the *sports world*. These people are involved not only in the production of art, but in selling it, collecting it, displaying it, writing about it, and teaching it. Their training, experience, and commitment give them the authority to make judgments.

Do these people ever make bad judgments? Yes. Some objects should have stayed in history museums. Some examples of experimental art should have been forgotten. But there are also many traditional paintings and sculptures that were misjudged by experts in the past. Most of those works now are out of sight, gathering dust in museum basements.

The art that you see in art galleries and art museums is called *fine art*. It is fine art that is reproduced and written about in newspapers, art magazines, and art books like this one. Sometimes the term fine art is used to contrast it with *folk art* and *commercial art*.

Folk art is art produced by amateur or untrained artists. Commercial art is the kind of art that you see everyday in the newspapers or on television.

Summary

Philosophers of art ask difficult questions about art to try to define what art is. It is almost impossible to define art by looking for traits that all artworks have in common. Most works possess good design, but not all do. Furthermore, many things besides art have good design. Artworks should provide an aesthetic experience. They are meant to be appreciated for their own sake. But many things besides art can be experienced this way. Therefore, neither good design nor the aesthetic experience is a complete test of what makes something a work of art.

One thing that all art has in common is human intention. Traditional paintings, sculptures, ancient objects, experimental forms of art, and even pieces of mounted driftwood can be called artworks if someone intended them to be art. The art world decides what can be called *fine art*, the kind we see in art galleries and museums.

Aesthetic Analysis 2.1

Why Is It Art?

Select an object from home that you can defend as an artwork. Is it old or new? Why is it art? How does it meet the conditions listed in this chapter? Bring your object to school. Defend your object as art. What reasons would you give? Can you *prove* that something, anything, is art?

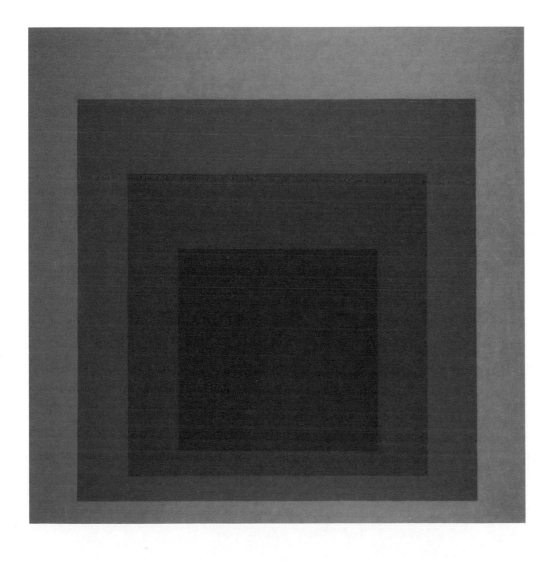

2–16 Josef Albers, *Homage to the Square: Glow*, 1966. Acrylic on fiberboard, 48″ x 48″ (122 x 122 cm). Hirshhorn Museum and Sculpture Garden, Smithsonian Institution, Gift of Joseph H. Hirshhorn, 1972.

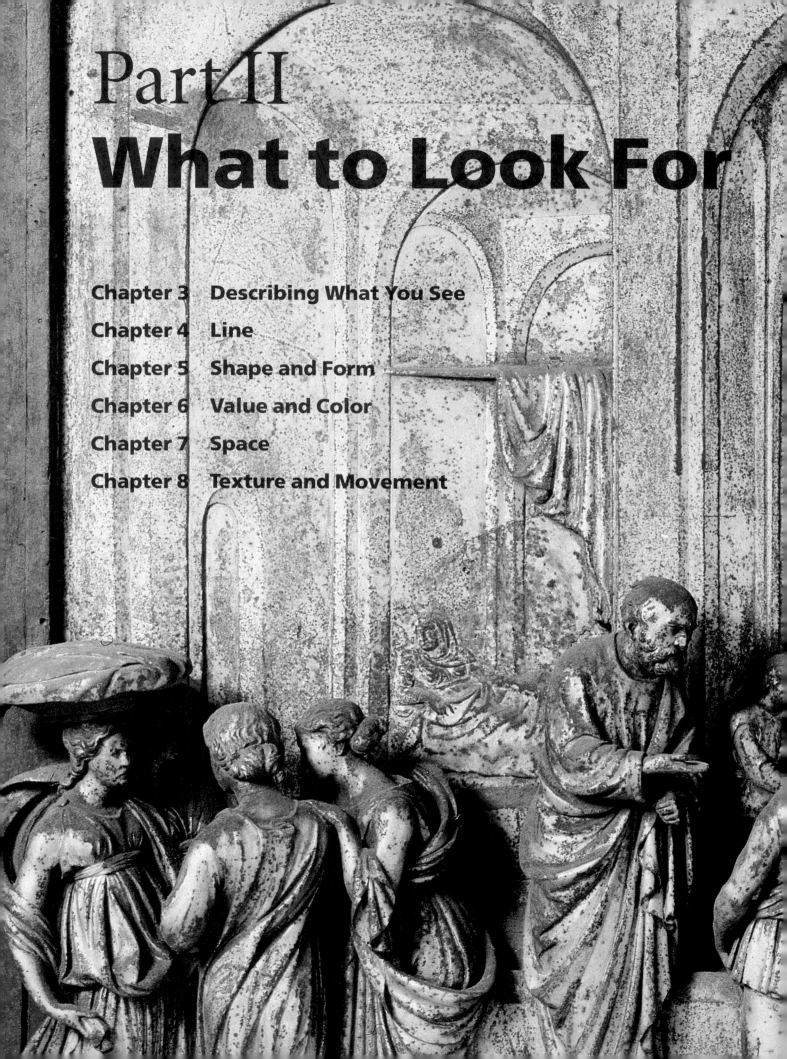

Part II
What to Look For

Lorenzo Ghiberti, *The Story of Jacob and Esau*, detail from *The Gates of Paradise*, ca. 1435. Gilt bronze, 31 1/4" (79 cm) square. Formella dell Porta del Paradiso. The Baptistry, Florence.

Chapter 3
Describing What You See

One way to open ourselves to art is by taking the time to *look* at an artwork. Our world is full of images, such as advertisements, illustrations, billboards, and photographs. We get into the habit of glancing and not really looking. This is unfortunate, especially when good pictures are involved.

To make sure that we are looking, and not just glancing, at a picture, we should try once in awhile to *describe* it.

Description

According to the dictionary, **describe** means "to tell or write about, to give a detailed account of." If you were to describe a work of art, first you would *look* at it closely. Then you would *tell* or *write* about what you saw. This kind of telling or writing is called *description*.

When writing a description you must stick to the **facts**. Include things like the objects, people, shapes, and colors that you and others can see. Do not include **opinions**, such as: "The man is wearing a *stupid* hat,"

3–1 There are many things in this painting: people, objects, colors, and textures, even a puppy. Pierre Auguste Renoir, *Luncheon of the Boating Party*, 1881. Oil on canvas, 51″ x 68″ (130 x 173 cm). © The Phillips Collection, Washington, DC.

"That is a *pretty* color," or "This picture is about people having *a lot of fun*." These statements may be true for you but not for others. They are opinions, not facts.

How well can you describe a painting? Look carefully at and write about *Luncheon of the Boating Party* (fig. 3–1) by Renoir. To make the job somewhat more challenging, give yourself only fifteen minutes to write your description.

Do not continue reading until you have finished the description.

Did you feel that you needed more time to describe the picture? If you said yes, you are right.

Your description probably explained that there are a number of young men and women. They are gathered on what appears to be a deck. Some are sitting and some are standing. Several seem to be talking to one another. You probably also noted the table, the food and drink on the table, the young woman at the table holding a little dog, the railing behind the table, the people leaning on the railing, the awning overhead, and the leafy foliage beyond the deck. Did you have time to write about the people's clothes, their hats, or what they are doing? Did you notice the sailboats in the distance?

If you mentioned all those things, you did quite well, but that is only a *beginning*. A good description would have pointed out several more things about the people. For example, some are nearer to the viewer than others. Those on the left seem spread apart, while those on the right seem crowded together. Some are looking to the right, some to the left, some toward the viewer, and some away from the viewer.

Both the table and the railing are on the left side of the picture, but both lead your eye to the right. A good description would have called attention to this.

Meet the Artist

Pierre Auguste Renoir
1841–1919

Warm red and yellow colors fill a tranquil scene of carefree vacationers gathered at an afternoon meal. Bold brush strokes define faces and figures leisurely mingling in the summer sun. Pierre Auguste Renoir developed a reputation for his talent in portraying light-hearted scenes like *Luncheon of the Boating Party*.

As one of five children of a tailor from Limoges, France, Renoir had to save every penny he earned as a porcelain painter to attend the School of Fine Arts in 1862. There he became friends with other aspiring artists, including Claude Monet and Alfred Sisley. These men influenced each other's painting. They began to work in similar styles, using brilliantly colored dabs of paint and often painting outdoors. These techniques were considered unique and revolutionary. Later, this group of artists and friends became known as the Impressionists.

Renoir soon attained great status as a portrait painter. Underneath this success, however, he was often dissatisfied with his work. He was also self-conscious about being a member of the working class and not a part of the middle class group who were the subjects of his paintings. But the public adored him. In his lifetime Renoir was paid to paint over two thousand portraits of wealthy art lovers.

Why did he paint such joyous scenes when he was really unhappy? "There are enough ugly things in life for us not to add to them," he once said. The happy images Renoir painted contrasted with his emotions.

From delicate work on porcelain and drawing from models in an art class, Renoir learned the techniques necessary to paint on canvas. Using these skills, Renoir presented colorful scenes filled with happiness and untroubled ease, a world he created with paint and brush.

3–2 What are some colors that you see in this "white" tablecloth? Pierre Auguste Renoir, *Luncheon of the Boating Party* (detail), 1881. Oil on canvas, 51″ x 68″ (130 x 173 cm). © The Phillips Collection, Washington, DC.

3–3 What other colors besides green do you see in this section of foliage? Pierre Auguste Renoir, *Luncheon of the Boating Party* (detail), 1881. Oil on canvas, 51″ x 68″ (130 x 173 cm). © The Phillips Collection, Washington, DC.

If you said *all* of these things, you did *very well*. But even so, you would have described only the people and objects in the painting. Your description would have left out some of the most important things. The various lines, shapes, colors, and textures should have been described.

We hope you said something about color. But did you note that the white tablecloth (fig. 3–2) is not a single color of white, or that the foliage (fig. 3–3) is not a single color of green? Did you point out that some colors are lighter (or darker) and that some are brighter (or duller)?

As you can see, if you were to write a good description, you would need a great deal of paper and a lot of time. It is not something that can be done in fifteen minutes.

Even if you had been given one hundred minutes, you probably would have left out many important things. To describe a work of art, you need more than just enough time. You also need to *know what to look for* and to have the appropriate *vocabulary*. You need the right words to describe what you do see.

Knowing What to Look For

You may see as much as, and as clearly as, the average human being. But being able to see normally does *not* mean that you are going to see all of the things you should in a work of art. You first need some knowledge about what you are looking at. You also need some practice.

Compared to Renoir's painting, the Sunday comics (fig. 3–4), television cartoons, and other pictures that you see all the time are very simple. Leaves are usually one shade of green, skies are blue, and clouds are white and puffy shaped. Houses have

3–4 Comic strip art is obviously not very demanding of your ability to describe shapes and colors. *Rex Morgan, M.D.*, DiPreta, ©1988. King Features Syndicate. Reprinted with special permission of North America Syndicate.

3–5 Can you name all the different colors in just this little section of Renoir's painting? Pierre Auguste Renoir, *Luncheon of the Boating Party* (detail), 1881. Oil on canvas, 51″ x 68″ (130 x 173 cm). © The Phillips Collection, Washington, DC.

pointed roofs and Santa Claus always has a round body and a red suit. Colors are plain and shapes are simple in this kind of everyday art.

As you can see, the shapes in *Luncheon of the Boating Party* are very complicated. The colors are even more so (fig. 3–5). For example, every item of clothing, whether it is a white shirt, a blue dress, or a brown suit, consists of different shades of white, blue, or brown. The leafy foliage consists of not only different shades of green, but also bits of yellow, blue, white, and brown. All of the colors in this painting come in different degrees of lightness and darkness. They vary in brightness and dullness. This quality is referred to as **shading**.

The complicated colors in *Luncheon of the Boating Party* are used to do more than just describe objects. The colors play an important role in providing unity and balance. They also add to the mood. The ways in which colors do this will be explained in later chapters. For now, when you look at pictures, pay more attention to colors. Look at line, shape, texture, and space.

Vocabulary

Probably the easiest thing for you to talk about in a picture is the *subject matter:* the people and objects. It may be more difficult for you to talk about colors and textures. You have not learned the right vocabulary for talking about art. For example, you may be able to recognize the color orange without knowing that it is a "secondary" color. You may not know how such a color relates to other colors. You may already be aware of the texture of a painting without having the words to describe it. On the other hand, you may not be aware of these things at all, until you first learn the words for them.

The Elements of Art

The *elements of art* are the beginning points for learning about art and art vocabulary. The elements of art are line, shape, form, value, color, space, and texture.

In a particular work of art, some elements may be less important than others. For example, look back at the wrapped coastline pictured in the first two chapters. Here color probably plays a less important role than shape. But the element of color is still there. All of the elements are present in some degree in all works of visual art.

By learning the elements, you will see things that you may not have noticed before. You will also learn the words for those things.

Try it Yourself

Save your description of *Luncheon of the Boating Party*. You may want to add to it as you learn more about art in the next chapters.

Look at a picture for a few minutes. Then put the picture away and write a description of it from memory. After you have finished, look at the picture again. Compare your description with the picture.

Summary

Describing is telling about what you see. A description of an artwork should stick to the facts.

It is not easy to describe a painting like *Luncheon of the Boating Party*. There are many things to look for. There is the subject matter—the people and objects. There are the visual elements—lines, shapes, colors, textures, and space. The visual elements will be discussed in the next five chapters. Knowledge of these elements should help you see things in art that you did not see before. This knowledge will also provide you with words for those things.

Criticism Experience 3.1

Describing an Artwork

Describe Grant Wood's *American Gothic* (page 25). Your teacher will give you guidelines that will help you complete your description.

Grant Wood, *American Gothic,* 1930. Oil on beaver board, 30″ x 25″ (76 cm x 63 cm). The Art Institute of Chicago, Friends of American Art.

Chapter 4
Line

The word **line** has many definitions in Webster's dictionary. You can *line* a ball in baseball, hit the *line* in football, memorize *lines* for a play, and avoid being last in *line* at the cafeteria. Even when the word is used to describe "long thin marks," there are many examples that fit this meaning.

Lines can be found in nature in such things as the veins of a leaf (fig. 4–1). The branches of trees in winter (fig. 4–2) and the wind-etched sands of a desert (fig. 4–3) have lines. Lines are everywhere in the world around you. On your way to school you probably saw telephone lines and electric power lines stretched between poles. If you looked down you probably saw the cracks of the sidewalk.

In fact, the printed letters and numbers you are reading right now are shapes made with lines. The letters *c* and *s* and the number 5 are made with single lines that are open at the ends. Some letters, like *f, t,* and *x,*

4–1 Wynn Bullock, *Leaves and Cobwebs,* 1968. Silverprint, 7 ½″ x 9 ¼″ (19 x 24 cm). © The Detroit Institute of Arts, Founders Society Purchase, Michigan State Council for the Arts Exhibition Fund.

4–2 Photograph: Barbara Caldwell.

4–3 *White Sands National Monument,* New Mexico. Photograph courtesy U.S. Dept. of the Interior, Washington, DC.

4–4 Photograph: Barbara Caldwell.

are made with lines that cross. Some, like *y* and *k*, are made with open lines that are connected in places. Many, like *a, b, e, 6,* and *9,* are made with lines that are partly open and partly closed. Of course, at least two—*o* and *8*—are made of single lines with no open ends. Isn't it amazing how many letters and numbers can be created by arranging or rearranging a few straight and curved lines (and dots to make *i* and *j*)?

4–5 Courtesy ©Color-Art, Inc., St. Louis, Missouri.

Try it Yourself

Look at the letters in other alphabets, such as Greek or Russian. Some alphabets, like Arabic, Hebrew, and Japanese, are very different from the English alphabet. Perhaps you can create your own alphabet.

A road map is another example of lines. Lines and shapes on a map are called *symbols.* They stand for other things. Figure 4–5 is a map of northern Illinois. The long lines stand for roads, highways, and rivers. On the roads and highways are dots (a little circle surrounded by a line) that stand for small towns. The little squares on Interstate Highways 80 and 39 stand for exits. The wandering blue line that runs beside Highway 6 is the Illinois River.

Art has as many kinds of lines as the lines you find in nature or in books and maps. Many lines in art are created by moving a tool such as a pencil, charcoal stick, pen, or brush. Did you know that some lines can even be made with light (fig. 4–6)?

4-6 Gjon Mili, *A Centaur Drawn with Light—Pablo Picasso at the Madoura Pottery in Vallauris, France.* Photograph. ©1984. Sotheby Parke Bernet, Inc., New York.

Studio Experience 4.1

Varieties of Line

Select five different drawing media such as crayons, pencils, felt-tip pens, ball-point pens, drawing pens, sticks, and brushes. Make five different kinds of lines drawn from top to bottom of the page, with each medium. Record the medium under each set of lines.

Studio Experience 4.2

Expressive Line Drawings

Use what you learned in Experience 4.1 to make an interpretive drawing of fall weeds.

Kay Dye.

4–7 Charles M. Schulz, *Charlie Brown and Snoopy*, 1973. *Peanuts* reprinted by permission of UFS, Inc.

4–9 Ben Shahn, *Dr. J. Robert Oppenheimer*, 1954. Brush and ink, 19 ½″ x 12 ¼″ (50 x 31 cm). The Museum of Modern Art, New York. Purchase.

Descriptive Lines

You have been making lines since the first time you picked up a pencil. At first you probably made scribbles. Eventually your lines turned into recognizable pictures. This use of lines—whether by a child or an artist—is called **descriptive**. Descriptive lines come in many varieties.

Outlines

The most basic kind of descriptive line is an outline. An **outline** is a line that surrounds a shape. Alphabet letters and map symbols are examples of outlines. In school you use outlines to make letters. You also use them when you make pictures.

Like you, comic strip artists use outlines to create their characters, such as Charlie Brown and Snoopy (fig. 4–7). The lines of an outline drawing are usually the same thickness throughout. Also, only the outer edges of the shapes are defined. For these reasons, an outline drawing seems to have little depth. Charlie Brown and Snoopy are almost as flat as cutouts.

Contour Lines

Contour lines also define the outer edges of shapes. Unlike outlines, however, contour lines vary in thickness and darkness. They also define the edges of shapes within a form. They give a greater sense of depth to the object. Notice the contour lines in the Persian drawing *A Portly Courtier* (fig. 4–8). These lines smoothly trace the man's belly and even some of the folds in his clothes.

Contrast the Persian artist's "relaxed" lines with the intense, scratchy lines of Ben Shahn's *Dr. J. Robert Oppenheimer* (fig. 4–9). How do the dark thick lines add interest and help describe the subject?

Diego Rivera used ink and brush to create lines that describe an Indian mother carrying her child (fig. 4–10). Some lines are narrow and some are quite wide. Some, like the one that shows the underside of the mother's arm, are both narrow and wide. Compare Rivera's two people to Charlie Brown and Snoopy. Which pair seems to you to be the most solid, the most three-dimensional? Which picture has the most variety in its lines?

4-8 *A Portly Courtier*, Persia, Tabriz, ca. 1535. Ink and gold on paper, 5″ x 4″ (13.5 x 10 cm). Courtesy of The Arthur M. Sackler Museum, Harvard University Art Museums, Gift of Mr. Henry B. Cabot, Mr. Walter Cabot, Mr. Edward W. Forbes, Mr. Eric Schroeder and the Annie S. Coburn Fund.

4-10 Diego Rivera, *Untitled (mother and child)*, 1936. Ink on paper, 12″ x 9 ¼″ (30 x 24 cm). San Francisco Museum of Modern Art, Albert M. Bender Collection, Gift of Albert M. Bender.

4–12 Wu Chen, *Bamboo*, Yuan dynasty, 1350 AD. Album leaf, ink on paper, 16″ x 21″ (41 x 53 cm). Collection of the National Palace Museum, Taipei, Taiwan, Republic of China.

Because of their variety, contour lines are more interesting and descriptive than outlines. Lines in drawings by professional artists are often called contour lines rather than outlines. When you draw, which kinds of lines do you use most often: outlines or contour lines?

Individual Lines

Just as a single line can represent the letter *S*, it can describe an individual strand of hair. Look at the close-up of a painting by Andrew Wyeth (fig. 4–11). Wu Chen used single strokes of an ink-loaded brush to describe the stalks and leaves of a bamboo plant (fig. 4–12). He also used individual strokes for each symbol of the Chinese writing on the left of the picture. This elegant writing is called *calligraphy*.

4–11 Andrew Wyeth, *Braids* (detail), tempera.

Contour Line

Produce a drawing using contour lines that describe the three-dimensional characteristics of an object.

a. The lines in this contour drawing accurately and sensitively describe the edges of forms, and the details and folds of the coat found within the major forms. Jean Auguste Dominique Ingres, *Portrait of a Young Man*, ca. 1815. Pencil, 11″ x 8″ (29 x 20 cm). Museum Boymans-van Beuningen, Rotterdam.

b. The outline of a hand is accurate, but appears flat and lacks information when compared with the contour drawing on the right.

Hatching

David Levine used contour lines to make a humorous drawing of a public person (fig. 4–13). But look closely at the lines in the face and coat. The artist used many thin, closely spaced, parallel lines called **hatching**. Hatching lines that cross, like those on the lower part of the head, are called **crosshatching**.

In hatching, the black lines are so thin and close together that they blend with the white of the paper. When this happens, they appear gray. This effect is called *optical mixing*. The mixing of black and white happens in the eye. When you look at Levine's picture, the black hatching lines are optically mixed in your vision. You see a variety of grays. These grays help to describe the nose, cheeks, chin, and jowls. The use of lighter and darker grays to make a form seem three-dimensional is known as *shading*. You will learn more about shading in the chapter on value and color.

4–13 David Levine, *Nixon as The Godfather*, 1972. Reprinted with permission from *The New York Review of Books*. ©1963–73, Nyrev, Inc.

Hatch and Crosshatch

Use pen and ink, black ball-point pen, or pencils to practice hatching and crosshatching. Make several drawings. Try to achieve a wide range of lights and darks.

a. Hatch and crosshatch techniques.

b. Student work.

c. Student work.

Implied Lines

The lines we have seen so far are just that: *seen* lines. They are visible. They have width and length. However, there are some lines that are not seen, at least not in the usual way. They are **implied**; that is, they are indicated indirectly. An actual line does not have to be present in order for a line to be suggested, or implied. Lines can be implied by *edges, closure,* and *lines of sight*.

Edges

Look at Renoir's painting of a boating party (fig. 4–14). Renoir did not use outlines or contour lines to set off one shape from another. Nevertheless, the lines are implied by **edges**. An edge exists where one shape ends and another begins. In Renoir's painting, an edge is

formed where an arm meets the railing and where the man's back on the right meets the chair. Another example of an edge is where the man's hand touches the railing. All these edges suggest the presence of lines. The lines are implied.

In a sculpture, an edge exists where the sculpture ends and the space around it begins. The edges of Elizabeth Catlett's carving of *Mother and Child #2* imply many graceful lines (fig. 4–15). If you were to draw her carving, the outside line would look almost like a rounded parallelogram. The curve of the mother's hand is repeated in the circle of the infant's head. What other curved lines and angles do you see in this sculpture?

4–14 Pierre Auguste Renoir, *Luncheon of the Boating Party*, 1881. Oil on canvas, 51″ x 68″ (130 x 173 cm). ©The Phillips Collection, Washington, DC.

The outer edges of a building or the roofline can also suggest lines. But lines also are suggested by the edges around window and door openings, and the edges of overhangs, ledges, balconies, railings, posts, and trim. In the Japanese villa (fig. 4–16), most of the lines are horizontal. They emphasize the width of the building rather than its height. Horizontal lines suggest a sense of stability and restfulness. We associate these qualities with home. By contrast, most of the lines of the Sears Tower (fig. 4–17) are vertical. They emphasize the height of the building. Because we associate height with power, the vertical lines symbolize the strength of a powerful corporation.

4–15 Elizabeth Catlett, *Mother and Child #2*, 1971. Walnut, 38″ (97 cm). Malcom Brown Gallery.

4–17 Skidmore, Owings and Merrill, Sears Tower, 1974. Chicago, Illinois. Rosenthal Art Slides, Inc., Chicago.

4–16 The Shoin, Katsura Imperial Villa.

4–20 Mokuan, *The Four Sleepers* (detail). Muromachi (mid-fourteenth century). Ink on paper, 28″ x 14″ (71 x 36 cm). Maeda Ikutokukai Foundation, Tokyo.

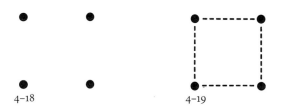

4–18

4–19

Closure

Lines can even be implied by a simple arrangement of dots. For example, there are no lines in figure 4–18. Nevertheless, we see this arrangement of dots as a square rather than as four separate dots. We connect the dots in our "mind's eye" (fig. 4–19). Our tendency to connect marks this way, or to "see" lines where none exist, is called ***closure***.

Closure is required to connect the loosely drawn and delicate lines in Mokuan's *The Four Sleepers* (fig. 4–20). Can you see the four sleepers? Would you agree that lack of clarity makes the picture more interesting and humorous? Why?

Closure is required even for viewing a photograph. The photograph in figure 4–21 provides limited "information." The student and the teacher are formed by just a few areas of black and white. The teacher's face has almost no outline or any other lines except a mouth.

Lines of Sight

Have you ever looked up when someone else looked up? Looking in the same direction as another person is a natural tendency. The lines along which people look are called **lines of sight**. In Renoir's *Luncheon of the Boating Party*, the merrymakers are looking at each other. It is very natural for the viewer to also look along the same lines of sight. It is similar to the process of closure. Artists often use lines of sight to connect different parts of a picture. Which of the many lines of sight do you think are the most important in *Luncheon*?

Expressive Use of Lines

We have seen that artists use lines to describe shapes or forms. They also use lines to indicate shading. We have also seen how painters, cartoonists, sculptors, and architects use implied lines.

In addition to these uses, lines are also used by artists to express feelings and ideas. Some examples of the expressive qualities of lines have been mentioned already. Recall the "relaxed" lines of the Persian drawing (fig. 4–8) and the "intense, scratchy" lines of Shahn (fig. 4–9). The implied lines of the Catlett sculpture (fig. 4–15) can be described as "graceful." The lines of

the Japanese villa suggest "restfulness and stability" (fig. 4–16), while the lines of the Sears Tower suggest "power and strength" (fig. 4–17). Lines—descriptive or implied—have their own "personalities."

Abstract Lines

Abstract lines are mainly found in abstract art. Abstract art can be nonrepresentational (also called *nonobjective*). There is little or no attempt to show a pictorial likeness or image. **Abstract lines** are not used to symbolize, to outline, or to look like shading. Abstract lines are expressive, not descriptive. As a viewer, you have little choice but to see abstract lines for what they are: lines.

4–22 Which lines of sight do you think are the most important? Pierre Auguste Renoir, *Luncheon of the Boating Party,* 1881. Oil on canvas, 51″ x 68″ (130 x 173 cm). ©The Phillips Collection, Washington, DC.

4–21

4–23 José Roberto Aguilar, *The Brazilian Myth (O Mito Brasileiro)*, 1981. Acrylic on canvas, 7´ x 13´ (2.4 x 4 m). Collection of Kim Esteve, São Paulo, Brazil.

Try it Yourself

Look at the examples of abstract art (figures 4–23, 4–24, 4–25, and 4–26). Come up with a word or two to describe the feeling that each work seems to express. You can use the words in the columns below or add your own words. Compare your set of words with your classmates' words. See if your choice of words agrees with theirs.

aggressive	delicate	soft
awkward	energetic	strong
balanced	explosive	swift
blunt	graceful	timid
bristling	nervous	unstable
brutal	powerful	weak
calm	restless	wild
chaotic	rhythmic	

4–25 Kazuaki Tanahashi, *Heki*, 1965. Ink on paper, 36˝ x 28˝ (92 x 71 cm). East-West Center, Honolulu.

4-26 James Feltner, *Chien.*

4-24 Ibsen Espada, *El Yunque,* 1985. Oil and ink on paper applied to canvas. 53 ¼″ x 63″ (135 x 160 cm). McMurtrey Gallery, Houston.

Line Personalities

If you did the Try it Yourself, you matched abstract lines with adjectives such as aggressive or calm. Could you match people you know with these adjectives?

How does a line acquire a personality? There is no single answer to this question. However, we tend to associate lines with other things in our experience. We associate certain feelings with a line's shape, movement, and direction.

Shape. Straight lines remind us of things like buildings that are strong or powerful. Curved lines remind us of people, animals, or plants that are soft, delicate, or graceful. Jagged lines suggest objects like broken glass, sawteeth, or lightning that are bristling, aggressive, or wild.

Movement. A line, as we explained, is often the record of real movement. We associate lines with the movements of animals, people, or even our own bodies. Straight lines may seem rigid or swift. Curved lines seem relaxed or graceful. Jagged lines seem nervous or awkward.

Direction. If a line has movement, it also has direction. Lines that move in vertical directions seem strong; horizontal lines seem calm or stable; and diagonal lines seem unstable (fig. 4–27).

These descriptions are *generalizations*. The personality of a particular line may be due to its shape, movement, and direction. But it can also be influenced by other elements in the artwork. For example, shapes, colors, textures, and even other lines in a work of art can affect the personality of a line. (The visual elements of shape, color, and texture are discussed in later chapters.)

Summary

There are many kinds of lines. We can see lines in nature and in our human-made environment. Letters and numbers on book pages are made up of lines. Lines appear on maps and even musical scores.

Lines in art also come in various forms. Lines can be *descriptive, implied,* and *abstract.* Descriptive lines are created with a variety of tools, and can be outlines, contour lines, single lines, or hatching. On the other hand, lines can be implied by the edges of forms in paintings, sculptures, and buildings. Lines can be implied by the process of closure and by lines of sight. Abstract lines, unlike descriptive lines, usually do not symbolize or represent anything except themselves.

All lines—whether descriptive, implied, or abstract—can express feelings and ideas. We can talk about lines as having personalities. We give personalities to lines by associating certain feelings with a line's shape, movement, and direction. The expressive qualities of lines are an important part of the aesthetic experience.

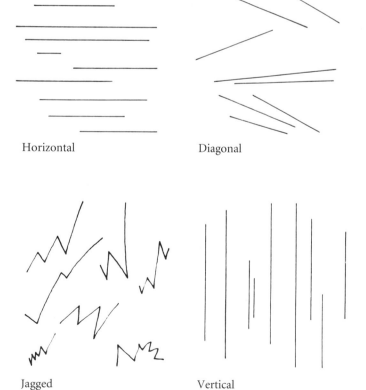

Horizontal   Diagonal

Straight   Curved   Jagged   Vertical

4–27

Lines Express Feelings

Artists communicate ideas and feelings through lines. Van Gogh's drawing of cypress trees shows how lines can express spiraling rhythm and energy. Create an abstract or nonobjective drawing. Try to show a particular idea or feeling through the lines you use.

a. Vincent van Gogh, *Grove of Cypresses*, 1889. Pen and ink over pencil on paper, 24″ x 18″ (61 x 46 cm). The Art Institute of Chicago, Illinois (Gift of Robert Allerton).

b. Leonardo da Vinci, *Study of a Tree.* The Royal Library, Windsor, England.

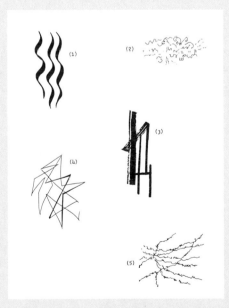

c. Match these words with the line drawings above. Timid, aggressive, strong, graceful, nervous.

d. Create abstract drawings in which lines communicate ideas or feelings.

Chapter 5
Shape and Form

Shape

A **shape** is a two-dimensional area with a recognizable boundary. You can make a shape by drawing or painting lines on paper. You can make a shape by cutting something out of paper. The edge of the shape implies a line. As you can see, there is a relationship between lines and shapes.

Here is a quiz for you to test your knowledge about shape. Choose the response that identifies the following figures:

Shape Quiz I

1. a. *a vase*
   b. *two faces*
   c. *either a or b*

2. a. *eight dots*
   b. *a circle*
   c. *two squares*
   d. *any of the above*

3. a. *a black and white pattern*
   b. *a locomotive*
   c. *either a or b*

Answers:
1. (c)
2. (d)
3. (c)

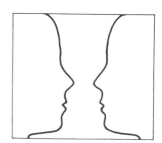

5–4 When you took the quiz, which did you see first: the vase or the faces? Did you see both? Can you see both at the same time? Does it matter whether the shapes are solid or outlined?

All of the shapes in the quiz can be seen in more than one way. Look again at the illustration for question 1 (fig. 5–4). It provides a good example of the tendency to see a **pattern** as two kinds of shapes: figure and ground. A **figure** appears to stand out, to be "on top of" a ground. A **ground**, on the other hand, appears to be underneath and surrounding a figure. The white shape in the illustration is the figure and the black shape around it is the ground *if you see the pattern as a vase*. However, the black shapes are figures and the white is the ground *if you see the pattern as two identical faces looking at each other*. Try to see it either way. Such a pattern can be "read" in two different ways, but not both ways at once. You can reverse the figure and ground. Artists use the term **positive shape** to refer to figure and **negative shape** to refer to ground.

Circle Limit IV by M. C. Escher (fig. 5–5) is an excellent example of figure-ground, or positive-negative, reversal in an artwork. Which is figure: black or white? Can you see it either way? Can you see it both ways simultaneously?

Maurits C. Escher

1898–1972

Devils link together and the spaces between them form angels. Or, do the spaces between the angels form devils? Maurits Cometis Escher experimented with many repeating patterns similar to the one in *Circle Limit IV*, in which the edges of one object help to form the shape of another.

Escher's fascination with the repetition of geometric shapes is just one aspect of his art. An accomplished printmaker, Escher first became interested in art in his high school in the Netherlands. There he learned to create designs by rolling ink on the textured surface of a carved linoleum plate, and imprinting this inked surface onto paper. This printmaking process could be repeated to make multiple copies of a single image.

Following formal training in graphic arts at college, Escher experimented with a range of subject matter for his prints. Early imagery included Escher's observations of the real world, especially scenes he recorded from visits to Italy and Spain. His interest in nature and reality gradually gave way to an obsession with invented landscapes—dreamy worlds filled with strange creatures and impossible perspectives.

Like the multiple patterns of devils and angels in *Circle Limit IV,* there are multiple levels on which to look at this artist: as a master printmaker, a master drawer, and as a man with a masterful sense of imagination and creativity.

5–5 What are the reversible figures in this print by Escher? In what ways does the meaning change when the figures are reversed? M. C. Escher, *Circle Limit IV,* 1960. Woodcut in two colors, diameter 13 ½″ (34 cm). ©1960 M. C. Escher Foundation, Baarn, Holland.

5-8 Did you see the locomotive when you took the quiz?

Return again to the quiz. Questions 2 and 3 involve *closure*. You learned about closure in the previous chapter. You probably saw the eight dots of question 2 as a circle (fig. 5–6). With some effort you could connect the dots to see them as forming two separate squares (fig. 5–7). It is much easier, however, to see a circle. The simplest shape is always the one that works best for closure.

Did you see question 3 as a random pattern of white shapes or as a locomotive (fig. 5–8)? At first you may not have seen the locomotive. But once your mind's eye connects the shapes, the locomotive stands out clearly.

At first glance, the cover of the 1938 issue of *Harper's Bazaar* (fig. 5–9) seems to be just some stripes that change color in the middle. A longer look reveals a few stars. The stars, together with the red and white stripes, remind us of the "stars and stripes," the American flag. Eventually, we see the image of a sewing machine. Because the sewing machine is not outlined, it is virtually a part of the black and lavender stripes. It is "embedded" in the background. It stands out from the background only because of a few changes in color and the addition of a spool of thread. The theme of the magazine is American fashion. In what ways does the cover express that theme? Do you think it is successful? Explain your answer.

The *Harper's* cover was influenced by early twentieth-century art, such as Picasso's *Three Musicians* (fig. 5–10). The painting can be read as an image of three musicians. Or it can be read as an abstract pattern of shapes. In fact, Picasso probably wanted you to appreciate the pattern more than the image, which is primarily humorous. The shapes of this painting are cleverly assembled. Although the shapes are not reversible, it is difficult to distinguish between figure and ground, or between positive and negative. Suppose this painting were an album cover. What kind of music would it be used for?

5-9 A. M. Cassandre, *Harper's Bazaar* magazine cover, March 1938, U.S.A. Courtesy *Harper's Bazaar*.

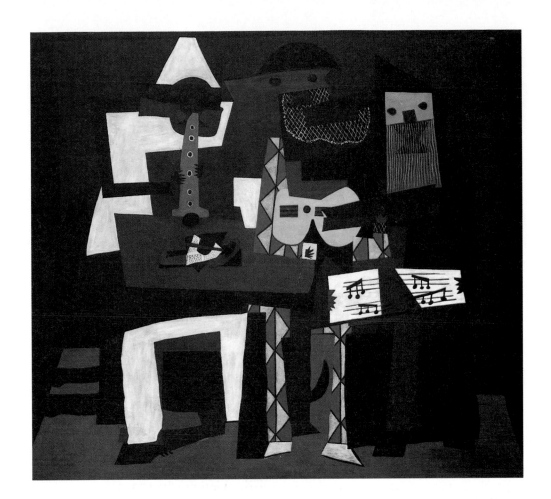

5–10 Pablo Picasso, *Three Musicians*, 1921. Oil on canvas, 6′ 7″ x 7′ 3 ¾″ (201 x 223 cm). The Museum of Modern Art, New York. Mrs. Simon Guggenheim Fund.

Studio Experience 5.1

Reversible Drawings

Produce an outline drawing in which figure and ground are reversible.

Studio Experience 5.2

Reversible Patterns

Create a reversible pattern. Cut an abstract figure out of construction paper. Then alternate the positive and negative shapes.

Kim Gass.

Chapter 5 *Shape and Form* 43

Form

Most of the things we use in everyday life are three-dimensional shapes, or **forms**. A form has height, width, and depth. The chair you are sitting on and the desk you are working at are good examples of forms.

Forms in Pictures

In this section we will cover forms in pictures, that is, the *representation of three-dimensional objects on a two-dimensional surface*.

Try this second quiz on shape. Answers to this quiz follow.

Shape Quiz II

1. a. an ellipse
   b. a football
   c. a top of a pop can
   d. any of the above

2. a. a trapezoid
   b. a blade of a knife
   c a side of a truck
   d. any of the above

5–13   5–14

5–18

5–19

5–20

5–21

5–15

5–16

5–17

You probably guessed that the answer for both questions was (d), any of the above. Like the examples used in the first quiz, these illustrations can be seen in different ways.

The example in question 1 is an ***ellipse*** (fig. 5–13). An ellipse is a curved shape that is longer in one dimension than it is in another.

But, in a picture, an ellipse can also represent a three-dimensional *ellipsoid* (fig. 5–14). A football is an ellipsoid. (Did you ever kick an ellipsoid? Did it bounce like a round ball, or *sphere*?) An ellipse can show the top of a pop can as seen from an angle (fig. 5–15). But as you know, the true shape of a pop can top is a circle (fig. 5–16).

You may think of the pop can top as being shaped like a circle, even when you see the top from an angle. This is an example of ***shape constancy***, or the tendency to see a shape as unchanging regardless of the angle at which you see it.

The artist who drew the ellipse wanted you to see it as a circle at an angle. He or she also wanted you to see the whole image as a three-dimensional *cylinder*. To make the pop can look as though it were on a table in front of you, the artist made the top look short in comparison with its width (fig. 5–17). The artist also curved the bottom edge of the can to match the curve of the ellipse at the top of the can. The object appears to be three-dimensional. Making a three-dimensional object in a picture appear to be seen at an angle by shortening one or two of its dimensions is called ***foreshortening***.

Now look at the shape in question 2 of the quiz (fig. 5–18). It is a *trapezoid* with four straight sides. Two of its sides are parallel. A trapezoid can easily be used to represent the flat blade of a utility knife (fig. 5–19). It can also represent the side of an eighteen-wheel truck that is coming toward you (fig. 5–20). Compare the foreshortened view of the truck with its full view (fig. 5–21). Because of shape constancy, you think of it as being the same truck.

The use of foreshortening to make objects appear three-dimensional is very common in traditional paintings. Virtually every item in Dirk Bouts's *Polyptych of the Last Supper* (fig. 5–22) has been foreshortened. Identify as many items as you can. Some of these have been diagramed to show how they appear in the picture as it is, and how they would appear if not foreshortened (fig. 5–23).

5-22 Dirk Bouts, *Polyptych of the Last Supper* (center panel), 1464–68. Oil on wood, 6′ x 5′ (183 x 153 cm). Louvain, Eglise de St. Pierre. Giraudon/Art Resource, NY.

5-23 Details of *Polyptych of the Last Supper*.

Not foreshortened

Foreshortened

5–24 Charles White, *Preacher,* 1952. Ink on cardboard, 21 3/8″ x 29 3/8″ (54 x 75 cm). Collection of The Whitney Museum of American Art (Purchase).

So far, we have seen examples of foreshortening in objects: pop cans, trucks, windows, and even floor tiles. Foreshortening can also be applied to people. Parts of Charles White's *Preacher* (fig. 5–24) are clearly foreshortened. Look at the lower part of his right arm, the upper part of his left arm, the palm and fingers of his right hand, and even his head. Notice how complicated the foreshortening is in both hands.

In Mary Cassatt's *The Bath* (fig. 5–25), both objects and people are foreshortened. This technique is readily seen in the forms of the basin and the pitcher. The effect of foreshortening is even more pronounced in the forms of mother and child. You may have noticed that their upper bodies, compared to their legs, are quite short. However, the most extreme effect of foreshortening occurs in their faces. Look at how close together the eyes and the mouth are in both faces.

Meet the Artist

Mary Cassatt

1844–1926

Ignoring the objections of her parents, in 1861 Mary Cassatt boldly enrolled at the Pennsylvania Academy of Fine Arts. With a strong independent nature and financial support she was able to complete four years of work at this important art school at a time when art was frowned upon as an occupation for women. Rather than remain quietly at home, Mary preferred a life full of adventure and art.

Her keen desire to learn brought Mary to Paris, the center of the art world in 1865. There she was able to pursue her studies of the great masters of the past, while meeting and working with the new and influential Impressionist artists. Mary learned unfamiliar artistic techniques from her new friends, such as printmaking and the use of colorful pastels to create soft images. She also explored Europe, enjoying museums and attending gallery exhibitions of international art, from as nearby as Italy to as far away as Japan.

Inspired by what she saw, Mary began to create paintings and prints with renewed enthusiasm. Her explorations on the subject of mother and child were numerous. The gentle caress of the mother as she washes her child in *The Bath* is just one example of the hundreds of maternal images which Mary created during her lifetime.

Throughout her travels, her years living in Europe, and those when she returned to the United States, Mary remained an independent woman. She never chose to marry or have children. Rather, Mary Cassatt focused her life on the pursuit of technical expertise in painting and printmaking, and on achieving a beauty in her life and art which is uniquely her own.

5–25 Mary Cassatt, *The Bath,* ca. 1891–92. Oil on canvas, 39 1/2″ x 26″ (100 x 66 cm). The Art Institute of Chicago, Robert A. Waller Fund.

5–26

5–27

Look at the illustration of the foreshortened truck (fig. 5–26). Did you notice that the back of the truck is shorter than the front? This is because the back is farther away. To make something appear farther away in a picture, the artist makes it smaller. To show something close, the artist makes it larger. We tend to think of an object's size as unchanging no matter how close or far away it is. This tendency is called *size constancy*. An illustration of size constancy can be seen in a picture of utility posts (fig. 5–27). The artist drew the farthest away post twice—once on the left-hand side and again on the right-hand side beside the nearest post. Were you surprised to learn how small the image of the farthest away post is?

Studio Experience 5.4

Distance

Study how distance affects the size of objects. Trace an outdoor scene on a windowpane. Notice how small the images are compared to their actual size. Then trace the drawing. Use ruled lines and shading to enhance the illusion of depth.

Studio Experience 5.3

Foreshortening

Create foreshortened shapes in drawings of geometric forms. Cut ellipses and trapezoids from paper to use as patterns.

5–28 Alexander Calder, *The Arch* (three views), 1975. Steel painted black, 56′ high. Storm King Art Center, Mountainville, New York. Photographs by Jerry Thompson. Purchase and by exchange.

Real Forms

So far we have been talking about three-dimensional forms *in pictures*. Technically, all the pictures in this book, even the photographs, have only two dimensions—height and width—even though they may represent depth. However, you are surrounded by real forms. You, the other students and the teacher, as well as tables, cupboards, equipment, books, and the room itself have height, width, and depth.

Sculpture, pottery, metalwork, and architecture are a few examples of three-dimensional art. When a person makes a sculpture, he or she is making a *real* form, not the picture of a form. Suppose you wanted to make a sculpture of a truck. You would not foreshorten the side to make it *seem* long. You would make it long in reality.

When you look at a sculpture, you need to move around it in order to see its different sides (fig. 5–28). The many-sided form of a sculpture does not have to be viewed just by the eyes. You can also "view" it by moving your hands across its different surfaces, edges, and corners.

Try it Yourself

Find a small object with an interesting shape—a tool, bowl, wood scrap, or small sculpture. Do not show your object to your classmates. Put all the objects into paper bags. Without looking inside the bags, "view" each object with your hands. Then draw pictures of the objects. Compare your drawings with the actual objects.

Studio Experience 5.5

Sculpting Without Seeing

Model a clay sculpture while blindfolded. Or conceal the clay in a paper bag. Form a mental image of the sculpture and use your sense of touch to shape the clay.

5–29 Organic Shapes and Forms.

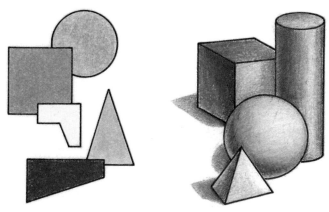

5–30 Geometric Shapes and Forms.

Expressive Qualities of Shapes and Forms

In Chapter 4 you learned about the expressive qualities of lines. For example, lines could be described as relaxed, excited, energetic, strong, or unstable. Shapes and forms also have expressive qualities. Artists typically classify shapes and forms as *organic* or *geometric* and *closed* or *open*.

Organic versus Geometric

Organic shapes and forms (fig. 5–29) are found throughout nature: earth, water, clouds, plants, animals, and people. Organic shapes tend to be irregular. Sometimes their edges are relatively straight, but never perfectly so. Sometimes their surfaces are relatively flat, but they are never perfect planes. Sometimes they are curved, but never perfectly round like a circle or a sphere.

Geometric shapes and forms (fig. 5–30) are typically found in things made by people, such as buildings, bridges, factories, and office machines. Unlike organic forms, geometric forms are very regular. Their edges and surfaces are straight or perfectly curved.

The forms of *The Mill* (fig. 5–31), a famous landscape painting by Rembrandt, are primarily organic. Even the few human-made objects, such as the mill and the rampart wall below the mill, show the effects of natural weathering and erosion. The edges of the forms are irregular.

Compare this painting to *House by the Railroad* (fig. 5–32) by Edward Hopper. The forms are primarily geometric. Except for the somewhat irregular lines of the roof and windows, the rest of the lines are fairly regular and straight. Note the vertical lines of the sides of the house. Horizontal lines are used for the eaves, the porch overhang, and the railroad track. Finally, notice the diagonal line of the shadow.

5–31 What do the geometric forms used in this painting seem to be expressing? Are the forms open or closed? Rembrandt van Rijn, *The Mill*, ca. 1650. Oil on canvas, 34 1/2″ x 41 5/8″ (0.88 x 1.06 m). ©1993 National Gallery of Art, Washington, Widener Collection.

5–32 As in the Rembrandt, can you tell what the geometric forms in this painting express? Are the forms open or closed? Edward Hopper, *House by the Railroad*, 1925. Oil on canvas, 24″ x 29″ (61 x 74 cm). Collection, The Museum of Modern Art, New York. Given anonymously.

Closed versus Open

The scenes by Rembrandt and Hopper are similar. Both consist of single buildings set against the sky. Both express loneliness. The geometric forms in *House by the Railroad* make the loneliness seem even "starker." Furthermore, the forms in both paintings seem solid and heavy. The mill and the land it rests on seem massive. Even though the house by the tracks has a few windows, it looks heavy and dense. These are **closed forms** in both paintings. Nothing can penetrate them.

Open shapes and forms, on the other hand, allow space to penetrate. Notice the forms in the landscape *Pine Trees* (fig. 5–33) by Hasegawa Tohaku. Unlike the forms of Rembrandt and Hopper, the Tohaku trees are so open they almost float. Indeed, space penetrates the entire landscape. The pines are surrounded by acres of mist and light. How do the ideas and feelings expressed in the Tohaku compare with those in the Rembrandt? the Hopper?

5-33 Hasegawa Tohaku, *Pine Trees*, Momoyama Period, Japan, 1539–1610. Ink on paper, 61″ (155 cm) high. Tokyo National Museum. (Photo courtesy the International Society for Educational Information, Inc.)

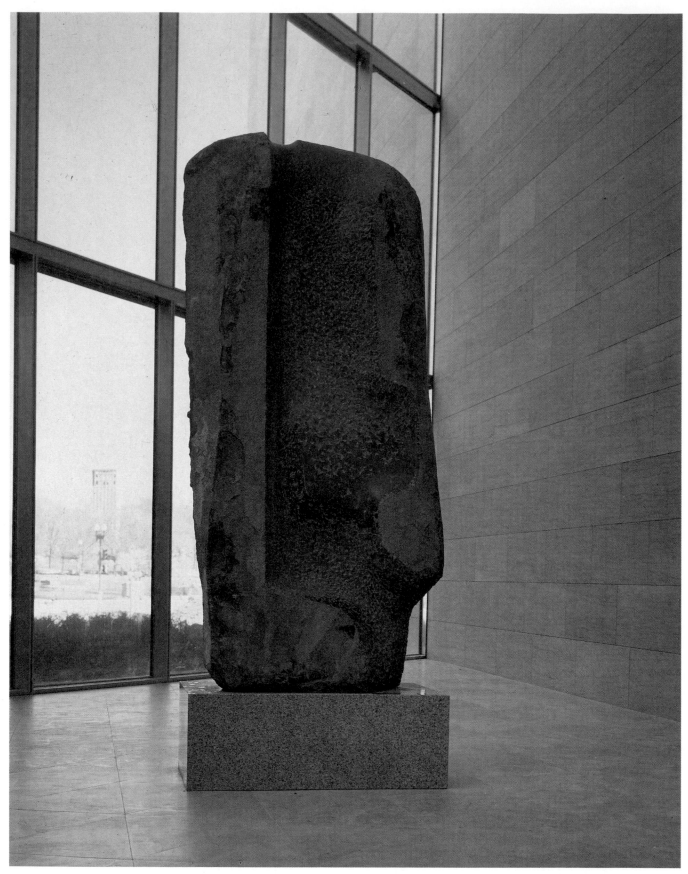

5–34 Isamu Noguchi, *Great Rock of Inner Seeking,* 1974. Basalt, 128″ x 63″ x 35″ (325 x 160 x 89 cm). ©1993 National Gallery of Art, Washington. Gift of Arthur M. Sackler, M.D. and Mortimer D. Sackler, M.D.

Forms in abstract art can also be described as organic or geometric and closed or open. The abstract sculpture in figure 5–34 by Isamu Noguchi is organic and closed. Abstract art does not represent things we see. However, it does express ideas. Noguchi's piece is called *Great Rock of Inner Seeking*. Do you think that it expresses the ideas suggested in the title? Explain your answer. Why did the artist use an organic form? a closed form?

Like the Noguchi piece, *Untitled* (fig. 5–35) by Doris Leeper is abstract. However, it is geometric and open. Even though it is open, does it seem as light as Tohaku's pines?

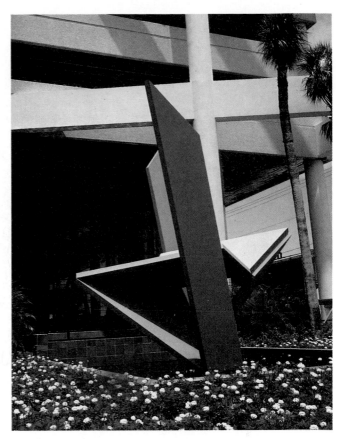

5–35 Doris Leeper, *Untitled*, 1984. Epoxy over aluminum, 15′ 3″ x 13′ 3″ x 12′ 9 ¼″. Barnett Centra, West Palm Beach, Florida. Photograph: David Zicki. Courtesy of the artist.

Try it Yourself

On a piece of paper, write a few sentences about the ideas and feelings that you think are expressed by Tohaku's *Pine Trees*, Noguchi's *Great Rock of Inner Seeking*, and Leeper's *Untitled*. Explain how the types of forms used in each work—organic or geometric, closed or open—affect the ideas and feelings that the work expresses.

Summary

Shapes, like the letters and pictures in this book, have height and width but no depth. Forms, on the other hand, have height, width, and depth. Most of the things in this world, like ourselves, are forms.

This chapter discussed our tendencies to see shapes in certain ways. We see shapes in terms of figure-ground, closure, shape constancy, and size constancy. Figure-ground and closure often occur when we look at pictures or simple two-dimensional patterns. Shape and size constancy affect what we see when we look at both real forms and pictures of forms.

An artist often uses foreshortening to represent three-dimensional objects in a picture. Furthermore, an artist will make an object larger or smaller in a picture to make it appear to be closer or farther away.

Artists who make sculptures or pottery, and who design buildings or interiors, deal with real forms. To see a three-dimensional artwork such as a sculpture in its entirety, a viewer must see its many sides. A sculpture can also be appreciated through the sense of touch.

Finally, it is possible to classify shapes and forms as organic or geometric and as closed or open. Organic shapes and forms are typical of forms found in nature. With the exception of the planets and stars in the sky, and some crystals on the earth, geometric forms are almost always human-made. Closed forms tend to be dense or massive. Open forms are penetrated with negative shapes or space.

Try it Yourself

Now that you have learned more about shape, go back to your description of Renoir's *Luncheon of the Boating Party*. Can you see in the painting any examples of foreshortening? Are some of the forms of people larger than others? Why? Which forms are organic? Which, if any, are geometric? Which are closed? Which are open?

6–1 Michelangelo, *God Separating Light from Darkness.* The Sistine Chapel, The Vatican, Rome. Scala/Art Resource, NY.

Chapter 6
Value and Color

Light and Dark

Without light we could not see lines, shapes, forms, or any objects. In fact, unless it is a source of light itself, an object is visible only to the extent that it *reflects* light.

Light, along with its opposite, dark, appears in the legends of most cultures. Among the episodes illus-trated on the Sistine Chapel ceiling by Michelangelo is the separation of light and dark (fig. 6–1). Light is often used to symbolize truth, hope, and new life. On the other hand, dark is often associated with evil, the fear of the unknown, and death. Have you ever seen the sky just before a storm when light turns to dark (fig. 6–2)? Light and dark are also important in art.

6–2 Light colors colliding with contrasting dark colors produce drama in a picture. Cynthia Stanton, *A Wild and Wicked Sky near Remus, Michigan,* August 16, 1988. Reprinted with permission of the Helen Dwight Reid Educational Foundation. Published by Heldref Publications, 1319 Eighteenth St., N.W., Washington, DC. 20036-1802. ©1988.

6–4 Value helps us to differentiate one form from another. Imagine what the world would be like if nothing had color. Pierre Auguste Renoir, *Luncheon of the Boating Party*, 1881. Oil on canvas, 51″ x 68″ (130 x 173 cm). © The Phillips Collection, Washington, DC.

Value

Imagine the possible ranges of light and dark in this world. One extreme might be looking directly at the noonday sun. The other might be experiencing the blackness of a deep cave. But in daily life the range of light and dark is much less dramatic than that.

In artwork, the range of light and dark (seen under normal light conditions) is known as *value*. Typically, values are represented on a nine-step scale (fig. 6–3). White is at one extreme and black is at the other. In "black-and-white" reproductions (fig. 6–4) everything consists of different values on the gray value scale. You are able to distinguish different objects because of their different values.

The lightness or darkness of a particular value is *relative*, depending on its context. In other words it is light or dark in comparison to its surroundings. For example, the banjo face in Henry O. Tanner's *The Banjo Lesson* (fig. 6–5) appears light when compared to the shadows around it. But compared to the light values in the background, it appears rather dark.

6–5 Henry O. Tanner, *The Banjo Lesson*, 1893. Oil on canvas. 4′ ½″ x 3′ 11″ (123 x 119 cm). Hampton University Museum, Hampton, Virginia.

6–6 What is the color of the egg: white or dark gray?

The amount of reflected light can make the value of an object seem lighter or darker. You see the egg in figure 6–6 as being very light—either white or off-white. Now cover the upper half of the egg with your hand. You see that the lower half of the form is not very light (or white) at all. Reflected light causes the difference in value between the top and bottom halves of the egg. In this case, the reflection is stronger on the top.

Artists often take reflected light into account when they want to make a form look solid. The artist made the polyhedron (fig. 6–7) look three-dimensional by making some surfaces darker than others. Using lighter and darker values to make something look three-dimensional is called **shading**. The technical term is **chiaroscuro** (kee-ah´-ro-skuh´-ro), an Italian word that literally means light-dark. Earlier, in Chapter 4, you saw an example of shading (fig. 4–13). Hatching and crosshatching was used to make the caricature of a celebrity look more three-dimensional.

Try it Yourself

Cut a ½" hole out of the middle of a piece of paper. Lay the paper over the drawing of the polyhedron. Move the paper around. Can you see that the values go from very light to very dark? Do the same with the picture of the egg.

Studio Experience 6.1

Value Contrasts

Create a black and white tempera painting of a still life. Shine a single light on the still life from one side. Use different values to suggest a mood and to make the objects appear three-dimensional.

a. Kristy Skully.

b. Maria Alvarez.

6–7 How many values did the artist use to make this polyhedron appear solid?

Value and Artistic Expression

Shading is a very effective way for an artist to create a mood. You may recall that light and dark often stand for good and evil. Artists will very often use value to express these moods. However, light and dark do not always stand for good and evil. Look back at two examples in Chapter 5. In Hopper's *House by the Railroad* (fig. 5–32), the light seems oppressive and depressing. In Rembrandt's *The Mill* (fig. 5–31), the darkness seems peaceful.

In *A Woman in White* (fig. 6–8), Picasso used mostly the middle range of the value scale. He kept the contrasts of light and dark to a minimum. The colors are neither very light nor very dark. The whole picture seems bathed in a bright, but soft light. This light gives a peaceful feeling. The woman herself looks peaceful and relaxed. In this painting, light seems to play a positive role. Do you think that the light was meant to symbolize something positive about womanhood? Why?

The artist used mostly the dark end of the value scale in *Mademoiselle Charlotte du Val d'Ognes* (fig. 6–9). However, very light values were used in places. A single source of light illuminates one side of the woman. The rest of the picture is left in relative darkness. The use of dark shading and strong contrast to create drama or establish a mood was very popular in the 1600s and 1700s. Like Picasso's woman, Mademoiselle Charlotte seems relaxed, though perhaps more solemn. Here, dark contributes to a somber mood, but not necessarily an evil one.

6–8 Pablo Picasso, *Woman in White*, 1923. Oil on canvas, 39″ x 31 ½″ (99 x 80 cm). The Metropolitan Museum of Art, Rogers Fund, 1951; from the Museum of Modern Art, Lizzie P. Bliss Collection.

6–9 French Painter, Unknown, Portrait of a Young Woman, called *Mademoiselle Charlotte du Val d'Ognes.* Oil on canvas, 63 ½″ x 50 ⅝″ (161 x 129 cm). The Metropolitan Museum of Art, Bequest of Isaac D. Fletcher, 1917. Mr. and Mrs. Isaac D. Fletcher Collection.

6–10 The visible spectrum.

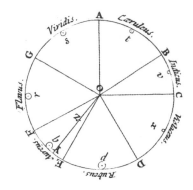

6–11 *Newton's Color Wheel*, from Isaac Newton, *Optice*, 1706. The British Library, London.

Color

Of all the visual elements, **color** is the most fascinating and puzzling. Because of its effects on people, color has been studied more than any of the other elements. To analyze color, we must return to the discussion of light.

In a famous experiment over three hundred years ago, Isaac Newton demonstrated that light is very complicated. He also showed that color is a property of light. When a beam of light passes through a glass object, called a prism, the light divides into the seven colors of the rainbow (fig. 6–10). Each of these colors represents a different ray of light. All seven rays—a small fraction of the total number of light rays—make up what is known as the *spectrum*. Newton demonstrated that white light includes all of the spectrum colors. Newton created a color circle to show the spectrum colors (fig. 6–11). Today we use a color wheel (fig. 6–15).

The average person thinks of color as belonging to objects. Strictly speaking, this is not true. There is a difference between light and *reflected* light. Light is the real source of color. Reflected light is the light given off by objects. When white light strikes a red apple, the apple looks red because it *absorbs* every color of light *except* red, which it reflects. A lemon absorbs all the colors except yellow (fig. 6–12). When light is totally absorbed by an object, the object appears black.

Color has three dimensions: hue, value, and saturation.

Hue

Hue identifies a color as blue, yellow, red, or green, and so on, as seen in the spectrum or the color wheel. In addition to the hues of the spectrum, an infinite number of hues can be created through intermixing.

At this point, however, a distinction must be made between colored light and pigment. Pigment is the col-

6–15 Color wheel.

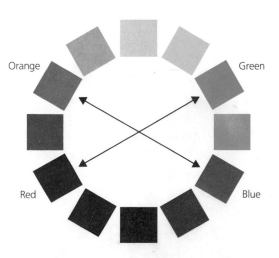

6–16 Complementary colors are opposite in hue and are also opposite each other on the color wheel.

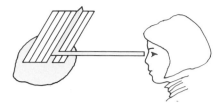

6–12 A lemon absorbs all the colors of light except yellow.

6–13 Primary and secondary hues in lights.

6–14 Primary and secondary hues in pigments.

oring matter found in such things as inks, crayons, paints, dyes, and glazes. Mixing colored lights is an *additive* process. When all colors are combined, the result is white (fig. 6–13). Mixing pigments, on the other hand, is *subtractive*. Pigments behave the same way as the surfaces of lemons or apples. They absorb all the colored rays except those we see.

Combining many different colors creates increasingly darker results—as you know if you've ever mixed paints. Theoretically if all three primaries are combined in the correct proportions, the final result would be black (fig. 6–14). A black surface absorbs all the spectrum colors. Since almost all artworks involve the use of pigments, the following discussion will focus on the behavior of pigment hues.

Red, yellow, and blue are called *primary colors*. Supposedly you can make any other hue with just these three, if you know how to mix them properly. Yellow and red make orange, yellow and blue make green, and red and blue make violet. Orange, green, and violet are called *secondary colors*. Notice that on the color wheel (fig. 6–15), each secondary color is placed midway between the primary colors that produced it. Lying between the primaries and secondaries are the ***intermediate colors***: yellow-orange, yellow-green, blue-green, blue-violet, red-violet, and red-orange. These are made by unequal mixing of primaries. For example, approximately two parts yellow mixed with one part red produces yellow-orange.

Hues directly opposite each other on the color wheel are called ***complementaries***: red and green, orange and blue, yellow-orange and blue-violet, and so on (fig. 6–16). In addition to being opposite geographically, they are exactly opposite in hue. For example, yellow, a primary color, has nothing in common with its complement, violet, which is composed of red and blue. Complementaries play a role in both *saturation* and *color harmonies* (discussions follow).

Studio Experience 6.2

Related Colors

Mix red, yellow, and blue tempera paint to create a picture using only secondary and intermediate colors.

Next try making a hue that lies between a secondary and an intermediate hue, such as bluish green (between green and blue-green).

Can you think of some fancy names—turquoise, aqua—for these in-between hues? Can you invent some new colors?

a. Ellen Zauke

b. Christopher Green.

Value

You have already learned about the element of value. Value can be associated with shades of gray. Black, white, and gray are sometimes called neutral colors, or *neutrals.* These three colors have no hues.

However, value is an aspect of all colors. Every color has a normal value, which is shown on the wheel. The value, or the lightness and darkness of a color, can be changed by adding white or black to the color. Different values of red (fig. 6–17), for example, can be shown on a value scale. Lighter values of a color are called *tints.* Darker values are called *shades.*

Artists sometimes create paintings that use tints and shades of just one color. Such paintings are called **monochromatic,** meaning one color.

Saturation

Saturation describes the brightness and dullness of a color. It is sometimes called **intensity**. A color's saturation can be represented on a scale from bright to gray or dull (fig. 6–18). All of the hues on the color wheel are bright (or as bright as the printer was able to make them).

Yellow, blue, or red paint straight from the bottle will be bright. Mixing any two of the primaries, as you saw earlier, produces a new color. Secondary or intermediate hues on the color wheel are also bright. But if you mix a color with its *complement,* the resulting color will be a duller one, because each color subtracts from the other. If you mix complementaries in the right proportions, not necessarily in equal amounts, the result may be a neutral gray (fig. 6–19).

6–17 Value scale of red. What color should be added to make a tint of red?

6–18 Saturation or intensity scales for orange and blue.

Studio Experience 6.3

Monochromatic Colors

Produce a monochromatic painting using a color and black and white. Use at least five values of the color you chose.

a. Roz Kellerman.

b. Mike Hernandez.

6–19 Mixing a color with its complement can produce a neutral gray.

Colors of low saturation that have identifiable hues can be just as beautiful as bright colors. Most of the colors in nature are of this type: the olive greens and forest greens of spring and summer, and the golden yellows, burnt oranges, and brown-reds of fall (fig. 6–20).

The colors of clothes are not always bright. They may be dulled reds, greens, and blues, as well as browns. The colors of woodwork also tend to be of low saturation: mahogany (deep reddish brown), oak (brownish yellow), and maple (brownish yellow-orange).

Studio Experience 6.4

Mixing Bright and Dull Colors

Use tempera paint to mix a color with its complement to produce a nine-step saturation scale. You should have a pure color at one end, three saturation changes, gray in the middle, three saturation changes, and the second color at the other end.

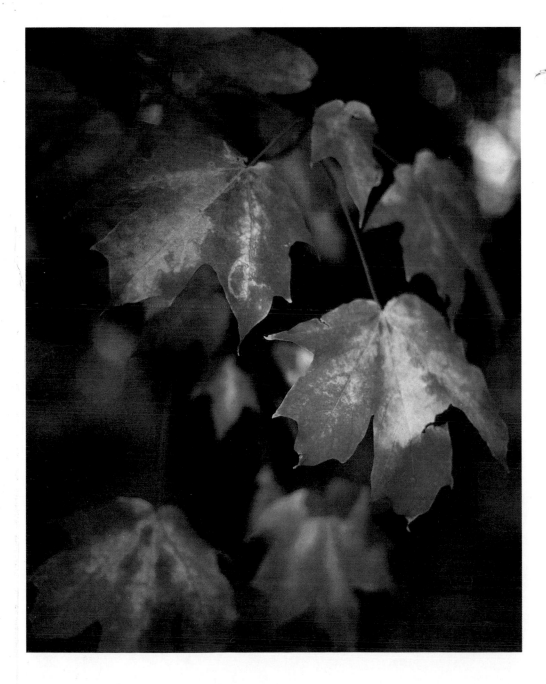

6–20 Which of the colors are saturated? Which are of low saturation? Photograph: Barbara Caldwell.

Matching Colors

Find some materials such as pieces of fabric, leaves, colored papers, labels, and wrappers. Mix paint to match their colors.

Judy Bertolotto.

Kelly Strufert.

6–21 Which of the smaller squares appears more orange? Why?

6–22 A tint appears much darker on which field of color?

6–23 Which of the smaller squares appears to be of brighter intensity?

Color Interactions

Colors can be affected by other colors. A particular color can look different when placed side-by-side or on top of another color. Its hue, value, or saturation can be affected, depending on the combination. The following illustrations provide some examples.

Hue Interaction. A patch of yellow-orange appears more orange on top of a square of yellow. On top of a square of orange, it appears more yellow (fig. 6–21).

Value Interaction. A tint appears much darker on light color than it does on black (fig. 6–22).

Intensity Interaction. A medium bright blue will appear brighter on top of a neutral than it does on top of a bright blue (fig. 6–23).

Color Harmonies

Color harmonies are combinations of colors that are considered satisfying, or that produce certain effects. In the discussion of *hue,* you learned some color groups: secondaries, complementaries, and so on. These color combinations can also be thought of as types of color harmonies, or color *schemes.*

Triad harmonies consist of three equidistant hues on the color wheel. The triad harmony shown in figure 6–24 is made up of the three secondary colors. Other triad harmonies would be the primaries or three of the intermediates. Because of their mutual dissimilarity, a triad of the primary colors would be the most daring combination. Secondary or intermediate hues, on the

6-25 Helen Frankenthaler, *Cravat,* 1973. Acrylic on canvas.
62 ½″ x 58 ¾″ (159 x 149 cm). Courtesy of the artist.

other hand, are apt to be more agreeable because of their shared colors. Perhaps that is why Helen Frankenthaler chose a triad harmony of secondary colors. She poured diluted colors of violet, green, and orange onto a white canvas (fig. 6–25).

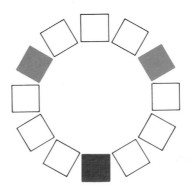

6-24 A triad scheme.

Complementary colors, as we have seen before, are opposite colors. Therefore, a *complementary combination* would provide the strongest contrast. There is a greater chance that the colors would "clash." For this reason, some designers prefer a **split complementary** scheme. They might choose one hue and combine it with hues on either side of its complement (fig. 6–26). This brings two of the colors closer together and tends to tone down the "violence" somewhat. The trim colors in Paris architect Jean Satosme's living room (fig.

6–27) consist of red against a variety of yellow-greens and blue-greens. These colors are split complementaries of red.

Analogous harmonies consist of adjacent hues on the color wheel, for example, yellow, yellow-green, green, and blue-green (fig. 6–28). Because of their strong "family resemblances," these kinds of hues are very agreeable. Yet they are different enough to provide interest. If necessary, contrast can be strengthened by varying the values. The inlaid colors decorating the

6–26 Split complementary scheme.

6–28 An analogous scheme.

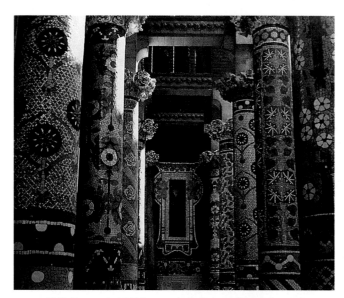

6–29 Llúis Domenèchi i Montaner, Balcony of the Palace of Catalan Music (Palau de la Musica Catalana), Barcelona. Art Resource, NY.

6–27 How do the neutral tones help soften the contrast in this interior?

balcony pillars of a music palace (fig. 6–29) range between red and blue-violet. The colors, along with the rich patterns, contribute significantly to the overall splendor.

Monochromatic combinations use tints and shades of one hue only (fig. 6–17). Because all the colors are the same hue, they go together very well. However, with the gain in harmony comes a loss of boldness. A monochromatic scheme risks being uninteresting because it is the least daring. However, Picasso's *The Old Guitarist* (fig. 6–30), which is mainly monochromatic, could not be called uninteresting. Because of the subject, the colors are very appropriate and contribute to the mood of sadness.

Expressive Qualities of Color

Why is blue appropriate for a picture with a sad mood? Imagine *The Old Guitarist* painted in tones of red, yellow, or orange. Given these alternatives, blue clearly seems to be the best choice. But this is not to say that blue always expresses sadness. In other contexts, blue can suggest such qualities as serenity, dignity, and elegance.

Color and its effects on people have been the subject of more research (and guesswork) than any other visual element. Red is said to raise blood pressure, while blue lowers it. Pink, a tint of red, has been shown to have a calming effect on violent children. In one experiment, factory workers thought that the building temperature had been raised after the colors of the walls were changed from blue and gray to red and brown. In fact, the temperature had remained at 70 degrees.

Artists are aware of the power of color. Artists divide colors into warm and cool categories. Reds, oranges, and yellows (the colors on the left side of the wheel) are considered *warm* colors. Blues, greens, and violets (the colors on the right) are considered *cool* colors (fig. 6–31). Reds and yellows make us think of such things as blood, fire, and the sun. Blues, greens, and violets remind us of sky, water, trees, grass, and shade. Whatever the reasons, the use of warm colors in a design is likely to excite us, while cool colors are likely to have a quieting effect.

Vincent van Gogh was one of the first artists to understand how color could be used for its own sake. He wrote about a painting in a letter to his brother, Theo: "I tried to express the terrible passions of humanity by means of red and green." Van Gogh often

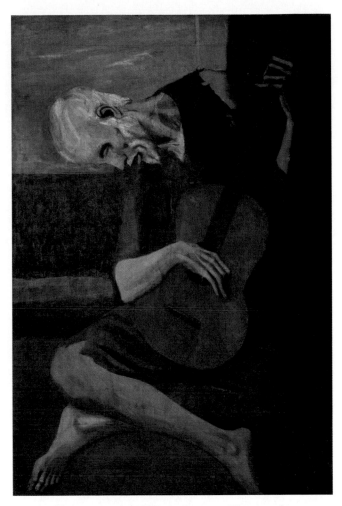

6–30 Pablo Picasso, *The Old Guitarist*, 1903. Oil on panel, 48″ x 32 ½″ (123 x 82 cm). The Art Institute of Chicago, Helen Birch Bartlett Memorial Collection.

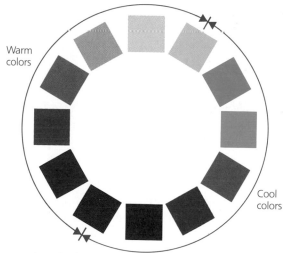

Warm colors

Cool colors

6–31 Color wheel.

6-32 Vincent van Gogh, *The Artist's Bedroom at Arles,* 1889. Oil on canvas, 28″ x 36″ (72 x 91 cm). Stedelijk Museum, Amsterdam.

used color as a cry of pain and anguish, but he also used it in more peaceful ways. Two paintings of his bedroom are shown here. One uses mostly warm colors (fig. 6-32). The other uses mostly cool colors (fig. 6-33). Almost everything in these pictures is similar except their colors.

Color is something that you have lived with all your life. Are you surprised to learn that color is so complicated? Actually this discussion barely scratches the surface. Entire books have been written about color theory and the variables of color. Artists and designers deal with these issues all the time.

Why learn more about color? In some tribal cultures, color is not very important. The people in those cultures have normal vision, but they do not recognize many hues. In one culture, the people had words only

for light and dark and the color red. In effect, the people could not "see" yellows, oranges, pinks, blues, and so forth.

Think what you would be missing if the only hue you could distinguish were red! Knowing more about color enables you to *see* more of it. This will help you to enjoy the infinite variety and rich possibilities of color in art, and also in life (fig. 6-34).

6-33 Vincent van Gogh, *The Bedroom*, 1888. Oil on canvas, 29″ x 36″ (74 x 91 cm). The Art Institute of Chicago, Helen Birch Bartlett Memorial Collection.

Meet the Artist

Vincent van Gogh

1853–1890

In 1988, Vincent van Gogh's colorful painting of irises sold for over fifty million dollars. But did you know that van Gogh died a penniless man? Van Gogh spent most of his life without money or possessions, choosing instead to devote his life to art.

Vincent was born in a small town in Holland near the border of Belgium. Throughout his life, Vincent maintained a strong relationship with his brother, Theo, who supported Vincent emotionally and financially throughout his career as an artist. There were times in Vincent's life when he was extremely depressed and experienced periods of mental illness. During these times, when he was staying at a hospital in St. Remy, France, and later when he moved to Auvers-sur-Oise, near Paris, Vincent was able to depend on Theo's love and assistance. Theo remained a source of support until the end of his brother's life, when Vincent committed suicide in 1890.

In a letter to his brother, Vincent once asked: "How…can I make myself useful, what end can I serve?" The answer to that question is in the bold brushstrokes, the brilliant colors, and the unique images which he portrayed in his paintings.

Describe the colors of both van Gogh paintings in terms of their hue, value, and saturation. Also describe your reactions to the colors of each. Which do you prefer, the warm or the cool painting? Why?

Imagine you are an interior decorator. What colors would you use to paint a hospital room? What colors would relax patients? cheer them up? Would your choice depend on the ages of the patients? Explain.

Imagine you are designing stage settings for a play. What colors would you use for a lively musical? a mystery set in England? a comedy?

Imagine you are a graphic designer. What colors would you use in a safety poster? an ecology poster? a travel poster?

Studio Experience 6.6

Warm and Cool Colors

To understand the expressive potential of color, create two pictures of one scene. Draw one picture in warm colors and one in cool colors. Use oil crayon on colored paper.

a. Mike Perrot.

b. Student work.

6-34 How do these colors contribute to the festive mood of the occasion? *Balloon Festival.* Photograph courtesy Ray Miller.

Summary

This chapter is about two related elements: value and color. The source of both value and color is light.

Value refers to the range of light and dark that can be seen in a work of art. This range can be represented in a value scale with white at one extreme and black at the other. An object's surfaces have lighter or darker values depending on the amount of light they reflect. Representing the surface light of an object is called shading or chiaroscuro.

Color, a powerful element in the hands of the artist, is a complicated subject. Usually, artists are involved with colors of pigments rather than colors of light. Pigments absorb light rays, reflecting only the colors not absorbed. Combining all pigments results in black, the absorption of all light rays.

Hue is the name of a color as seen in the spectrum or color wheel. Hues can be divided into groupings such as primary, secondary, and complementary.

Value applies to the lightness or darkness of a color on a scale from white to black.

Saturation describes the brightness or dullness of a color on a scale from bright to gray.

Hue, value, and saturation are affected by color interaction. Certain color combinations, or color schemes, are used often by artists and designers.

Color affects people. It is a powerful tool for expression and for prompting aesthetic responses. Artists divide hues into warm and cool categories, each with certain expressive and aesthetic potentials.

Try it Yourself

Now that you have learned more about color, go back to your description of Renoir's *Luncheon of the Boating Party*. Can you add anything new about the colors? For example, how would you identify the color of the stripes of the awning in terms of hue, value, and saturation? Would you describe the colors in this picture as being mostly light or mostly dark? mostly bright or mostly dull? mostly warm or mostly cool? Why?

Chapter 7
Space

Answer these true–false questions before reading about space.

Space Quiz

1. Space is empty. (T–F)
2. Space is always invisible. (T–F)
3. Unlike shape or form, space cannot be measured. (T–F)
4. The experience of space can be related to the sense of movement. (T–F)
5. Spatial is the adjective form of the word space. (T–F)

7–1 Claude Monet, *La Gare St. Lazare, Paris*, 1877. Oil on canvas, 32 ½″ x 39 ¾″ (83 x 101 cm). Fogg Art Museum, Cambridge, Massachusetts (Maurice Wertheim Collection).

Space in Our Environment

We often think of *space* as the emptiness that surrounds objects, or the emptiness inside of hollow shapes such as boxes or buildings. Also, we think of space as being invisible. So, why is it considered one of the visual elements? There are at least two answers to that question.

First, space on this earth is not really empty. It is filled with oxygen and other gases we call air. And as you know, air is not always clean and clear. Sometimes it is full of smoke, dust, or *pollution* (fig. 7–1) that can be seen. Sometimes it is full of particles of water and dust that we call *clouds* (fig. 7–2) or *fog,* which can also be seen. So, space is not always invisible.

Second, we "see" space by seeing its *boundaries.* The space inside a room has size and form. For example, the ceiling, floor, and walls of a room (fig. 7–3) determine the size and form of a space. Interior space in a room is often called **volume.** Outdoors, the size and form of a space is determined by buildings, plants, reflecting pools, and other objects (fig. 7–4). We could say that space is "empty form."

You can sense, or experience, space around you through movement. While sitting at your desk, you can sense the space under the desk simply by moving your legs and feet. You can sense the size and volume of your classroom, or its **spatial** aspects, by walking around in it. (You can also sense the spatial aspects by just looking around the room.)

How did you do on the quiz? The correct answers are:

1.F, 2.F, 3.F, 4.T, 5.T.

Try it Yourself

How well do you know the location of things in your room at home? Stand in the center of the room. Then, with your eyes closed, try to find the middle drawer of your dresser. Can you sense the correct direction, distance, and height of the drawer (or other object)?

7–2 Photograph: Barbara Caldwell.

7–3 The Hasso-no-seki tea room, Konchi-in temple, Kyoto.

7–4 Foreign Office Building, Brasilia.

7–5 *East Building of the National Gallery of Art, Washington.*
©1993 National Gallery of Art, Washington, opened 1978,
I. M. Pei, architect.

7–6 *West Building of the National Gallery of Art, Washington.*
©1993 National Gallery of Art, Washington, opened 1941,
John Russell Pope, architect.

Space in Three-Dimensional Art

To the architect, space is probably the most important visual element. An architect must design pleasing and interesting spaces in which people live, work, or play. The architect I. M. Pei did just that in 1978 when he designed the central court of the East Building of the National Gallery of Art (fig. 7-5). The spaces in the central court vary in size, form, and even level. These spaces provide an exciting environment for strolling and viewing art.

The interior of the National Gallery's rotunda (fig. 7–6) is very different. The rotunda was designed by John Russell Pope and completed in 1941. The rotunda is a large, circular area defined by huge columns. It does not have the same variety of Pei's central court.

Yet the rotunda is as dramatic as the newer interior. Pope's design is formal. It follows the traditional rules of architecture. Pei's design is modern and informal.

The courtyard of a library (fig. 7–7) in San Juan Capistrano, California, is rather formal even though it is quite new. The courtyard was designed by Michael Graves in 1983. The rectangular space of the courtyard is *symmetrical*, or identical on both sides. It is less dramatic than either of the interiors at the National Gallery, but it is no less beautiful. And it is very appropriate for the peace and quiet of a library. Which of the three spaces do you prefer? Why?

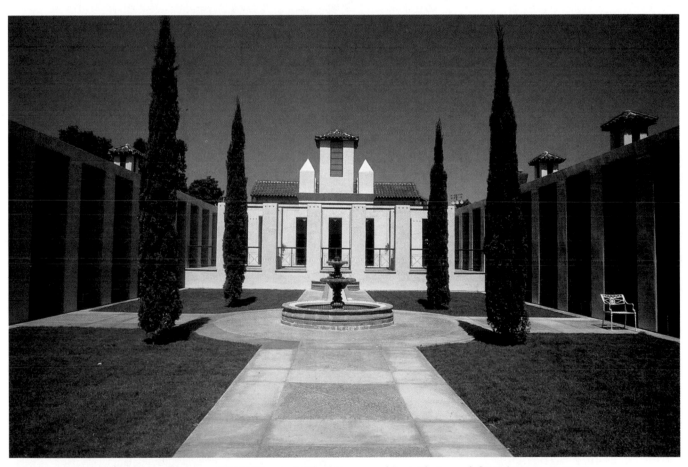

7–7 San Juan Capistrano Regional Library; SJC, California. Michael Graves, architect. Photograph ©1986 by Bruce Iverson.

7–8 Barbara Hepworth, *Pendour*, 1947. Painted wood, 12 ⅛″ x 28 ⅜″ x 9 ⅜″ (31 x 72 x 24 cm). Hirshhorn Museum and Sculpture Garden, Smithsonian Institution, Gift of Joseph H. Hirshhorn, 1966.

Space is also important to the sculptor. Modern sculptors often work with open forms, as Doris Leeper did in her sculpture *Untitled* (fig. 5–35). Barbara Hepworth's *Pendour* (fig. 7–8) is carved wood. The artist intentionally carved openings in it to create a unique relationship between form and space, or positive and negative.

A more extreme example of open form is *Linear Construction* (fig. 7–9) by Naum Gabo. Made of a plastic frame and nylon strings, it is more like a harp than a traditional sculpture. On a much larger scale is Alexander Calder's huge *mobile*. Part of this mobile can be seen in figure 7–5. The mobile hangs in the East Building of the National Gallery.

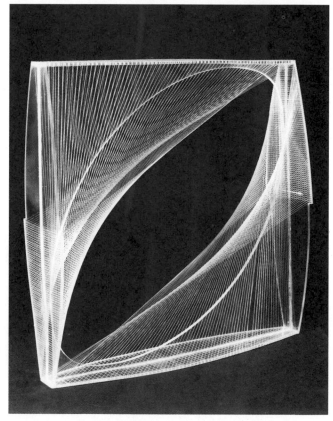

7–9 Naum Gabo, *Linear Construction*, 1942–43. Plastic with plastic threads, 14″ x 13 ⅝″ x 3 ½″ (36 x 35 x 9 cm). The Tate Gallery, London/Art Resource, NY.

Red Grooms

1937–

Beneath layers of plastic, acrylic and brilliantly colored paint hides a wire armature, or skeleton base, draped with canvas and burlap. These materials, molded into bucking horses, high-riding cowgirls and cowboys, and gymnastic clowns, fill a fifty-foot long space.

Red Grooms decided to create *Ruckus Rodeo* after visiting a state fair in Fort Worth, Texas. In this sculptured environment, the artist has re-created certain events which you might see at a rodeo, but has exaggerated and distorted the details. A green horse with a yellow mane throws his rider in the air. A sixteen-foot-tall yellow bull sports six-foot-long horns. Cowboys wrestle steers and ride bareback broncos while fans cheer and hats are enthusiastically waved in the air. The sizes, colors, and actions of the people and animals in *Ruckus Rodeo* are unrealistic and imaginary.

This life-size walk-in sculpture of a western rodeo has been termed a **sculpto-pictorama,** and its artist, Charles Rogers Grooms, has been nicknamed "Red." Red has created other sculpto-pictoramas including *City of Chicago* and *Ruckus Manhattan,* which memorialize major cities in the United States.

Born in Nashville, Tennessee, in 1937, Red Grooms was encouraged by his parents to pursue his early talent and interest in art. Influenced by visits to the Tennessee State Fair and the Ringling Brothers and Barnum and Bailey Circus, Red began to create unique versions of imaginary circuses in his backyard. From performing original skits for his classmates to working at a local art gallery after school, Red was committed to a career as an artist. In fact, by the age of eighteen he had already exhibited his paintings at a gallery in his hometown.

Red has spent most of his career in New York City. There he has worked collaboratively with other artists since 1957 to create skit-like performances known as "happenings," and sculpto-pictoramas like the dramatic and colorful *Ruckus Rodeo.* With this colorful city and its inhabitants as his subjects, Red Grooms has devoted his life to pursuing an art filled with humor and activity, teeming with excitement and life.

Red Grooms, *Ruckus Rodeo,* 1975–1976. Sculpture wire, celastic, acrylic, canvas and burlap, 174″ x 606″ x 294″ (442 x 1539 x 747 cm). Commissioned by the Modern Art Museum of Fort Worth. Museum purchase with funds from the National Endowment for the Arts and the Benjamin J. Tillar Memorial Trust.

7-10 Piet Mondrian, *Composition in Black, White and Red*, 1936. Oil on canvas, 40 ¼″ x 41″ (102 x 104 cm). The Museum of Modern Art, New York. Gift of the Advisory Committee.

7-11 Senabu Oloyede, Oshogbo, Nigeria. Wall hanging, starch resist on cotton. 33 ¼″ x 75″ (85 x 191 cm). Gift to Field Museum of Natural History from Robert Plant Armstrong.

Space and the Picture Plane

So far in this chapter, the word *space* has been used to mean a three-dimensional area. Some artists, however, use the term to refer to the flat, two-dimensional surface of a painting. The flat surface of a painting or drawing is sometimes called the **picture plane.** Modern artists, especially those who paint abstract pictures, take great care in deciding where to place shapes on the picture plane. For example, they may place shapes high or low, or to the left or the right on the picture plane.

Piet Mondrian was a very skilled abstract artist. He took great care in arranging each line, shape, and color on the picture plane. The space in his *Composition in Black, White and Red* (fig. 7–10) is very balanced.

Artists sometimes define space as being the unfilled areas of the picture plane. They also use space to refer to the "background" of the painting or to the ground of a figure–ground relationship. (A "figure" stands out on top of a ground. A "ground" appears to be underneath and surrounding a figure.) These areas are sometimes called *negative space.* In the Mondrian painting, negative space would be the white areas. In the wall hanging by Senabu Oloyede (fig. 7–11), it would be the black areas.

Representing Three-Dimensional Space in Two-Dimensional Art

Many pictures, especially those we call "realistic," appear to have the three dimensions of height, width, and depth. Of course, these pictures do not have actual depth. In Chapter 5, you learned that depth can be created by shading and foreshortening (figures 7–12, 7–13). These methods make an object seem solid and three-dimensional. Depth can also be created by changing the size of an object to make it appear closer or farther away (fig. 7–14).

In this chapter, you will learn four more ways to create a sense of depth: *overlapping, high and low placement, linear perspective,* and *aerial perspective.* Bouts's *Polyptych of the Last Supper* (fig. 7–15) will be used to illustrate the first three methods.

Overlapping

A simple way to suggest depth in a picture is by having things overlap. An object is placed in front of and partially covering something else (fig. 7–16). In the Bouts

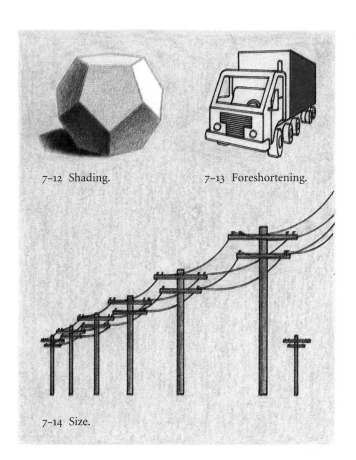

7–12 Shading.

7–13 Foreshortening.

7–14 Size.

7–15 Dirk Bouts, *Polyptych of the Last Supper* (center panel), 1464–68. Oil on wood, 6′ x 5′ (183 x 153 cm). Louvain, Eglise de St. Pierre. Giraudon/Art Resource, NY.

painting, the two men that overlap the table appear to be closer to us than the table itself. The table is closer to us than the central figure of Jesus.

High and Low Placement

Usually, something that is lower in a picture appears closer to us than something that is higher (fig. 7–17). The two men on "our" side of the table are lower in the picture than Jesus. Therefore, they are closer to us than Jesus is. Their cups are lower than Jesus' cup and therefore closer.

7–16 Overlapping forms.

7–17 Which of these objects (higher or lower) appears to be closer to us?

Try it Yourself

Take a blank sheet of paper. Think of the surface of the paper as "space." In the middle of this space, place a cutout of a house or tree. This image becomes a "frame of reference." Now take a cutout of an animal or person and place it below the frame of reference. Does it appear small? When placed above the frame of reference, it should appear large (fig. 7–18). What causes this "magical" effect? (For an answer, reread page 48 on size constancy in Chapter 5.)

7–18 Which of these forms appears larger?

Depth in Collage

Cut out images from magazines, catalogs, and newspapers. Arrange them in a collage to suggest depth. Use overlap, large and small shapes, and low or high placement in the picture.

a. Corinna Carey.   b. Mark Gardener.

Linear Perspective

Linear perspective is the most complicated method for showing depth. Look at the drawing of a basketball court (fig. 7–19). Vertical lines are used for the posts supporting the backboards. Horizontal lines are used for the sidelines. The center and end lines appear to be parallel in the drawing (as they are in real life). But in fact, they are not. They *converge*, or come together, at a point in the distance. This is called the *vanishing point*. When all these lines are extended by dotted lines they meet at the point. This type of perspective is called **one-point perspective.**

Polyptych of the Last Supper also has one-point perspective. Look at the diagram in figure 7–20. Many lines are vertical or horizontal. Many more lines converge: the ends of the table, most of the lines in the floor pattern, and most of the beams in the ceiling.

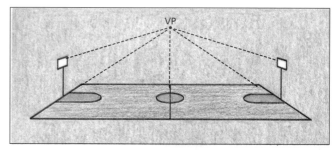

7–19 One-point perspective uses horizontal, vertical, and converging lines.

7–21 Two-point perspective uses vertical lines and two sets of converging lines, but no horizontal lines. Therefore, there are two vanishing points.

7–22 One-point perspective with the vanishing point located above eye level.

7–20 In artwork using one-point perspective, many lines converge at a single vanishing point that appears to be in the distance.

Look at the men sitting at each end of the table, as well as the tops and bottoms of the two windows. Dotted lines from the men and the windows converge.

Two-point linear perspective is used in the second drawing of a basketball court (fig. 7–21). There are vertical lines and *two* sets of converging lines. There are no horizontal lines. The converging lines of the center line, end lines, and edges of the backboards go to the left vanishing point. The sidelines, which are the other set of converging lines, go to the right point.

Compare the drawing of the basketball court in figure 7–22 with figures 7–19 and 7–21. Figure 7–22 has one-point perspective. However, the viewer seems to be standing on the floor. In the first and second drawings, the viewer seems to be sitting in the bleachers. The *eye level* is different. Eye level refers to the height of the viewer's eyes relative to the ground. In the third picture, the eye level is below the height of the backboards. In the first two pictures, the eye level is above. Usually the vanishing point (or points) is on the eye level.

Where is the eye level in relationship to the men in *Polyptych of the Last Supper?* Would the viewer be sitting, standing on the floor, or standing on a stepladder?

Try it Yourself

Choose a photograph or picture. Lay a ruler along any of the lines of the picture. Try to find the vanishing point or points. (See the example in figure 7–23.) WARNING: One or both of the points may be out of the picture. If so, glue the picture to a large piece of paper if you need to draw lines outside of the picture.

Try to find the vanishing point and eye level of *The Country School* (fig. 7–30). (TIP: Lay your ruler along the lines formed by the benches on either side of the room, the top edge of the window on the left, and the top edge of the wall on the right.)

Studio Experience 7.2

Identifying One-Point Perspective

Draw three cubes in one-point perspective. Place one cube above the eye level, one overlapping the eye level, and one below the eye level. Place the vanishing point in the center. Then draw three cubes that are off to one side of the vanishing point.

7–23 Can you locate the vanishing point of this picture?

Applying One-Point Perspective

Find a photograph of a structure with one-point perspective. Create a drawing of it. Show converging lines, a vanishing point, and eye level.

a. Sarah Johnson.

b. Malcolm Ferguson.

Identifying Two-Point Perspective

Draw two rectangular forms using two-point perspective. Draw one form overlapping the eye level, and the other above the eye level.

Applying Two-Point Perspective

Photocopy a photograph of a building that has two-point perspective. Glue the copy onto a piece of drawing paper. Extend the picture beyond its original boundaries by drawing your own additions. Locate the vanishing points by extending the lines that appear in the photograph.

Try it Yourself

Study the picture *Frontispiece to "Kirby's Perspective"* (fig. 7–24) by William Hogarth. This picture does not represent depth using the methods discussed in this chapter. How many violations or inconsistencies of size, overlapping, high–low placement, and linear perspectives can you see? Make a list. Compare your list with a classmate's.

7-24 William Hogarth, *Frontispiece to "Kirby's Perspective"* (Joshua Kirby's edition of Dr. Brook Taylor's *Method of Perspective*), 1753. Engraving, 8 ¼" x 6 ¾" (21 x 17 cm). Reproduced Courtesy of the Trustees of the British Museum.

7–25 George Caleb Bingham, *Fur Traders Descending the Missouri*. Oil on canvas, 1845. 29″ x 36 ½″ (74 x 93 cm). The Metropolitan Museum of Art, Morris K. Jesup Fund, 1933.

Aerial Perspective

Recall that air is often filled with fog, smog, or air pollution. When the air is filled with particles, objects become less visible. Notice how indistinct the buildings in the distance are in Claude Monet's *La Gare St. Lazare* (fig. 7–1).

But even in the country, and on clear days, moisture in the air can affect the appearance and color of things in the distance. When an object is far away, its colors become lighter, cooler, and duller. The colors lack hue or value contrast. The object's outlines and details become less distinct. In a picture, this effect is known as **aerial perspective.** Notice how George Caleb Bingham used colors to create aerial perspective in *Fur Traders Descending the Missouri* (fig. 7–25). The colors create four layers in the scene. Each layer appears at a

greater distance. Notice the boat, a hazy island behind the boat, a hazier island beyond it, and the still hazier riverbank in the background.

In traditional Chinese ink painting, aerial perspective is used to create glowing mountain scenes. In *Bare Willows and Distant Mountains* (fig. 7–26), the artist was able to suggest various degrees of distance. Although the ink technique is monochromatic (Chapter 4), the Chinese artist controlled the values and clarity of details. The trees in the lower right are relatively dark and distinct. The trees and houses across the river are hazy and shrouded in mist. The mountains in the background almost disappear.

A Landscape with Aerial Perspective

Create a simple landscape that has aerial perspective. Use values of black and white tempera paint to create this effect. Use lighter values and contrasts to make shapes seem farther away.

Mick Carreras.

7–26 Ma Yuan, *Bare Willows and Distant Mountains*, China, Southern Song dynasty, about 1200. Round album leaf; ink and colors on silk, 9˝ x 8˝ (24 x 21 cm). Chinese and Japanese Special Fund. Courtesy, Museum of Fine Arts, Boston.

7–27 Andrew Tsinajinnie, *Pastoral Scene,* Navajo. Tempera, 20 ½″ x 32″ R. C. Cline Land Co., Inc.

7–29 I. Rice Pereira, *Oblique Progression,* 1948. Oil on canvas, 50″ x 40″ (127 x 102 cm). Collection of Whitney Museum of American Art, New York. (Purchase).

Three-Dimensional Space in Abstract Painting

People tend to think that abstract art does not have spatial depth. But this is not true. Painters of abstract works are concerned with more than just the two-dimensional space of the picture plane. For some abstract painters, the suggestion of three-dimensional space is also important.

Look at the depth in Andrew Tsinajinnie's stylized and semiabstract picture of a Navajo settlement, *Pastoral Scene* (fig. 7–27). Depth is conveyed through variations of size, overlapping, high–low placement, and even some foreshortening.

Hans Hofmann used some overlapping in *Flowering Swamp* (fig. 7–28). He created depth, however, mainly through *color variation.* Notice how the warm colors tend to come toward the viewer. The cool colors tend to go back.

Foreshortening, overlapping, size variation, and color variation create depth in Irene Rice Pereira's abstract *Oblique Progression* (fig. 7–29). The sense of movement through and around lines and shapes in space is quite vivid.

7–28 Hans Hofmann, *Flowering Swamp,* 1957. Oil on wood, 48 ˝ x 36 ˝ (122 x 91 cm). Hirshhorn Museum and Sculpture Garden, Smithsonian Institution, Gift of the Joseph H. Hirshhorn Foundation, 1966.

7–30 Winslow Homer, *The Country School*, 1871. Oil on canvas, 21 ³⁄₈″ x 38 ³⁄₈″ (54 x 98 cm). The Saint Louis Art Museum (Purchase).

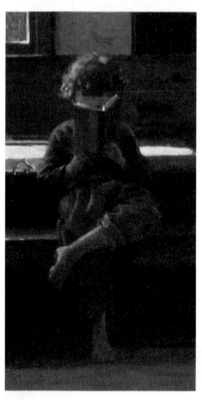

7–31 Creating a close-up is one result of changing the frame of a picture. Winslow Homer, *The Country School* (detail).

Framing

Framing establishes the limits of what is seen in a picture. Winslow Homer framed *The Country School* (fig. 7–30) so that we see almost the entire one-room school. Because of the teacher's size and location, she is the most important person in the picture. But she, along with the students, is relatively small in comparison to the size of the painting. Therefore, she appears to be relatively far away.

Framing can affect the point of view and the meaning of a scene. Look at the single boy sitting to the left of the teacher. He is one of the farthest-away people. Suppose that we reframe the picture so that we see only him. In the new frame (fig. 7–31), he is much larger in comparison to the size of the picture. Therefore, he appears to be very close. Pictures like this that are framed very close to the central image are sometimes called *close-ups*.

In the new picture, the focus is just on the boy and what he is doing. In the original, he was merely a small part of a large scene. In what ways do you think the story has been changed? Is the new story more interesting or less interesting than the original?

Cut out two "L" shapes (at least five inches for one leg and three inches for the other). Use the L's to make an adjustable frame (a). Move the frame across a picture. Stop when you come to an interesting part. Adjust the size of the frame by sliding the two L's as needed to create a close-up (b). See how many new pictures with different stories you can make out of the original. If possible, use a photocopying machine to enlarge each of your new pictures.

a.

b.

c.

Summary

The size and form of a space can be determined by its boundaries and the objects it touches. The interior spaces of hollow objects and buildings are referred to as volume.

We sense the form and size of a space not only with our eyes but also by our bodily movements.

Space is very important to artists who deal with three-dimensional artworks. Architects, especially, have to consider space when they design buildings and interiors. Modern sculptors often include holes in their works to create added space. They may make open sculptures out of strong lightweight materials.

Artists who make paintings and drawings often use the word *space* to refer to the two-dimensional area of the picture plane.

Artists who make realistic pictures are representing depth on a two-dimensional surface. They create the illusion of three-dimensional objects and people surrounded by three-dimensional space. Depth is created by shading, foreshortening, and making objects large or small. These methods were explained in Chapter 5. Depth can also be created by overlapping, high and low placement, linear perspective, and aerial perspective. Color variation is also used in abstract art to create depth.

Framing means deciding the borders of a picture. Framing affects the space shown in the picture. It can also determine the point of view and meaning of a picture.

Now that you have learned about space, go back to your description of Renoir's *Luncheon of the Boating Party.* Can you recognize examples of high and low placement or overlapping? Can you locate the vanishing point and eye level? Is the eye level high, low, or average with respect to a standing person?

The framing of *Luncheon* allows us to see the whole party on the deck. Try changing the space and the scene by reframing the painting.

Chapter 8
Texture and Movement

8–1

8–3

8–2

8–4 Photographs: Barbara Caldwell.

Texture

Texture refers to how the *surface* of something feels to the touch: rough, smooth, hard, soft, gritty, slick, and so forth. Texture is everywhere (figures 8–1, 8–2, 8–3, 8–4). In art, texture is described as *glossy* and *matte*. *Glossy* means slippery, like the surface of a newly waxed floor. *Matte* means smooth but nonslippery, like the surface of a chalkboard.

Although texture is related to touch, we do not always have to touch something to sense its texture. At times we can feel texture just by looking at it.

Try it Yourself

List some things in the classroom, such as the chalkboard, woodwork, a countertop, or the ceiling.

Describe the texture of each item in a few words. Then touch some of these items. Did you discover additional qualities about their textures? If so, change or add to your descriptions. Can you sense the texture of the ceiling by just looking at it and "touching" it in your imagination?

Texture in our daily lives is very important. It is more important than we often realize. Take eating out, for example. The atmosphere of a restaurant depends a great deal on the textures. Examples of glossy textures include plates, cups, silverware, glasses, countertops, coffee machines, and mirrors. Matte textures include napkins, place mats, tablecloths, carpeting, and drapes. Rough textures may be found in such things as unvarnished paneling and brick planters.

What about the food (fig. 8–5)? Flavor is important. But so is the texture of the food, or the way it feels in the mouth. You would be very disappointed in a hamburger bun that was not "fresh." It should have the correct balance between softness and firmness, and between moistness and dryness. The same, of course, is true for everything inside the bun.

Texture in Art

All art objects have texture. In a photograph, it is not the glossy texture of the photograph itself that is important. It is the texture we see in the picture. In *Migrant Mother* (fig. 8–6), a photograph by Dorothea Lange, we see the textures of the lined face of the

8–5

8–6 Dorothea Lange, *Migrant Mother, Nipomo, California,* 1936. Photograph: Dorothea Lange Collection, The Oakland Museum.

mother, her hair, the hair of her children, and the material of their tattered clothes. Such textures are called *simulated textures.* They relate to the images in the photograph and not its surface. You cannot touch them, but they are nevertheless vivid. The textures in *Migrant Mother* play an important role in telling a story about the sad conditions of migrant families in the 1930s.

Like photographs, realistic paintings have simulated textures. For example, look at the painting of a longhorn steer (fig. 8-7). Don Nice captured the colors of the animal's hide as well as its texture—right down to the little bristles of hair.

8-7 Don Nice, *Longhorn Steer, Western Series, American Predella #6*, 1975. Acrylic on canvas and watercolor on paper, 91″ x 120″ (231 x 305 cm). Delaware Art Museum, Wilmington.

8-8 Jean Dubuffet, *The Cow with the Subtile Nose*, 1954. From the Cows, Grass, Foliage series. Oil and enamel on canvas, 35″ x 45 ¾″ (89 x 116 cm). The Museum of Modern Art, New York. Benjamin Scharps and David Scharps Fund.

8–9 Edouard Manet, *Oysters*, 1862. Oil on canvas, 15 ⅜″ x 18 ⅜″ (41 x 48 cm). ©1993 National Gallery, Washington, Gift of the Adele R. Levy Fund, Inc.

Simulated texture is either nonexistent or unimportant in abstract or semiabstract painting. The texture seen in *The Cow with the Subtile Nose* (fig. 8–8) was not intended to resemble cowhide. The artist, Jean Dubuffet, wanted you to sense the texture of the paint itself. He mixed oil and enamel paints, applied them thickly, and worked them to create a spotted effect. If you saw this work in the Museum of Modern Art, you might be tempted to feel the bumps and ridges—the actual texture—of its paint.

In some paintings, like Edouard Manet's *Oysters* (fig. 8–9), both kinds of textures play roles. The textures of the oysters, along with the lemons, are perhaps realistic enough to make you hungry. The texture of the thick strokes of paint used to create the oysters is also visible. This painting gives you the best of both "worlds": simulated and actual textures. It appeals not only to your sense of sight and touch, but also to your imagination of food.

8–12   Viola M. Wood, *Festival Form*, 1975. Ceramic, 12″ x 8″ x 4″ (30 x 20 x 10 cm). Collection of the artist.

8–10   Michelangelo, *Pietà*, 1498–1500. Marble, 5´ 9″ (2 m) high. St. Peter's, Vatican State. Erich Lessing/Art Resource, NY.

8–11   Marilyn Levine, *Trent's Jacket*, 1976. Ceramic, wood and metal hooks, 35″ x 18″ x 8″ (89 x 46 cm x 20 cm). Private Collection. O. K. Harris Works of Art.

Look at Michelangelo's famous sculpture of the Pietà (Italian for *pity*) in figure 8–10. It is made out of polished marble. The actual texture is smooth and hard. But, like Manet's painting, the sculpture lets you experience the simulated textures of the flesh and clothing of Jesus and Mary. The gown clings to Mary in some places and gathers in heavy folds in other places. Yet you never lose sight of the fact that it is stone.

Can you tell what material Marilyn Levine used to make *Trent's Jacket* (fig. 8–11)? Even if you saw the piece in the gallery you would probably not guess. The "jacket" is not leather but *ceramic* (the material of which bricks are made). Levine succeeded so well in making a hard material resemble a soft material that she has fooled the viewer. Works like this are sometimes called "fool-the-eye" art. However, do you think *Trent's Jacket* could fool your *touch*?

There are no simulated textures in the ceramic vase by Viola M. Wood (fig. 8–12). The only important textures are the actual ones. The artist varied the texture by scratching the clay and adding pieces of clay. Note how the rough surfaces are contrasted with the smooth surfaces. Everything about this piece—its textures, its colors, even its weight—appeals to the senses. It invites us to pick it up and hold it.

Try it Yourself

At home look at some of your favorite objects, such as clothing, jewelry, a watch; or old toys, dolls, teddy bears, games. Do you like these things because of their textures? Is the texture of a teddy bear actual or simulated, or both?

Find a natural object from outdoors and a human-made object, such as a brick, a weathered board, or a rusty nail. Bring them to class. Describe the texture of each object.

Studio Experience 8.1

Simulated Textures

Use magazine photographs with simulated textures to create a Surrealistic paper collage of imaginative objects and figures.

Marie Ramirez.

Studio Experience 8.2

Textures in Clay

Produce five different textures on a clay tile. Use three of these methods: pushing and pinching with fingers, pressing clay on clay, incising and impressing with a tool.

Tim Ziegler.

Movement

Although not considered one of the visual elements, movement is an important factor in the experience of art, and should be discussed before we leave Part II. A sculpture is best experienced by moving around it. You can experience Wood's vase (fig. 8-12) by rotating it in your hands. Even two-dimensional art involves movement. When you studied the textures in *Oysters* (fig. 8-9), your eyes probably moved from one object to the next.

Each of these instances could be considered examples of viewer movement. The viewer, not the art object, moved. Viewer movement, even if it involves only the eyes, is a necessary part of experiencing art. But there are other relationships between visual art and movement. They are: *implied movement, optical movement, actual movement,* and *sequence.*

Implied Movement

An image, whether a picture or a sculpture, captures a moment in time. By stopping time, it implies a relationship to time, and also to movement. The subject may be as motionless as the oysters in Manet's still life. Or the subject can be frozen in action. In the scene from the movie *North by Northwest* (fig. 8–13), the airplane is frozen in midair. The man is clearly running. The photograph implies a great deal of movement. In this case it is implied by the subject matter. Whether you have ever seen the movie or not, you immediately know that the man is in danger. You have a basic knowledge of aircraft. You know that this one—even if it is a slow crop duster—is too close for comfort. Indeed, with some imagination, you can hear its propeller and feel the pounding heart of the man.

8–13 Cary Grant in a scene from *North by Northwest,* directed by Alfred Hitchcock. ©1959 Loew's Inc. Ren. 1987 Turner Entertainment Co.

8–14　George Bellows, *Stag at Sharkey's*, 1909. Oil on canvas, 36 ¼″ x 48 ¼″ (92 cm x 123 cm). ©The Cleveland Museum of Art, Hinman B. Hurlbut Collection.

In *Stag at Sharkey's* (fig. 8–14) by George Bellows, movement is implied by the subject of boxing and by Bellows' style of painting. Bellows used diagonals in the men's bodies, exaggerated postures, and lively brushwork to imply movement. Two boxers are flailing away at each other at close range. The one on the right is ready to deliver a punch with his free arm. Although the next moment is not shown, you can easily imagine the punch landing and the sweat flying.

Studio Experience 8.3

Suggesting Movement in Clay

Create an abstract clay sculpture. Use shape and placement of forms to suggest movement. Use textures for surface contrasts.

Linda Ortiz.

8–15 Umberto Boccioni, *Unique Forms of Continuity in Space,* 1913. Bronze (cast 1931), 43 ⅞″ x 34 ⅞″ x 15 ¾″
(111 x 89 x 40 cm). The Museum of Modern Art, New York. Acquired through the Lillie P. Bliss Bequest.

The title of Umberto Boccioni's *Unique Forms of Continuity in Space* (fig. 8–15) suggests movement, and for good reason. The artist was a member of the *Futurists.* The aim of this group in Italy was to express the speed and motion of modern society. Boccioni's sculpture is abstract. However, we can clearly tell that it is a figure walking with determination. The figure is striding to the left. The forward tilt of the trunk, the bend of the forward leg, and the extension of the rear leg resemble the movements of a walker. Even the swollen thighs suggest vigorous striding. But in some places the forms are disrupted and broken up. In other places they seem to sprout fins. These suggest that the figure is striding through a wind tunnel. Boccioni's sculpture is more than just an illustration of a walking person. It is a symbol of dynamic movement.

Claes Oldenburg
1929–

You've seen it a hundred times: someone dumping french fries out of a little paper sack. But Claes Oldenburg has frozen the act in time and space, and *Shoestring Potatoes Spilling From a Bag* becomes a gravity-defying performance, a large-scale example of implied movement.

Many of Oldenburg's works are large sculptures of commonplace household objects. In works such as *Shoestring Potatoes Spilling From a Bag* or the artist's 1988 work, *Spoon Bridge and Cherry* (the bridge-sized spoon that spans a body of water in Minneapolis), the sheer size of the sculpture shows us movement we might not have noticed in the object itself. In all his art, Oldenburg challenges the viewer to look at ordinary things—a typewriter, a slice of pie—in an extraordinary manner.

Claes Thure Oldenburg was born in Stockholm, Sweden, in 1929. His father was a member of the Swedish foreign service and the family traveled a great deal between Sweden, Norway, and the United States before settling in Chicago in 1936. By the time he was seven years old, Oldenburg had lived in three different countries and experienced many unique environments. Beginning in his childhood and continuing throughout his life, Oldenburg has recorded his daily experiences in these different places in both drawings and notes. These notations have become source books for ideas for some of his artwork.

Though Oldenburg has expressed his ideas with many different art media, including film, printmaking, drawing and painting, he is best known for his oversized sculptures which monumentalize American life. In each medium explored, Oldenburg has attempted to communicate something about art and about life by examining the everyday, ordinary aspects of our lives in new and exciting ways. "I am for an art that takes its form from the lines of life itself, that twists and extends and accumulates and spits and drips, and is heavy and coarse and blunt and sweet and stupid as life itself."

Claes Oldenburg, *Shoestring Potatoes Spilling From a Bag*, 1966. Canvas, kapok, glue, acrylic, 108″ x 46″ x 42″ (274 x 117 x 107 cm). Collection Walker Art Center, Minneapolis, Gift of the T. B. Walker Foundation, 1966.

Optical Movement

So far, movement has only been implied in the examples. The works have been static and motionless. They imply movement because of their subject matters, their forms, or a combination of the two. Some static works known as *Op Art* (or Optical Art) seem, almost

8–16 Victor Vasarely, *Edetta*, 1984. Acrylic on canvas, 39 ¾″ x 39 ¾″ (101 x 101 cm). Courtesy Circle Fine Art Corporation, Chicago, Illinois.

miraculously, to move. *Optical movement* is an illusion, a response by the eyes to lines, shapes, and colors arranged in certain ways. The viewer may feel dizzy after staring at the art. Stare for a few seconds at *Edetta* (fig. 8–16) by Victor Vasarely. Does the pattern of shapes shift between being a checkerboard and a network of diagonals? Does it tend to swell and contract almost as if it were inhaling and exhaling? Did you have different sensations? How would you describe them?

The compact pattern in *Current* (fig. 8–17) by Bridget Riley is even more interesting, or disturbing. The monotony of the bending lines seems infinite. There are no places for the eye to stop and focus. Notice that the lines, especially those along the narrow valleys where the bending of the lines is tightest, seem actually to vibrate.

Actual Movement

Although the lines and shapes created by Vasarely and Riley seem to move, their works are static. Some works, called **kinetic art**, actually move. Some kinetic works are connected by pulleys and chains to electric motors. Some are installed outdoors and are set in motion by the wind. Still others, called *mobiles,* hang from ceilings and slowly move with the currents of air

8–17 Bridget Riley, *Current,* 1964. Synthetic polymer paint on composition board, 58 ⅜ ″ x 58 ⅞″ (148 x 150 cm). The Museum of Modern Art, New York, Philip Johnson Fund.

8–18 Julio Le Parc, *Continual Mobile, Continual Light,* 1963. Steel and nylon, 63″ (160 cm) high. The Tate Gallery, London/Art Resource, NY.

8–19 Eadweard Muybridge, *Attitudes of Animals in Motion.* Courtesy of Sotheby's Inc., 1987.

8–20 Milton Caniff, *Terry and the Pirates,* 1943. Reprinted by permission: Tribune Media Services.

in a room. Recall Alexander Calder's huge mobile in the East Building of the National Gallery (fig. 7–5).

Julio Le Parc's *Continual Mobile, Continual Light* (fig. 8–18) consists of nothing more than pieces of polished metal hung on nylon threads. Because of their light weight, the metal pieces move rather freely. But the main movement is due to their reflections that dance off walls and ceiling. The motions of *Continual Mobile, Continual Light* are random. They have no particular order. This is true of most kinetic art.

Sequence

Comics and movies involve **sequence.** One thing follows after another in logical order. For example, the words on this page are arranged in a certain sequence for you to read.

Using a number of cameras, Eadweard Muybridge produced a sequence of still pictures. The sequence illustrates the positions of a horse and rider as they leap over a hurdle (fig. 8–19). In fact, the series is "read" like a page in a book, from left to right and from top to bottom. Each scene shows a slightly different position. Because of the many repeated scenes, the suggestion of actual movement is very strong.

Like a series by Muybridge, a comic strip also uses a sequence of pictures called *frames.* However, a comic strip is not intended to be a study of movement. It is intended to tell a story, like the sequence of *Terry and the Pirates* (fig. 8–20) by Milton Caniff. One frame follows another, each showing a scene or slice of action representing a new stage in the story. Conversation, or *dialogue,* is printed in "balloons" above the characters' heads. Because comic strips mix dialogue with pictures while telling stories, they are sometimes referred to as *narrative* art.

The character Terry was a pilot of a fighter plane during World War II. The *Terry and the Pirates* sequence shown here is a very short part, or *episode,* of a long story about Terry's adventures. The dialogue takes place on the radio between Terry and the pilot of a war-damaged cargo plane. Notice how both the drawing and dialogue contribute to the story. To make the sequence as dramatic as possible, Caniff used a variety of framing and points of view. The first frame is a close-up of the inside of Terry's cockpit. It shows the action from the young hero's point of view. The second shows it from the cargo pilot's point of view. The third frame is a distant view of both planes flying over mountains. The final frame, a close-up of Terry's plane at an odd angle, ends the episode.

Try it Yourself

Continue the story of *Terry and the Pirates.* Does the damaged cargo plane make it over the mountain? Does Terry radio for help? Does he return to base? Does either plane encounter enemy fighter planes?

Like a comic strip, a movie, or *film,* relies on sequence to tell its story. But unlike a comic strip, a film is a picture that actually *moves.* The viewer has no control over its movement or speed. He or she cannot look ahead to see what is going to happen nor look back to see what was missed (unless, of course, the viewer is watching it on a VCR).

A sequence in a film is a series of shots. A **shot** is like a frame of a comic strip, except it contains action. If the *Terry and the Pirates* episode were on film, the first shot would be of Terry in his cockpit, the second of his friend in the cargo plane, and so forth. Each shot would last perhaps five seconds. In the viewing of a film, a shot is an unbroken segment of a scene or action. Direct connections between shots are called *cuts.*

Like comic strip frames, film shots can show distant views or close-ups, as well as different points of view and angles. A camera can *tilt* (pivot up and down from a stationary position), **pan** (pivot sideways from a stationary position), **track** (move to follow an action), and *zoom* (make an image appear nearer or farther by means of a zoom lens). Finally, a camera can remain in a fixed position, with movement coming entirely from the action of the scene.

In the opening scenes of *Star Wars,* Princess Leia's starship is captured by a spaceship of the evil Galactic Empire. Following the capture, empire troops blow up the main bulkhead of Leia's ship and attack the defending rebel troops. The battle sequence, which takes less than fifty-nine seconds of viewing time, requires thirty-two shots. (The average length of a shot is less than 1.9 seconds.) Eight of those shots are described here. Almost all were filmed with cameras in stationary positions at chest height.

Studio Experience 8.4

Movement in a Comic Strip

Draw a comic strip with four or five panels. You can base the comic strip on a joke or story. Use a sequence of frames and visual cues to suggest movement.

Alex Blaine.

8–21 Artoo-Detoo and See-Threepio helplessly watch rebel troops defend the rebel blockade runner in the film *Star Wars*.
™ & © Lucasfilm Ltd. (LFL) 1977. All Rights Reserved. Courtesy of Lucasfilm Ltd.

Shot	Length of shot/ Camera position	Shot	Length of shot/ Camera position
Rebel soldiers retreat to corridor where Artoo-Detoo and See-Threepio are hiding.	3 seconds/Fixed camera at chest level	*cut to:*	
		Close-up of See-Threepio.	1 second
cut to:		*cut to:*	
The robots watch help-lessly as rebel troops are fired on (fig. 8–21).	1 second	Rebel troops killing and being killed.	1 second/Waist level
		cut to:	
cut to:		Robots move to other side of corridor, followed by explosion.	4–5 seconds/Camera pans to follow robots.
Close-up of See-Threepio.	1 second		
cut to:		*cut to:*	
Empire troops killing and being killed.	1 second	Smoke. Rebel troops in full retreat.	1 second

8–22 Artists are often called upon to make storyboards for movies like *Star Wars*. This illustration represents one shot of a sequence.
™ & © Lucasfilm Ltd. (LFL) 1977. All Rights Reserved. Courtesy of Lucasfilm Ltd.

The battle sequence ends with Darth Vader surveying the battle results. (The camera is at waist level to emphasize the evil commander's size.) Because of the shortness of the shots and the confusion of a pitched battle, odd angles of view were not used. A panning camera was used only once. Otherwise, the sequence would have been too hard to follow.

Movies like *Star Wars* contain complicated action. For these movies, artists are hired to make *storyboards*. A storyboard looks much like a comic strip. Each frame (fig. 8–22) represents a shot. A storyboard helps the director and the camera people to visualize a sequence before the actual shooting begins. The storyboard picture in figure 8–22 corresponds to the first shot in the listed description. Notice that the eye level in the picture is very low (about at the knees), while the position of the camera in the film is chest level.

Sound

Sound is an important element in film. In battle sequences the sounds of explosions and zapping weapons add to the realism. Music is often used to establish mood. In this case, it is used to increase the feeling of tension during the moments before the bulkhead is attacked. In *Star Wars*, as in *Terry and the Pirates*, dialogue is very important to clarify the action. In the scenes before the battle, See-Threepio explains to Artoo-Detoo that the pursuing ship knocked out their ship's main reactor. Seconds later, he says, "We're doomed! There'll be no escape for the Princess this time." What would film be like without sound? You have probably seen "silent" movies. You may recall that the action had to be interrupted every so often to show printed dialogues on the screen.

Try it Yourself

Add a sequence of your own to **Star Wars.** Make two columns. Explain the action in the left column. Indicate the point of view and position of the camera in the right-hand column. Tell whether the camera is stationary, tilting, panning, tracking, or zooming.

Closely observe a movie, either in a theater or on a VCR at home. See how an idea is developed by a sequence of shots. Take notes on what you see and hear.

Take notes on a commercial. What kinds of shots are used to make the product look appealing?

REMEMBER: With a VCR, you can reverse the tape and replay a sequence.

Making a Storyboard

Make a storyboard for a short video.

Try it Yourself

Now that you have completed this series of chapters on the elements of art, rewrite your description of Renoir's *Luncheon of the Boating Party.*

Summary

Texture refers to how the surface of something feels to the touch. All artworks, like all objects, have actual textures. Photographs, realistic paintings, and realistic sculptures also have textures that can be seen but not felt. This kind of texture is called simulated texture. In artworks that do not have simulated textures, such as crafts or abstract paintings and sculptures, the only important textures are the actual ones.

Although not a visual element, movement can be considered a factor in the experience of static art like paintings and sculptures. At the very least, a viewer must move his or her eyes to appreciate an artwork. An artwork can capture a subject in a moment in time. In such cases, the movement is implied. Optical movement is the illusion of movement. The patterns of lines and colors typically found in Op Art appear to move when the viewer stares at them. Actual movement is found in kinetic art. Parts of a kinetic artwork can be set in motion by a motor or by wind or air. Kinetic art is not static.

Comics and movies rely on sequence. In a comic, the sequence of viewing is from left to right (and also from top to bottom in the Sunday comics), but the viewer is free to skip around and move his or her eyes at any speed. In a film, the movement is actual. Both the movement and the sequence are determined by the film, not the viewer. A sequence is made up of a series of shots. Each shot consists of an unbroken view of a scene of action.

Part III
How Is It Organized?

Mantle. Detail: three figures. Wool, embroidered with colored wools. Peru, pre-Inca period, Early Nazca, ca. 600. The Metropolitan Museum of Art, Gift of George D. Pratt, 1932.

Chapter 9
Analyzing What You See

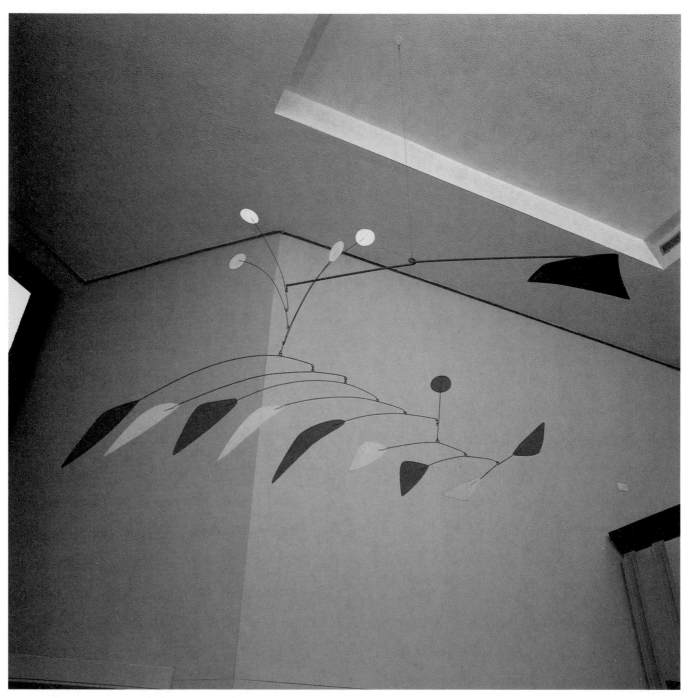

9–1 Alexander Calder, *Spring Blossoms*, 1965. The Pennsylvania State University.

9-2 Judy Chicago, *Virginia Woolf*, 1973. Sprayed acrylic on canvas, 5´ x 5´ (153 x 153 cm). Courtesy of the artist.

Now that you have completed Part II you should be able to identify and describe many things in an artwork. The purpose of this chapter is to teach you how to *analyze* a work of art. Analyzing is somewhat different from describing. But before going further, look at the following four statements. Each is a short *analysis* of one of the four artworks shown (figs. 9–1, 9–2, 9–3, 9–4). See if you can match the right statement with the right picture.

A. Although they differ in size and color, most of the shapes are similar in being rectilinear. The dominant feature is the post in the center.

B. Because it consists of a series of identical boxlike shapes separated by equal spaces, this artwork lacks not only variety but dominance.

C. A series of wavy lines, which are identical in size and shape, provide rhythm but little variety for this artwork. The dominant feature seems to be the center from which the lines radiate.

D. This work consists of a number of similar shapes of different sizes that form a rhythmic pattern.

9-3 Donald Judd, *Untitled*, 1985. ½˝ aluminum and ⅛˝ blue plexiglass over ⅛˝ black plexiglass, 6 units each ½ x 1 x ½ meters, overall 4 ½ x 1 x ½ meters. Courtesy Leo Castelli Gallery, New York.

(Answers: A = fig. 9-4, B = fig. 9-3, C = fig. 9-2, D = fig. 9-1)

How well did you do in the matching exercise? Were you confused by terms such as "rhythm" and "dominance"? Perhaps certain descriptive words, like "wavy lines" and "boxlike shapes," gave you enough clues to match the statement with the correct work. These short statements show how words, if used well, can both *describe* and *analyze* an artwork. Describing has to do with pointing out facts about the lines, shapes, and colors. Analyzing has to do with pointing out the *relationships* among these things.

Composition

The chapters of Part II covered each of the visual elements separately. In Chapters 9 and 10, we will see how the elements work together to make a complete work of art.

Composition refers to the way that lines, shapes, and colors have been put together. The artist, of course, is the person who has to put these things together. This task is called **composing.** The final result of composing a painting or a sculpture is called a composition.

Analyzing the Composition

Even though you, the viewer, do not do the composing, it sometimes helps if you know *how* a work of art was composed. In order to see how it was organized, to see what makes it tick, you have to break it down or "*decompose*" it. This is called **analyzing,** or *analysis.*

Analyzing an artwork means finding relationships in the composition. Two or more things in a work may have something in common. They can be related to each other.

Consider people, for example. Usually, when we talk about being related to somebody, we think of families. You are related to your uncle even though you may have nothing else in common with him. But there are other kinds of relationships besides family relationships. You are related to your classmates because you are all in the same classroom and being taught by the same teacher. You can be related to others because you are a fan of the Dallas Cowboys, like to ride horses, have brown eyes, and so on.

When you stop to think about it, everybody is related to everybody in some ways; everybody also is different from everybody in some ways. Often an analysis points out both differences and relationships. For example, Jenny likes indoor activities and Susie likes outdoor activities. Yet both are members of 4-H.

Try it Yourself

Think of one or two of your friends. List the things you have in common. You can list likes and dislikes, as well as appearance. Also list things that are different about the two (or three) of you.

Like people, colors and shapes in an artwork are often related in some ways and different in some ways. Look at Statements A and D on page 111. These statements point out both differences and relationships within an artwork. Statement A, in analyzing the composition of the painting in figure 9-4, says, "Although they differ in size and color, most of the shapes are similar in being rectilinear." Statement D, which is about the mobile (fig. 9-1), says, "This work consists of a number of similar shapes of different sizes."

Another kind of relationship has to do with one thing being more important than another thing. For example, a leader is more important than a follower. In a group that has a leader, all group members are related to each other. But also each follower is related to the leader in a special way and vice versa. Have you ever been a leader? Have you ever been a follower?

This kind of relationship in art is pointed out in the second sentence of statement A: "The dominant feature is the post in the center." The second sentence of statement C (about the abstract painting in figure 9-2) also speaks of dominance: "The dominant feature seems to be the center from which the lines radiate." You will learn about dominance in the next chapter.

In fact, Chapter 10 will discuss in detail several visual relationships. By being able to recognize these relationships and by learning the vocabulary for them, you will be able to analyze an artwork.

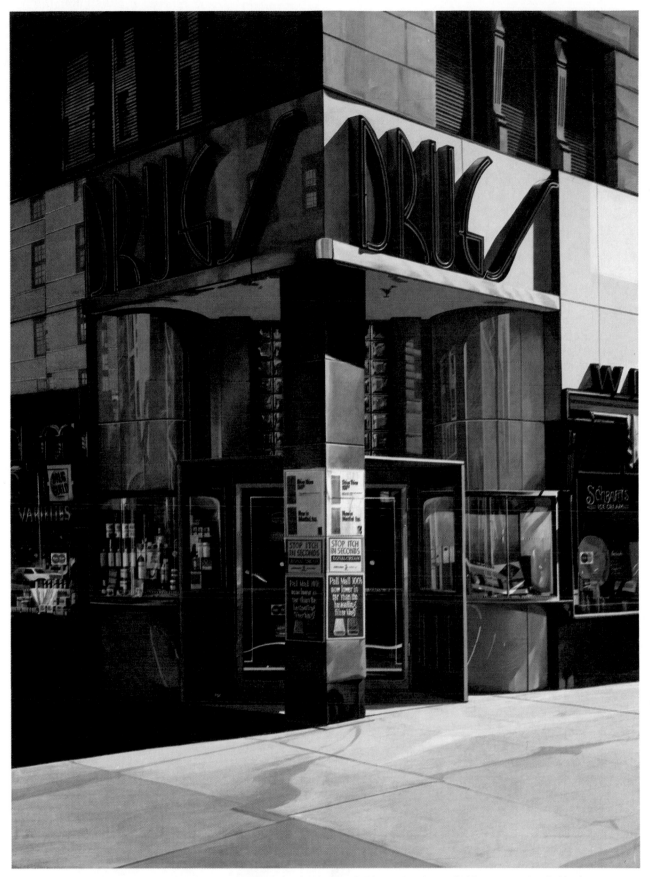

9-4 Richard Estes, *Drugstore*, 1970. Oil on canvas, 60″ x 44″ (152 x 113 cm). The Art Institute of Chicago, Restricted gift of Edgar Kaufmann.

Analyzing *American Gothic*

Analyze *American Gothic* by Grant Wood using the following guidelines, or more detailed guidelines provided by your teacher.

Procedure: In Chapter 3, you described *American Gothic*. However, you only included facts, the things about the painting that could be named and described with certainty. *Analyzing* involves identifying the relationship between things in the painting. How did the artist organize subject matter and elements including line, shape, texture, colors, and space so they interrelate as a composition? Take fifteen or twenty minutes to answer the following questions about *American Gothic*.

1. What similarities can you find among elements such as shape, colors, lines, patterns, size, direction of lines, and shapes?

2. Are there contrasts of elements such as color, shapes, forms, texture, direction, or size?

3. Are there elements in the picture that are repeated in some systematic way?

4. Are there elements that lead your eye through the composition?

5. Is there some element or area in the painting that is dominant or that seems most important?

6. What makes the painting seem to be balanced?

7. Can you describe a relationship between the subject and the way the artist used the medium (oil paint)?

Grant Wood, *American Gothic*, 1930. Oil on beaver board, 30″ x 25″ (76 x 63 cm). The Art Institute of Chicago, Friends of American Art Collection.

Grant Wood
1891–1942

Few paintings have achieved as powerful a hold on the imagination of an entire country as Grant Wood's *American Gothic.* A spinsterish woman wearing proper clothing and a serious expression is posed beside a stern man, gripping a pitchfork and staring intently at the viewer. A few strands of hair escape from the woman's tidy bun and fall down her neck emphasizing her otherwise immaculate appearance; the dark jacket suggests that this stoic farmer is dressed to attend church.

The posed figures standing before a white building, with their stiff posture, reserved manner, stony faces and unblinking eyes, have become symbols of the American family. *American Gothic* has come to symbolize farm life and traditional work values in the midwest United States.

Grant Wood was born in 1891 on a small farm in rural Iowa. There he lived a quiet childhood for the first ten years of his life, without telephones, radios, televisions or cars. He was educated in a one-room schoolhouse, and spent his free time drawing on scraps of cardboard from cracker boxes which his mother saved for him. In 1901, Grant's father died suddenly; the Wood family sold their farm and moved to the nearby city of Cedar Rapids to be close to relatives. During the next forty-one years of his life, Grant traveled and spent time in Europe, but always returned to live and paint in this Iowa city.

Grant Wood, *Self-Portrait*, 1932–41. Oil on masonite 14 ¾″ x 12 ⅜″ (38 x 31 cm). Davenport Museum of Art.

Though the time he spent on the family farm was brief, strong memories of his early experiences became the subjects of his paintings. From hayrides in the fields to the midday meal, Grant painted the types of people and the landscapes which he recalled from his childhood. During the prime of his career in the 1930s, he painted very little of the life he observed from the window of his Cedar Rapids home. Grant Wood chose instead to paint a romanticized version of rural Iowa as he remembered it from his youth.

Summary

Composing is what the artist does when he or she puts all the elements together to make a work of art.

Analyzing means figuring out how the work was composed. An analysis points out the relationships between and among the elements in a composition.

Chapter 10 will cover more about composing an artwork. It will also discuss what kinds of relationships to look for in a composition.

Chapter 10
Design

10–1 Georges Seurat, *Bathing at Asnières*, 1883–1884. Oil on canvas, 6′ 7″ x 9′ 11″ (201 x 302 cm). Reproduced by courtesy of the Trustees, The National Gallery, London.

In Chapter 9, you learned that artists compose elements to create a work of art. The final result is called a composition. The artist follows a plan, or **design**, to organize the composition. In the final composition, the different elements should all work together.

There are no exact rules for achieving good composition in works of art. However, there are some principles of design that can be followed. The principles of *unity, variety, dominance, rhythm and movement*, and *balance* can be helpful in seeing how the various elements are organized and how they work together.

Unity

Unity in art can be compared with teamwork in sports. A basketball team needs five players. But to be successful, the coach must make the five members play as a unit. Likewise, if an artwork is to be successful, the artist must make the elements work together as a unit. If a work of art does not have unity, it will appear to be a collection of individual parts. If the composition is successful, you are aware of the whole work of art before looking at individual parts. The main purpose of the artist's plan is unity.

Several aspects of design contribute to unity. They can be demonstrated by examining Georges Seurat's painting, *Bathing at Asnières* (fig. 10–1).

Proximity

One way to make separate objects look unified is to place them close together, or in *proximity.* In Seurat's painting there are groups of people and objects. There are the three boys on the right. A pile of clothing is by the large boy. The man and dog form a group of two. There are groupings of trees and buildings in the distance. Notice how the individual figures and objects along the riverbank are tied together by their proximity. Your eye moves from one to another.

Similarity

A second way to achieve unity is to make things *similar* in color, texture, shape, or form. Several objects in the painting, even those that are distant from each other, are connected by their similarity in color. Red-orange, for example, appears in the dog, the hat of the boy in the water, and his shorts. Can you identify some other items with red-orange? What other colors are repeated in Seurat's painting?

Several objects in the painting have similar shapes. For example, the dome shape occurs in the hats, the heads of the two hatless bathers, and even in some of the trees. There are many triangle shapes. For example, look at the bent legs of the persons sitting on the bank. The arms of the boy holding his hands to his mouth are bent in a triangle. Look for a triangle in the back of the reclining man, and in the shadow behind the large boy's arm. The boat sails are also triangular. Can you identify some other repeated shapes in the painting?

Continuation

When you view an artwork, your eye often follows a certain path. The flow of vision can be caused by a line, edges of shapes, or the arrangement of objects. This is called *continuation.* The edge of the riverbank in Seurat's painting is a good example of a line that directs the flow of vision. The riverbank continues from the lower right corner to the upper left side. Another is the line of the bridge and buildings.

Continuation is often reinforced by the similarity and placement of the forms. For example, your vision tends to move from the large figures in front to the small ones at the far end of the riverbank. Then you look along the buildings, past the boat sail reflected in the water, and back down to the boy with cupped hands. The continuation in *Bathing at Asnières* is shown in figure 10–2.

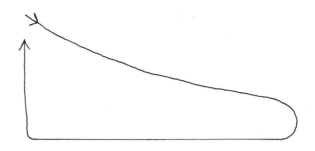

10–2 Diagram of continuation in Seurat's *Bathing*.

Studio Experience 10.1

Movement and Unity in Sculpture

Construct a three-dimensional sculpture. Choose wood scraps and organize them to create visual movement and unity throughout the form.

Kay Dye.

Faith Ringgold

1930–

As a child, Faith Ringgold suffered from asthma. She spent many days at home with her mother, Willi Posey Jones, who was a fashion designer and dressmaker. To keep Faith entertained while she was ill, she would give her fabrics, thread, crayons, and watercolors to play with. Without knowing it, Willi was helping her daughter to become an artist.

Faith Ringgold grew up in Harlem, New York, during the Great Depression. This was a difficult time when many people were unemployed and struggling to provide food and clothing for their families. Faith remembers that time as a very important part of her life which influenced her later artwork: "Mostly, I remember people. Faces of people. Everything about people. And…early on, I got involved with the souls of people."

Faith studied art education in college and taught in the New York City Public Schools. Together, she and her students explored African heritage and culture through art. From this experience Faith developed a sense of pride in being a black American.

1972 was a year of change for Faith. While teaching African crafts at a New York college, she had a retrospective exhibition of her paintings of the previous ten years. One of her students expressed disappointment in Faith's artwork: "I didn't see any of the techniques you teach us… beading, tie-dyeing. Why aren't you using the techniques of African women?" Faith could not answer her student's question. She began to realize that fabric and beads had been part of her life since childhood; perhaps she should use these materials and techniques in her artwork. Faith's childhood experiences, her youth in the Harlem community, and her interest in African culture could be combined to form a new type of art.

Faith began using cloth, beads, rope, thread, and ribbon to create unusual sculptures of people. Some of these sculptures were of people she remembered from growing up in Harlem. Others were of famous people like Wilt Chamberlain and Martin Luther King, Jr. Some of her sculptures are small, while others are larger than life. A small sculpture, *Lena*, requires that you look closely to learn about this little person who lives on the street, while *Martin Luther King* is larger than life-size, emphasizing Dr. King's importance to Faith and to all people.

Today Faith continues to work with a variety of traditionally African materials in her art, using them in sculptures of unique individuals, quilts which tell stories of people, and even performances which involve singing and dancing. Faith Ringgold's artwork portrays both her passion for people and her understanding of the struggles of modern life.

Faith Ringgold, *Lena*, 1978. Mixed Media. ©Faith Ringgold.

Variety

A composition can be so unified that it is uninteresting. A good example is the pattern in a tile floor. All of the tiles are the same color, in close proximity, and constantly repeated. The floor is very unified, but not very exciting.

Variety refers to differences. Variety may involve different materials and objects, and different forms of the same thing. Contrasts of values, textures, and colors also provide variety. Seurat's *Bathing* has a lot of variety. People of varied sizes, who are dressed differently, are doing different things. There are sailboats, buildings, trees, a dog, a river and a riverbank. There is also a variety of colors, lines, textures, and shapes.

Even with all of this variety, *Bathing* is a peaceful and relaxed scene. Seurat used related colors (yellow-greens and blues). The figures are posed in relaxed positions. Variety contributes interest to a picture, or to anything in life. Too much variety, however, can be disorderly and confusing. Therefore, variety in *Bathing* has been brought under control by unity.

Once in a while, an artist may use unrelieved repetition on purpose. In *100 Cans* (fig. 10–3) Andy Warhol repeated the same soup can one hundred times. Perhaps the work is a critical comment on the monotony of repeated commercial images that are forced upon us every day. By comparison, Joseph Cornell's *Object ("Roses des vents")* has a great deal of variety (fig. 10–4). It includes many different objects: maps, charts, rocks, compasses, a spring, seeds, and pictures. Cornell has pushed variety to the limit in this sculptural work. Perhaps the work is a comment on our tendency to gather and keep collections of odds and ends.

Dominance

When one element appears to be more important or attracts the most attention, we say it is **dominant.** The dominant element or form is usually a focal point in a composition. We tend to look at it first. In Seurat's painting, the large boy sitting on the bank by the pile of clothing dominates the picture. The boy is a focal point to which our eyes keep returning. Why does he dominate? One reason is his size. He is the second largest figure in the painting. Another reason is his location, which is near the center. The warm colors in his hair, flesh, and shorts contrast with the cool color of the water.

10–3 Andy Warhol, *100 Cans*, 1962. Oil on canvas, 72″ x 52″ (183 x 132 cm). Albright-Knox Art Gallery, Buffalo, New York, Gift of Seymour H. Knox, 1963.

10–4 Joseph Cornell, *Object ("Roses des vents")*, 1942–1953. Wooden box with twenty-one compasses set into a wooden tray resting on plexiglass-topped and partitioned section, divided into seventeen compartments containing small, miscellaneous objects and three-part hinged lid covered inside with parts of maps of New Guinea and Australia, 2 5/8″ x 21 1/4″ x 10 3/8″ (7 x 54 x 26 cm). The Museum of Modern Art, New York. Mr. and Mrs. Gerald Murphy Fund.

10–6   John Steuart Curry, *Baptism in Kansas,* 1928. Oil on canvas, 40″ x 50″ (102 x 127 cm). Collection of Whitney Museum of American Art. Gift of Gertrude Vanderbilt Whitney.

10–5   Richard Estes, *Nedick's,* 1969–1970. Oil, 48″ x 66″ (122 x 168 cm). Private collection.

An element does not have to be large or in the center of the artwork in order to dominate. An element may dominate because it is different from everything else. For example, the Coca-Cola sign in the painting by Richard Estes (fig. 10–5) stands out because it is the only major circular shape. The composition is filled with mostly rectangular shapes.

The preacher and the young woman are the dominant figures in John Steuart Curry's *Baptism in Kansas* (fig. 10–6). The two figures are centrally located at the hub of two circles. One circle is formed by the water trough. The other circle is formed by the ring of onlookers. This kind of composition is called *radial design.* Most of the people are looking at the central pair of figures. This fact is especially important to this radial design. They draw our attention to the pair. (This kind of direction, called *lines of sight,* was defined in Chapter 4.) Have you often looked where other people are looking or pointing?

Studio Experience 10.2

Dominance in Low-Relief

Arrange lightweight cardboard shapes around a heavy dominant form on a piece of cardboard. Glue in place. Stretch aluminum foil over the work to make a low-relief sculpture.

Cardboard shapes glued in place.

Finished work by Nick Capodice.

10–7 Edvard Munch, *The Scream,* 1893. Oil on canvas, 36″ x 29″ (91 x 74 cm). ©Munch Museum, Oslo 1993.

Rhythm and Movement

When you think of rhythm, you may think of the beat in music or the movements of a dancer. A painting also has **rhythm** and **movement.** Controlled repetition of shapes and lines, or the alternation of light and dark areas, creates a sense of movement. This is called rhythm. Although continuation contributes to visual movement, rhythm is a more powerful way to create movement.

There are three methods for creating rhythm. First, rhythm can be created by repeating the *same* element, such as a shape or a figure, with little or no variation. Secondly, it can be created by repeating two or more elements on an *alternating* basis, such as circle-square, circle-square. Thirdly, it can be created by *progressive* repetition, in which an element changes gradually from large to small, dark to light, and so on.

Most artworks include more than one kind of rhythm. Andy Warhol's *100 Cans* (fig. 10–3) shows unvarying repetition in the vertical rows of cans. In the horizontal rows, rhythm comes from the alternation of red and white on the label.

The Scream by Edvard Munch (fig. 10–7) involves a rhythm of curved shapes and lines that become progressively larger from the upper left to the lower right. Our eyes follow their movement toward the main figure. Then the converging lines of the bridge provide a progression of shapes from large to small. These lines direct us back into the left part of the picture. Do you experience a movement in and out of the painting that suggests the echoing of a scream?

10-8   Claude Monet, *Waterloo Bridge*, 1903. Oil on canvas, 25 ¾″ x 36 ⅝″ (65 x 93 cm). Worcester Art Museum, Massachusetts.

You can see all three types of rhythm in Claude Monet's painting, *Waterloo Bridge* (fig. 10–8). The negative spaces beneath the arches *alternate* with the positive forms of the arches, creating a rhythmical movement diagonally across the picture. The arches become *progressively* smaller from left to right, reinforcing the visual movement across the painting. Monet also created a progression of colors from light and bright in the foreground water, to the dark of the bridge, to the grayed or dull colors in the background. *Repeated* white and light green brush strokes on a dark color suggest waves and reflections in the water.

You can find rhythm in Seurat's *Bathing*, but it is more subtle. The curved line along the head, neck, and back is repeated in all of the seated figures, and in the boy in the water with cupped hands. The edge of the riverbank provides a continuous flow of line that brings our eyes to progressively smaller forms. Look closely at the reflections in the water for rhythmic light and dark alternations. The light is coming from the right of the painting. It causes an alternation of light and dark values on all of the figures and objects. Can you identify more examples of alternation and repetition in the background?

Balance

Look at the two examples of the painting *Going Home* by Jacob Lawrence (fig. 10–9A, B). Which one do you like better? Most people choose example (A) as more satisfying than (B). Before reading further, can you explain what was affected by removing the seated figure in the striped pants and the reclining figure from the left front of the picture? Why?

10-9A Jacob Lawrence, *Going Home*, 1946. Gouache on board. Collection IBM Corporation, Armonk, New York.

10-9B This version of Jacob Lawrence's painting has been photographically altered. Which do you think is better balanced?

Removing the figures in Jacob Lawrence's painting made the right side of the picture appear heavier than the left. It affected the balance of the composition. **Balance** in a composition refers to an equal distribution of *visual weight* on either side of a composition's center. The visual weight of images and objects in a painting depends on their relative size, brightness of color, contrasts of value or texture, complexity of shapes, and distance from the center of the composition.

The unchanged reproduction of *Going Home* (A) is *asymmetrically* balanced because the artist achieved a feeling of equally distributed visual weights with figures and objects that are different. The figure that is putting the bag on the shelf creates a forceful diagonal thrust to the right. This thrust and the weight of the figures in the lower right foreground are balanced by the weight of the figures that are in the lower left foreground of the picture. Lawrence carefully positioned all of the figures and objects in *Going Home* to create a "felt" equalization of visual weights.

Symmetrical balance is simpler to achieve and easier to analyze. The decorative symbols woven into the seventh century Peruvian mantle (fig. 10–10) are arranged in symmetrical balance. Identical elements are equally distributed on either side of a vertical axis in the center of the composition. Robert Indiana's *The X-5* (fig. 10–11) is a contemporary example of pure symmetrical balance. In this very precise painting, one side of the composition is a mirror image of the other.

Sometimes the two sides of a composition are similar enough to imply a vertical central axis, and varied just enough to challenge you to identify the differences. This kind of balance is called *approximate symmetry*. You can see it in the painting called *Mae West* by Salvador Dali (fig. 10–12). At first glance, this appears to be a purely symmetrical painting. But look closely and you will discover a number of differences between the two sides. Do you think the painting looks like a portrait, a room interior, or both?

10–11 Robert Indiana, *The X-5*, 1963. Oil on canvas, 108″ x 108″ (274 x 274 cm). Each of five panels is 36″ x 36″ (91 x 91 cm). Collection of Whitney Museum of American Art. Purchase.

10–10 Mantle. Detail: three figures. Wool, embroidered with colored wools. Peru, pre-Inca period, Early Nazca, ca. 600. The Metropolitan Museum of Art, Gift of George D. Pratt, 1932.

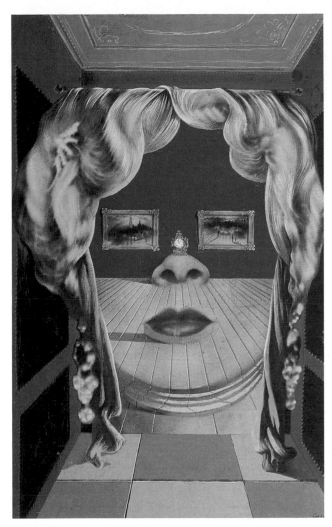

10–12 Salvador Dali, *Mae West*, ca. 1934. Gouache, 11″ x 7″ (28 x 18 cm). The Art Institute of Chicago, Gift of Gilbert W. Chapman in memory of Charles B. Goodspeed, 1949.

10–13 Pomo storage basket. California. Nineteenth century. Coiled basketry, 13 ½″ x 21″ (34 x 53 cm). Courtesy of The National Museum of the American Indian/Smithsonian Institution. (1332g).

10–14 Tadasky, *A-101*, 1964. Synthetic polymer paint on canvas, 52″ x 52″ (132 x 132 cm). The Museum of Modern Art. New York. Larry Aldrich Foundation Fund.

Radial balance results from the repetitive placement of two or more identical or very similar elements around a central point. The Pomo Indians of northern California wove into their baskets geometric designs that radiate outward from a central point (fig. 10–13). The radial balance causes a spiraling movement over inner and outer surfaces of the basket. *A-101* (fig. 10–14) by Tadasky is a radially balanced optical painting. The painting is designed to create the illusion of movement. Try staring at the center of the concentric circles until the black lines begin to whirl.

John Curry's *Baptism in Kansas* demonstrates a more subtle use of radial balance (fig. 10–6). The figures of the preacher and young woman are a central point. Around them are circles of people and automobiles. Even the placement of the house and barn suggests a larger circle that goes off the page.

Look again at Seurat's *Bathing at Asnières* (fig. 10–1) to analyze how it is balanced. You will have no trouble recognizing that it is asymmetrical and well balanced. When you begin to analyze the distribution of visual weights, however, you discover that most of the people are on the left. Even the man lying down, who is the largest figure of all, is on the left. The large man, the placement of the figures, and the diagonal thrust of the riverbank direct attention to the upper left. But on further analysis, you discover that this left-ward tilt is counterbalanced by several things: the right-of-center placement of the large boy, the warm-cool color contrasts between the blue water and the orange hair, shorts, and hat of the boys on the right, and the fact that almost everyone is looking to the right.

Studio Experience 10.3

Drawings with Balance

Make three contour drawings of five or six objects. In each drawing, make one object dominant. Arrange the other objects to show symmetrical, asymmetrical, and radial balance.

Seurat was very concerned about such things as unity and balance. His *Bathing at Asnières* demonstrates all of the design principles. However, some of the other examples included in this chapter do not. Andy Warhol's *100 Cans* (fig. 10–3) has unity, but very little variety and no dominance. Cornell's work of art (fig. 10–4) has variety in the objects. It also has some unity because of a network of horizontal and vertical lines on the upper maps, the compartments in the box, and the rows and columns of compasses. However, it lacks dominance and rhythmical movement. Both Robert Indiana's *The X-5* (fig. 10–11) and Tadasky's *A-101* (fig. 10–14) have little variety.

Some works of art seem to defy all of the principles of design. *Black Painting* by Ad Reinhardt (fig. 10–15) appears to be simply a large black square. If you look at it long and hard, you may see the shape of a cross. Even if you do see the shape, however, there is little variety, no focal point, no rhythm, and no visual movement. Since there are no visual weights, there is nothing on which to base decisions about balance. Black dominates the painting.

The **principles of design** are based on the fundamentals of vision—on how we see everything in our environment. (Recall the discussions on perception of color and shape, object size, figure and ground, and space in Chapters 4, 5, 6, and 7.) They are apparent in most artworks. They give us a way to analyze a composition. The principles of design also help us understand how parts of an artwork are organized.

Summary

The artist is always aware that a whole work of art is more important than any single part. Therefore, he or she must have a plan for organizing all of the elements that make up an art form. This plan, or design, can be analyzed in terms of certain principles: *unity, variety, dominance, rhythm and movement,* and *balance.*

Unity is described as a sense of wholeness or oneness that is present when all parts of an art form work together. When a composition is unified, you find your vision moving easily over the objects, shapes, and elements. Your concern is for the total form rather than individual parts. Although unity is dependent upon all of the design principles, it is especially enhanced by *proximity, similarity,* and *continuation.*

Too much unity can result in monotony. Therefore, the artist includes some *variety.* Contrasts of colors, different shapes, and variations of lines or

10–15 In some nonrepresentational works, one element is totally dominant. Black dominates this painting and the viewer's perception of it. What meanings are suggested by a large black square? Ad Reinhardt, *Black Painting*, 1960. Oil on canvas, 60″ x 60″ (152 x 152 cm). Photograph courtesy of The Pace Gallery.

textures can create some interest and excitement. Look for examples of unity with variety in your environment, such as the design of a building, a shopping mall, or a landscaped park.

Sometimes an element or area of an artwork appears to be *dominant*. It attracts your immediate attention. Other parts of the composition may be emphasized in varying degrees. These contrasts help to direct visual movement from an initial focal point to other parts of the artwork.

Rhythm and movement result from the organized repetition of an element or elements in a work of art. Three methods of creating rhythm are repetition, alternation, and progression.

Balance is a feeling of equilibrium among all the parts of a composition. Balance in an artwork may be symmetrical, approximately symmetrical, asymmetrical, or radial.

The principles of design are very interdependent. Artists use them all, and in many different ways. These principles will help you to analyze and appreciate a variety of art forms. You may also find them helpful in creating your own works of art.

Criticism Experience 10.4

Analyzing an Advertisement

Use the analysis guidelines in Chapter 9 and Experience 9.1 to analyze an advertisement. Cover the principles of design in your analysis.

Lauri Lazar.

Part IV
What Is It Made Of?

Mary Miss, *Field Rotation*, 1981. Wood, concrete, steel, earth and water. Structure 7' x 56' x 56' (2m x 17m x 17m), centered in 4¹/₂ acre site.

Chapter 11
Introduction to Media

The word **medium** is the singular form of media. It has two meanings that apply to art. Medium can refer to the material used for making an artwork. It can also refer to the liquid ingredient of a paint, such as water, linseed oil or egg yolk, in which pigment is suspended. For this discussion, we are interested in the first use of the term.

The following chapters will introduce you to a variety of two- and three-dimensional art forms, and the media associated with each of them. For example, painting is a **two-dimensional** art form. The media used for painting include oil, watercolor, acrylic, and tempera. Media for sculpture, a **three-dimensional** art form, include welded and cast metal, wood, stone, plaster, and plastic. As you will see, the various media are used to make different kinds of art. They are also used for different expressive purposes.

A medium is not always a material that does just what the artist wishes. Think of the artist's work with the medium as a contest. The artist wants to use the medium for a certain purpose. The medium, however, may not have the capabilities to support the purpose. Each medium has special capabilities and limitations. The artist learns through trial and error what the material can do. The artist then uses that information to achieve his or her purpose. The more an artist knows about a medium, the greater his or her mastery of the medium will be.

The artist's choice of medium is often related to the **subject matter,** what is represented in the work. For example, carved stone would not be a very good medium for expressing the qualities of a landscape. Oil paint, on the other hand, is excellent for representing colors, tones, sky, clouds, hills, and trees in a landscape.

Both the sculptor and the painter can do portraits, however. For example, Charles Peale portrayed George Washington in an oil painting as a victorious Revolutionary War general (fig. 11–1). Horatio Greenough used marble to produce a larger-than-life sculpture of Washington that looks like a Roman emperor seated on a throne (fig. 11–2).

11–2 Horatio Greenough, *George Washington,* 1840. Marble, approx. 11′4″ (347 cm) high. National Museum of American Art, Washington, DC, USA/Art Resource, NY.

11–1 This portrait of George Washington expresses the American feeling of the nationalism and confidence which sustained the country during the Revolutionary War. Charles Wilson Peale, *George Washington at the Battle of Princeton,* 1780–1781. Oil on canvas. Yale University Art Gallery (Gift of the Associated in Fine Arts and Mrs. Henry B. Loomis, in memory of Henry Bradford Loomis, B.A. 1875).

Each portrait of Washington contains its own information. Peale's painting gives the illusion of depth. The figure, cannon, and other objects look three-dimensional. An apparently confident General Washington, wearing a Continental Army uniform, leans against a cannon. Behind him are the American battle flag and his waiting horse. The banners of the defeated British troops (Hessian mercenaries) are at his feet. In the background, American soldiers take British prisoners away. The figures and objects, colors and textures are placed in an environmental setting, which contributes to the meaning of the artwork. Do you think the painting expresses the confidence of a general, or the confidence of a young republic capable of winning and defending its freedom?

In contrast to the painting, Greenough's sculpture of Washington has real depth and textures. You can both see *and* feel the rounded three-dimensional forms and the different textures. The viewer can move around the sculpture and see it from different angles to get more information. Greenough's sculpture was originally created for the Capitol rotunda in Washington, DC. However, the American public demanded that it be removed. Americans objected to seeing a former president portrayed as a partially nude Roman emperor.

The medium is also the artist's means of expressing ideas. For example, Greenough designed and carved the marble sculpture to express his ideas about George Washington as a great, powerful, and heroic leader of our country. By comparison, the form that Alberto Giacometti gave the sculpture called *Man Pointing* (fig. 11–3) would not be practical for carving in marble. Nor would stone be as effective for expressing his ideas about the human condition. Giacometti used bronze casting to produce this spindly, seven-foot-tall figure that does not appear heroic or powerful. Greenough's massive sculpture of Washington displaces space and suggests great strength. *Man Pointing* is so slender that the figure seems lost in space—perhaps even threatened by the surrounding emptiness. The bronze casting medium seems well suited to expressing ideas such as man's frailty.

More often than not, the artist already has a form or idea in mind before he or she selects a medium. Then the artist chooses the medium that will best express that idea or form. When analyzing a work of art, we look for good relationships among the medium, subject matter, and expression. In Chapters 12 and 13, you will learn about many artworks in many different media. Studying the examples and working with your own art materials will help you understand the interaction between the medium and expression of ideas.

Analysis Experience 11.1

Choosing Media

Look at Greenough's sculpture of Washington (fig. 11–2). Write down as many reasons as you can think of for making the sculpture in marble, rather than in wood, concrete or papier-mâché.

Try it Yourself

How do you think the public would react if, say, Jimmy Carter or George Bush were portrayed as a Greek god or Roman emperor? How would you react? If you don't think that kind of sculpture would be appropriate, what kind of symbolism would you suggest for a portrait of a modern president?

11–3 Alberto Giacometti, *Man Pointing*, 1947. Bronze, 70 ½″ (179 cm) high, at base 12″ x 13 ¼″ (30 x 34 cm). The Museum of Modern Art, New York. Gift of Mrs. John D. Rockefeller, III.

Chapter 12
Two-Dimensional Media

12–1 *Hall of Bulls*, left wall, Lascaux, ca. 15,000–13,000 BC. Dordogne, France. Courtesy of Scala/Art Resource, NY.

Chapter 11 suggested that working with a medium is like a contest. When you play tennis, it helps if you know something about your opponent. In the same way, it helps if you know the capabilities and limitations of your medium when making a picture. Also, in order to appreciate an artwork, it helps to know what a medium is and something about it. This chapter describes various two-dimensional media: drawing, painting, mosaic, printmaking, photography and film, video arts, computer art, and mixed media.

Drawing
Monochromatic Drawing Media

When you draw, you make controlled marks on paper with a tool such as charcoal, pen and ink, pencil, crayon, or felt marker. These tools are drawing media. Some of these tools date back thousands of years. During the Ice Age (around 12,000 BC), hunter-artists used pieces of charcoal on cave walls to outline shapes of animals (fig. 12–1). As early as 2500 BC, Egyptian scribes used ink on sheets of *papyrus,* made from a plant that still grows along the Nile. In the 1400s, European artists began using pencils.

You have been using some of these tools since you were a child. However, that does not mean that drawing is necessarily easy. Sometimes drawing media require more skill than other kinds of media to produce good results. Usually, the artist has only two colors to work with—the color of the tool and the color of the paper.

You learned about values and shading in Chapter 6. You can often get different values in a drawing just by changing the amount of pressure on the pencil or drawing tool. If you rub a stick of charcoal hard, it makes very dark tones. The marks conceal the white of the paper. If you rub the stick lightly, it makes lighter tones. The marks allow tiny bits of white paper to show through and mix optically with the black grains of the charcoal. Observe how Käthe Kollwitz varied the pressure on the charcoal tool to create her self-portrait (fig. 12–2). In some places, like the extended arm, the strokes are broad and dark. In others, like the face and head, they are quite delicate.

Variety like this also can be produced by certain kinds of pencils. The pencil contains a combination of clay and graphite rather than lead. The amount of graphite in the pencil determines the type of line it can make. A hard pencil produces thin, light lines (fig. 12–3). A soft pencil produces thicker, darker lines (fig. 12–4). (Pencils used in school are usually 2B, or medium soft.) With just a few pencil strokes, Felix Klee, Paul's son, captured the quality of a sleeping kitten (fig. 12–5). Did he press harder in some places than others, use more than one type of pencil, or both?

12–2 Käthe Kollwitz, *Self-Portrait, Drawing*, 1933. Charcoal on brown laid Ingres paper, 18 ¾″ x 24 ⅞″ (48 x 63 cm). ©1993 National Gallery of Art, Washington, Rosenwald Collection.

12–3 Hard pencils, such as 2H, produce thin and light lines.

12–4 Soft pencils, such as 3B, produce thick and dark lines.

12–5 Notice how the thicker lines create darker values than the thin lines. Felix Klee, *Fritzi*, 1919. Pencil, 7 ⅝″ x 10 ⅝″ (19 x 27 cm). Collection, The Museum of Modern Art, New York. Gift of Mrs. Donald B. Straus.

Try it Yourself

Try to obtain pencils with different grades, like 2H (medium hard), 5H (very hard), and 5B (very soft). Discover the different kinds of lines they make.

Different values can also be obtained from India ink. Ink poured directly from the bottle is *opaque,* that is, not transparent. When applied to paper, it completely masks the color of the paper. The pen and ink drawing (fig. 12–6) uses shading to show details and rounded forms. The different values were made by hatching (Chapter 4). Notice how bold the strokes are and how they go in different directions.

12–6 The different values apparent in this pen and ink drawing were obtained by various hatching techniques. Vincent van Gogh, *Pollarded Birches,* 1884. Pencil, ink and paint on wove paper, 16″ x 22″ (40 x 55 cm). Rijksmuseum, Amsterdam.

Japanese artist Shin'cihi used ink in a different way to create shaded effects and depth. In his work (fig. 12–7), the artist used *ink washes,* which are films of water-thinned ink spread with a brush. An ink wash is semitransparent, or *translucent.* It allows the white of the paper to show through and produce gray. To control the values, Shin'cihi controlled the amount of the water in the mixture and overlapped some of the washes. Notice how the thinnest washes were used for the lighter parts of the scene (where the sun shines in the morning mist). The white of the paper itself represents the lightest part of all.

Colored Chalk or Pastel

Colored *chalks* lie somewhere between drawing and painting media. Like charcoal sticks or pencils, sticks of colored chalk can be applied directly to paper. But unlike most drawing media, colored chalks are multi-colored. Hunter-artists may have used an early form of colored chalk. They mixed clay with iron oxide, a pigment that produces brownish reds and yellows.

Pastels are a high-quality form of chalk with a wide range of hues. They were introduced in the 1700s. At that time they were especially popular with portrait painters. Pastels allow the artist to use a variety of colors without needing to mix paints or prepare canvas. However, they are quite fragile. The surface of a picture made with chalk or pastel can be easily smeared or dusted away. Pastel drawings must be sprayed with shellac mixed with alcohol or framed under glass.

Studio Experience 12.1

Contrasts in Chalk Drawing

Produce a drawing of a jacket that has descriptive contrasts of light and dark. Use black and white and one or two colors of chalk in your drawing.

Cathy Geno.

12–7 Shin'cihi, *Hisamatsu*, 1971.

12–8 The first stages of a watercolor painting by Dong Kingman. *Chinatown, San Francisco*. Watercolor, 18″ x 22″ (46 x 56 cm). Collection of Rocky Aoki.

Painting

Mention the word art, and most people think of painting. All painting media consist of colored powders called *pigments* and a liquid in which the pigments are mixed. This liquid is called the *vehicle*. The paint is applied to a surface, such as a wall, board, paper or canvas, called the *support*.

Watercolor

Watercolors consist of pigments mixed with water. They are applied with a brush to white paper. Like ink, watercolors have been around for centuries. At first they were used only to add a little color to drawings. In the early 1800s watercolors came into their own. At that time, their potentials were discovered and developed by English watercolorists. Since then, this medium has been very popular, especially for colorful, lively outdoor scenes.

The methods of working with watercolors are similar to those used for ink washes. In developing a composition, watercolorist Dong Kingman works in stages. He first lays in the lighter washes, then adds and overlaps more light washes. Finally, he applies darker washes, bright colors, and opaque strokes (figures 12–8, 12–9, 12–10). Among other procedures, Kingman also first wets the paper and stretches it. Then he blocks out the whites (sometimes with rubber cement, which is later removed).

Despite his years of experience, Kingman plans carefully before touching brush to paper. But in the end, Kingman's pictures, like all good watercolors, are fresh and spontaneous looking. They catch the spirit of the subject with an ease that comes from long practice.

12–9 Second stage.

12–10 Finished watercolor painting.

Watercolor Washes

Produce watercolor washes that are *flat* (uniform, unchanging), *graded* (light to dark), and *mixed* (varied hues and intensities). Then paint opaque lines over the washes.

a. Flat washes.

b. Graded washes.

c. Mixed washes.

d. Opaque lines over washes.

Tempera

Tempera is applied to paper, wood, or canvas. The medium of tempera consists of pigments mixed with an *emulsion.* An emulsion is a watery liquid with droplets of oil suspended in it. Egg yolk, a natural emulsion, has been the traditional emulsion used in tempera. Today there are many different emulsions. They can be based on casein (a milk product), gum arabic, plastic, and wax.

Unlike watercolors, which are thin and relatively transparent, tempera is creamy and opaque. To make an area white, the artist may use white paint or the paper. To lighten a color, the artist adds white paint, not water. Water is used as a thinner to make the paint flow better or to make it transparent. It is also used to clean brushes.

Tempera was used by the Greeks and Romans. It reached its peak in the late Middle Ages, between 1100 and 1500. During this period, tempera was the favorite medium for paintings on wooden panels, like *The Adoration of the Magi* (fig. 12–11) by Gentile da Fabriano. Tempera dries quickly with a soft matte finish and lends itself to fine detail. Because it is opaque, tempera allows the artist to paint over previously painted areas. The artist can continually improve effects of shading or texture. (This method does not work very well with watercolors.)

The *Adoration* has a greeting-card charm that is due to the medium of tempera. Note the delicate colors in the painting. In many places the colors are enhanced with gold foil. Note also the detail of the many figures and animals, especially the decoration of the Magi's crowns and splendid costumes.

The advantages of tempera for some kinds of painting, however, are disadvantages for other kinds. Rapid drying prevents the easy blending of colors. Tempera produces delicate effects instead of lively, spontaneous-looking effects. Furthermore, tempera colors tend to change while drying, making it difficult to predict the final results. Tempera gave way to oil in the 1400s and 1500s as the most popular medium. Still, some artists, notably Andrew Wyeth, use it to this day. When painting subjects like *Braids* (fig. 12–12), Wyeth finds the characteristics of tempera to be ideal for his purposes.

12–11 Gentile da Fabriano, *The Adoration of the Magi*, 1423. Tempera on wood panel, approx. 9´ 11˝ x 9´ 3˝ (302 x 282 cm). Galleria degli Uffizi, Florence.

12–12 Andrew Wyeth, *Braids*. Tempera.

A Tempera Painting

Create a tempera painting based on an artwork that portrays a situation. In *your* painting, show what happens next.

a. Darrell Wu.

b. Sue Musselman.

12–13 Emilio Cruz, *Past Pastures,* 1983. Oil on canvas, 72″ x 48″ (183 x 122 cm). Collection of the artist. Photograph: John Majjiotto.

Oil

Oil is the star attraction, not just of paint, but of all media. It is made up of pigments mixed with linseed oil. Turpentine is the thinner or solvent. The popularity of oil dates back to the 1400s. It was first used for colored *glazes,* which are thin films of transparent varnish. Glazes were brushed over tempera paintings to give them more luster. Somewhat later, at about the time of Leonardo da Vinci, artists began using oil paint from start to finish. Later still, in the middle of the 1500s, canvas replaced wood as the principal type of support. To this day, *oil on canvas* is perhaps the most popular medium of all.

Oil is much more flexible than tempera. It can be opaque or translucent, as thick as plaster or as thin as watercolor. Most importantly, it dries slowly. It allows an artist more freedom to blend colors and create a great variety of effects. You have seen some of that variety in the paintings in this book. How does the dry brushwork of Hopper's *House by the Railroad* (fig. 5–32) differ from the fluid brushwork of Bellows's *Stag at Sharkey's* (fig. 8–14)?

For more examples of oil paint's variety, compare and contrast the styles of Rembrandt (fig. 5–31), the unknown painter of *Mademoiselle Charlotte du Val d'Ognes* (fig. 6–9), Renoir (fig. 3–1), and Mondrian (fig. 7–10). The works of contemporary painter Emilio Cruz are especially representative of the medium. The word *exuberance* (full of life and high spirits) is often used to describe his paintings. Look at Cruz's *Past Pastures* (fig. 12–13). Exuberance is obviously expressed in the subject matter, especially in the terrifying head. But it is also expressed in the rich creamy paint and the iridescent colors. Cruz transformed paint into explosive energy.

Canvas is the most common support for oil paintings. It has several advantages for the artist. For one thing, it is very light. A large oil painting can be carried by one person. If thoroughly dry, a painting can even be removed from its thin wooden frame *(stretchers),* rolled, and shipped in a mailing tube. The same size painting on wood would be heavy and very awkward to handle or ship. It may surprise you to know, however, that oil rots fabric, including canvas fabric. To prevent canvases from rotting, artists have had to coat them with a layer or two of a special glue or gesso (a plaster-like substance) before applying paints. Today synthetic products are available for preparing canvases.

12–14 Helen Frankenthaler, *Canal,* 1963. Acrylic on canvas, 81″ x 57 ½″ (206 x 146 cm). Purchased with the aid of funds from the National Endowment for the Arts in Washington, DC, a Federal Agency; Matching gift, Evelyn Sharp. Photograph: David Heald ©The Solomon R. Guggenheim Foundation, New York.

Acrylic

Acrylic is a synthetic medium that came into use after World War II. Acrylic paints are made from plastic material suspended in a water-soluble liquid, or polymer. Acrylic can be applied to anything, including canvas. Acrylic is the most versatile medium we've covered so far. When thinned with water, it acts like watercolors. When its colors are extended with liquid polymer, they can be used as glazes. Special materials can be added to acrylic to make it thicker than oils. Normally fast drying, it can be made to dry slowly by the addition of "retarders." Most importantly, it can be applied directly to canvas without rotting it.

Helen Frankenthaler has taken advantage of this capability by pouring water-thinned acrylics onto raw canvas. This is a new approach to painting called *stained canvas.* The results of colors spreading, mixing, and sinking into the canvas are visible in *Canal* (fig. 12–14). Sometimes the canvas is warped or tilted in different directions during the process.

12–15 Diego Rivera, *Detroit Industry*, 1932–1933. Fresco, mural. ©The Detroit Institute of Arts, Founders Society Purchase, Edsel B. Ford Fund and Gift of Edsel B. Ford.

Fresco

If acrylic is the newest paint medium, fresco is one of the oldest. It is used to make paintings, or murals, on walls. Fresco painting consists of mixing pigments in water, spreading wet plaster onto a wall or ceiling, and applying the colors to the plaster before it dries. (Many cultures painted on a wall or ceiling after the plaster had dried, a method called secco.)

The first people to use fresco were probably the Minoans. Their seafaring culture flourished on the island of Crete around 1500 BC. The most famous examples of fresco were made by Italian artists from the early 1300s to the mid-1500s.

As you know, plaster dries quickly. Therefore the artist must plan ahead when spreading plaster. The artist must be able to paint the area within a few hours. A large mural, such as Diego Rivera's *Detroit Industry* (fig. 12–15), had to be painted in sections. To avoid leaving a water mark, Rivera probably ended each section at the edge of a figure or object, rather than in the middle. Possibly Rivera could do only a few of the

12–16 Diego Rivera, *Detroit Industry* (detail), 1932–1933. Fresco, mural. The Detroit Institute of Arts, Founders Society Purchase, Edsel B. Ford Fund and Gift of Edsel B. Ford.

laborers or one machine at a time in *Detroit Industry* (fig. 12–16). Because of the difficulties of working with the fresco method, the artist cannot easily make in-process changes or add fussy details. Perhaps this is why Rivera made the forms in his mural so bold.

Fresco does have two advantages: durability and permanence. It is *in* the plaster, not a film of paint *on* the plaster. Fresco can better withstand the effects of air pollution and wear and tear in general. A fresco is part of a wall or ceiling, and will survive as long as that wall or ceiling does.

Mosaic

A mosaic is a design or picture made from many pieces of stone or glass. These pieces, called *tesserae,* are set in cement. Mosaics are typically used to decorate a wall, ceiling, or floor. An artist must piece together thousands of individual bits of tesserae to complete a mosaic. In some ways a mosaic is more like a jigsaw puzzle than a drawing or painting. A mosaic has been called a "painting in stone." Mosaic is colorful, durable, and part of a wall or ceiling. In these ways it is similar to fresco.

Mosaics have not been very popular since the 1300s, but they were once more popular than frescos. The Romans, who embedded mosaic designs in floors and walls, used tesserae made of stone cubes. The Early Christians covered the walls and ceilings of their churches with mosaics made from pieces of glass.

Because glass reflects, and because tesserae do not lie on a uniformly flat plane, the mosaics reflect in all directions. Imagine the glittering effect inside a church filled with mosaics like *Emperor Justinian and Attendants* (fig. 12–17). Note the simplicity of both the composition and the individual figures. Even more than fresco, the medium of mosaic forces the artist to think in terms of large bold images. But the severity of the design is tempered by the sparkle of its surface.

Printmaking

Like drawings, prints are produced on paper, but with an important difference. A print can be *re*produced several times. The major techniques of printmaking involve the use of ink, paper, and a *plate.* A plate is the surface on which the picture or design is made. A plate is often a piece of wood or copper. To produce a print, a piece of paper is pressed against an inked plate. This process can be repeated many times to make many prints of one image.

Relief Prints

A *relief print* is so called because the image on the plate is in *relief,* that is, it projects or sticks up from the surface of the plate (fig. 12–18). The *woodcut* was devel-

12–18 A cross section of a relief plate.

oped in the 1300s to produce large quantities of religious pictures. The woodcut is still the most common kind of relief printing. (Linoleum is also used.) The artist draws on a block of wood, then cuts away the areas that are to remain white. The parts that will be printed are raised from the background. Black ink is rolled across the plate and clings to those parts that are in relief. When paper is pressed against the plate, the black ink is transferred to the paper, making the finished print.

Albrecht Dürer was a skilled sixteenth-century German artist. Study his *The Riders on the Four Horses from the Apocalypse* (fig. 12–19). Every black line that

12–19 Albrecht Dürer, *The Riders on the Four Horses from the Apocalypse,* ca. 1496. Woodcut, 15 ¼″ x 11″ (39 x 28 cm). The Metropolitan Museum of Art, New York, Gift of Junius S. Morgan, 1919. (19.73.209)

12–20 Elizabeth Catlett, *The Survivor,* 1983. Linocut, 11″ x 10″ (28 x 26 cm). Courtesy Malcolm Brown Gallery, Cleveland, Ohio.

describes shape or detail is exact. Dürer had to cut around each of these lines when carving the wooden block. It is hard to believe that this complex image is a woodcut.

Elizabeth Catlett has a different approach. In her *The Survivor* (fig. 12–20), the marks of the cutting tool are much more evident. Like many other twentieth-century artists, Catlett believes that the qualities of a medium should be visible, even celebrated, in every work of art.

Try it Yourself

Do you prefer Dürer's type of woodcut or Catlett's? People who like traditional art appreciate the great skill as shown by Dürer's approach. People who like modern art prefer works like Catlett's. Catlett's woodcuts may seem somewhat primitive, but they bring out the qualities of the medium. Are you a traditionalist or a modernist? Perhaps you appreciate both approaches, realizing that different standards must be applied to each. In any case, explain your position.

Elizabeth Catlett

1919–

African American painter and sculptor Elizabeth Catlett has focused her life and her art on civil rights. "I have always wanted my art to service Black people—to reflect us, to relate to us, to stimulate us, to make us aware of our potential." (Samella S. Lewis, *Art: African American.* New York: Harcourt Brace Jovanovich, 1978, p. 125).

Catlett's first experience with discrimination occurred when she was rejected from an art college which had never before accepted a black student. Bitter but determined, she entered Howard University, a predominantly black school, and pursued her studies with several famous black art professors.

In 1938, following in her father's footsteps, Catlett became an art teacher. Her first job in North Carolina paid only $59 each month, half the salary paid to white teachers. Recognizing the injustice in this system, Catlett helped campaign for equal wages for both black and white teachers.

Catlett went on to receive a master's degree in sculpture, to direct the art department at a university in New Orleans, and to teach at two schools in New York. Her dedication to the civil rights movement continued, reflecting itself in her politically active life and her emotionally vibrant artwork. During her first visit to Mexico in 1946 at the age of 27, Catlett decided to stay in this country to work on her linoleum prints with other printmakers; she remained there to marry, raise three children, and pursue her career as an artist. She became a naturalized citizen of Mexico in 1962.

Elizabeth Catlett's devotion to black people and to the citizens of Mexico remains an important aspect of her work today. This dedication is apparent in the intensity of the characters in her prints and sculptures. Strong-willed, determined and proud, these figures, like the artist who created them, illustrate the powerful impact of a life dedicated to art.

A Linoleum Block Print

Produce a three-color print using the linoleum reduction block procedure.

Chris Listello.

Intaglio Prints

Intaglio (in TAH lee-oh; Italian for "to cut in") is the opposite of relief printing. Rather than being above the surface, an intaglio image is below it (fig. 12–21). The lines, unlike relief printing, do not project. The artist cuts the lines that are to print *into* the plate. An intaglio plate is usually a sheet of copper or zinc. Sheet plastic is sometimes used.

12–21 A cross section of an intaglio plate.

Three kinds of intaglio are *engraving*, *etching*, and *aquatint*. To do engraving, the artist cuts lines into the plate using a special gouge called a *burin*. To do etching, the artist first covers the plate with a layer of wax, called a *ground*. Then the artist draws in the wax with a needle. When the plate is placed in acid, the exposed lines are eaten by the acid. To do aquatint, the artist bonds particles of resin to the plate, then blocks out those areas that are not to be eaten by the acid with a coat of shellac. When placed in acid, only the very small spaces between the resin particles are eaten.

All three intaglio methods use the same printing technique. Black ink is rubbed into the etched lines or areas. These inked areas are transferred to a piece of paper under the extreme pressure of an intaglio press. Engraved lines look hard and brittle. Etched lines appear softer. Aquatint produces gritty-textured areas of gray.

To make *Todd* (fig. 12–22) Xiaowen Chen used etching and aquatint. Some of the thinner, lighter lines on Todd's desk have been etched once or twice. The darker lines were made by drawing and "biting" the lines with acid several times. The gray areas on this side of the desk are the result of aquatint. The dark shadows around Todd and especially behind his left shoulder are the result of a combination of aquatint and densely hatched etched lines. Chen's print shows how the medium can be used to achieve variety in tone and texture.

12–22 Xiaowen Chen, *Todd*. Etching and aquatint.

12–24 Käthe Kollwitz, *Death Seizing a Woman*, 1934, Plate IV from the series *Death*, 1934–1936. Lithograph, 20″ x 14″ (51 x 36 cm). Collection, The Museum of Modern Art, New York. Purchase Fund.

Planographic Prints

In planographic printing, the image is *on* the surface of the plate (fig. 12–23). *Lithography* is one of the most widely used of all printmaking methods. It is based on the principle that oil and water do not mix. The artist draws on the flat surface of a block of limestone with a grease crayon. Then the surface is dampened with water. Of course, the grease lines do not absorb the water. When the artist rolls oily ink onto the plate, the damp part of the surface repels the ink. The ink is received by the crayon lines. These lines are then transferred to the paper.

12–23 A cross section of a planographic plate.

A lithograph tends to look like a drawing made with crayon or charcoal. Compare Kollwitz's lithograph *Death Seizing a Woman* (fig. 12–24) with her charcoal self-portrait (fig. 12–2). The brisk lines in the lithograph seem as spontaneous and direct as those done in charcoal.

Screen Prints

Screen printing is the newest printmaking medium. It is a stenciling process. The stencil is placed on a screen made of nylon or polyester, stretched tightly over a frame (fig. 12–25). The stencil can be made of paper or other blockout or resist materials. Ink is forced through the open areas with a squeegee. A separate screen is needed for each color printed. Screen prints do not reverse the image. They do not need heavy pressure, and can be printed on most surfaces.

12–25 Silk screen.

12–26 Pulling a squeegee across the silk screen.

Studio Experience 12.5

A One-Color Screen Print

Design a paper stencil for a one-color silk screen, using line and shape to express a subject of your choice.

Ellen Zauke.

Photography and Film
Photography

Photography has become the modern *folk* medium, or art of the common people. Probably you and your friends have all used cameras at some time. However, you may not know much about the technology of photography.

Like printmaking, identical copies, called prints, can be produced by photography. A photographer captures a scene from life onto light-sensitive film with a camera. A camera is simply a dark box with a *lens* that lets in light when the photographer trips its *shutter,* which opens and closes rapidly. To make the image of the scene visible, the film must be *developed.* This involves immersing it in special chemicals. At this stage the film has become a *negative.* A negative is a semitransparent image of the scene in which the lights and darks are reversed. In a black-and-white film negative, the whites are opaque and blacks are clear. Light grays are barely translucent and dark grays are semitransparent (fig. 12–27).

To make a print of the image, the photographer passes light through the film negative onto light-sensitized paper, which is then developed. This becomes the final product. The print is a positive image of the original scene (fig. 12–28).

So far we have discussed the basics. The photographer can control some things such as lighting, time of day, point of view, and distance. The photographer can also control film speed, width of the lens opening, focus, shutter speed, and flash. The time and temperature of the chemical bath and length of exposure on the contact paper can also affect the final photograph.

Using available light is very important. For example, suppose a subject is very dark and the photographer does not have a flash. He or she would need to use fast film (which is the most sensitive to light), a wide lens opening to let in as much light as possible, and a slow shutter speed.

A most interesting variable is the *focal length* of the lens. This is the distance between the lens and the plane of the film in the back of the camera. By changing the focal length, the photographer can control the composition of the subject within the frame. The longer the focal length, the larger the subject appears to be and the more it fills the frame (fig. 12–29). Lenses with short focal lengths are sometimes called *wide-angle* lenses. They are good for indoor scenes or situations where the photographer is close to the subject and wants to make it appear farther away (fig. 12–30). *Telephoto* lenses have long focal lengths. They are good for enlarging subjects that are in the distance (fig. 12–31). Expensive cameras come with interchangeable lenses. Some lenses have fixed focal lengths. Some have changeable focal lengths called *zoom* lenses.

Consider the decisions that Ansel Adams made when he photographed *Half Dome, Merced River, Winter, Yosemite Valley* (fig. 12–32). Did he journey some distance to locate the subject? Did he search for the spot from which to shoot it? Did he try different lenses to compose the scene within the frame? Did he wait long for the light and the cloud formations to appear before shooting? Did he take a number of shots? Could you have achieved the same results with this subject with your camera?

12–27 Black and white film negative.

12–28 The positive image print.

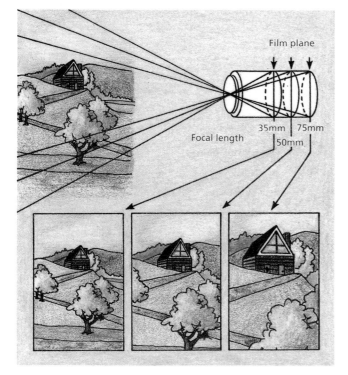

12–29 Focal length.

Try it Yourself

Look for interesting photographs in magazines like *National Geographic, Smithsonian, Life,* and *Sports Illustrated.* Identify those with interesting points of view, such as low eye level, high eye level, and close-ups. Identify pictures taken with wide-angle lenses or telephoto lenses. Can you tell which is which?

12–30 Wide-angle lens. Photographs: Barbara Caldwell.

12–31 Telephoto lens.

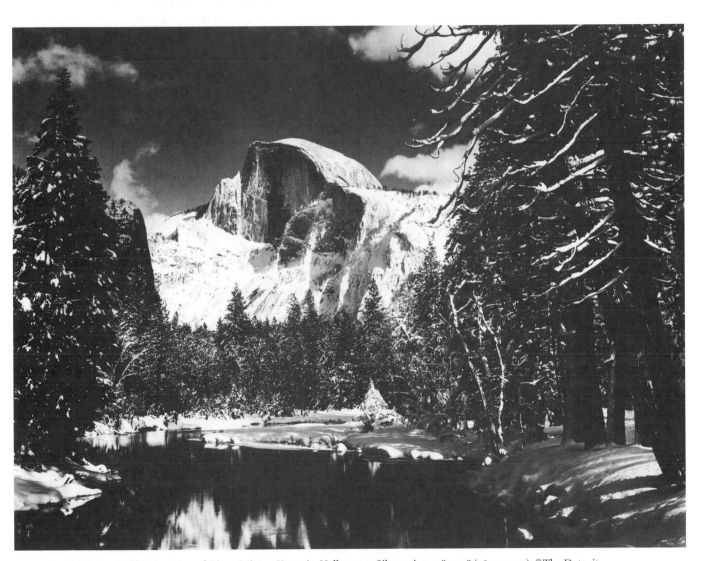

12–32 Ansel Adams, *Half Dome, Merced River, Winter, Yosemite Valley*, 1971. Silverprint, 15˝ x 19˝ (38 x 49 cm). ©The Detroit Institute of Arts.

12–33 The mutoscope.

12–34 The 35mm Mitchell NC.

12–35 The moviola.

Film

People have always been fascinated by moving pictures. The "peep show" (fig. 12–33) created the illusion of motion. The viewer turned a crank to move a series of photographs. Each photograph showed a slightly different motion. If the viewer turned the crank rapidly, the images appeared to be moving. If the viewer turned the crank too slowly, the viewer saw only the individual still pictures. The illusion of motion disappeared. Today's movie projector is based on the same principle of still pictures moving in rapid succession. Of course, the pictures are printed on long strips of film and projected onto a screen for all to see.

The film camera, like a still-photography camera, is an enclosed box (fig. 12–34). The film is contained in large reels called film *magazines*. The film has holes on both sides; sprockets on the camera hold the film in place. The film is fed through the camera in a rapid stop-and-go motion. A single frame of film is pulled into position behind the shutter, the film stops, the shutter opens, and a single image is exposed. This is repeated twenty-four times a second. This is the standard rate of speed for sound film.

Like the photographer, the filmmaker must consider lighting and the placement of people and objects within a frame. In addition, the filmmaker must also consider the movement of people and objects, as well as the movement of the camera. Recall what you learned about film shots and sequence in Chapter 8.

After the film has been shot, the scenes are cut and put together into the final product. This stage of filmmaking is called editing. The editor does not use all the film that was taken. The one-minute battle sequence in *Star Wars* described in Chapter 8 may have been edited from several minutes of film. When first developed, the shots of rebel troops were much longer than one second each. They were probably not in the same order as they appeared in the final sequence. To identify segments and rearrange their sequence, the editor uses a *moviola* (fig. 12–35). A moviola is a machine that runs the film at various speeds.

Commercial films like *Star Wars* are the creation of a *director* who supervises an army of people: writers, artists, musicians, carpenters, camera operators, sound technicians, editors, stunt men and women, not to mention actors and actresses. Think of it. All of these people are involved in the making of an *illusion*.

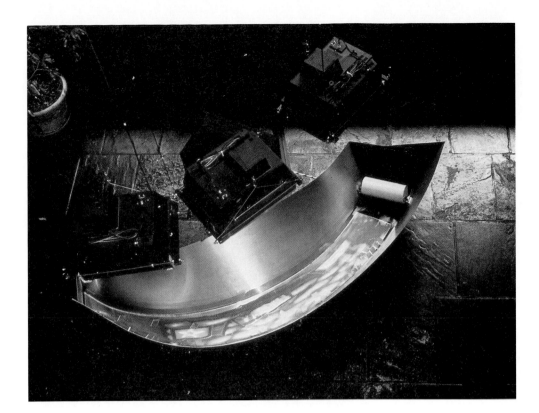

12–36 Shigeko Kubota,
River, 1979–1981.
Photograph ©1983
Peter Moore.

Video Art

Video refers to the picture portion of television. The images seen on television are created by electronic signals. (The images seen on film are created by chemical means.) A video camera is a tube with a lens and a photosensitive electronic plate in the back. The image on the plate is converted to electric signals by a scanner. The scanner reads the image from left to right and line by line from top to bottom in one-thirtieth of a second. The signals are transmitted through the air or carried by cable to a television. There, the signals are converted back to the original image by a "gun" that fires them at the screen. These signals are exactly the same as those read by the scanner. Television signals can also be stored on magnetic tape that can be played back at any time.

Because of recent breakthroughs in technology, many artists now use video instead of film. They use *camcorders*. Camcorders are hand-held units that combine the functions of camera and recorder. Camcorders are small, easy to operate, and relatively inexpensive. They also produce high-quality images. Thus for the individual artist, video has distinct advantages over film. Video tape is cheaper than film. The artist can play it back immediately on a camcorder instead of waiting for a film to be processed in a labo-ratory, threaded through a projector, and viewed in a darkened room.

Nam June Paik was one of the pioneers of video art. He began making works for galleries and public television as early as the late 1950s, long before camcorders hit the market. He manipulated images electronically to create moving geometric patterns. Some have jokingly called these patterns "moving wallpaper." He also used television sets to make novel sculptures.

A good example of a mixed media art is *River* (fig. 12–36) by Paik's wife, Shigeko Kubota. (Mixed media is discussed later in this chapter.) *River* consists of three television sets suspended from the ceiling. The images on the television sets are reflected in a stainless steel trough containing water and a motorized wave machine. Gallery-goers can see the images on the sets, the reflections of the images in the moving water, or the reflections of their reflections bouncing up into space. Critic Brooks Adams compared Kubota's *River* to "a fountain, an indoor garden, a reflecting pool."

Computer Art

Like video, computer art is electronic. The technology for computer art is developing rapidly. Presently, two-dimensional images in color can be produced with personal computers. Three-dimensional images and animated art can be produced on large systems that only government, industries, and universities can afford.

The brain of the computer, the central processing unit (CPU), basically is a board with electrical circuits and transistors. The smallest unit of information for the CPU is a *bit,* or *binary* digit. Binary refers to two numbers: 1 and 0. Think of a bit as an electrical switch: 1 is on, 0 is off. A string of binary numbers, that is, a pattern of on–off switches, makes up a *pixel.* A pixel can be translated into a dot in a specific location on the video screen. Of course, dots can be extended into lines, and lines can form images.

Most people type on a keyboard when they use computers. But an artist-operator draws his or her lines with a *light pen* on a *digitizing* tablet (fig. 12–37). If the computer and video monitor have color capability, the artist can make lines in color. British painter David Hockney was invited to create an "electronic painting" soon after this technology was invented. His *Untitled* (fig. 12–38) is the delightful result.

To create three-dimensional art, the artist uses foreshortening, perspective, aerial perspective, shading, texture, cast shadows, and reflections. Special programs are required to create these effects on a

12–37 Artists working with computers can access thousands of colors in a split second. Courtesy Invision.

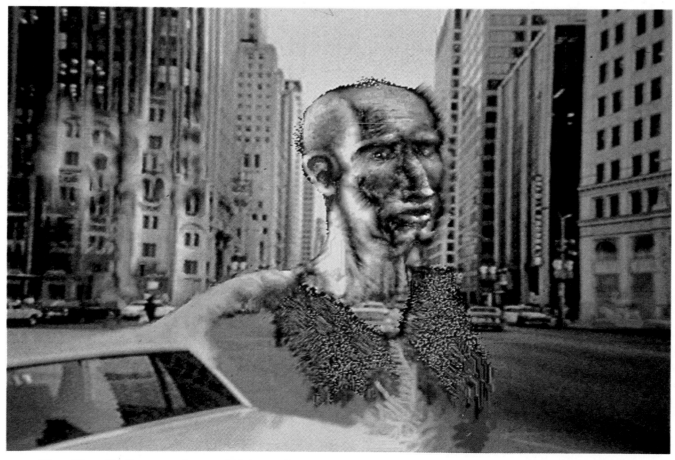

12–39 Hiromi Ono, *City Faces,* 1987. Courtesy SIGGRAPH '88.

12–38 David Hockney, *Untitled* from Painting with Light Series. The artist spent eight hours straight on a sophisticated computer to create such images. Courtesy Invision.

computer. *Programs* are sets of instructions for a computer to perform. And each of these programs contains long columns of mathematical calculations. Even longer programs are required to create animation, the illusion of objects moving through space. Television commercials often use computer-generated animation. For example, you have probably seen three-dimensional images of company trademarks rotating and zooming through space in commercials. Such an animation, even if it lasted only ten seconds, would require the efforts of a team of designers and engineers working with a powerful computer.

Hiromi Ono, a computer artist, uses computer graphics programs to create original art. Ono worked with digitized video images to produce a ghostly interpretation of the urban landscape in *City Faces* (fig. 12–39).

Try it Yourself

Look for examples of computer-generated art on television. Take notes on both their three-dimensional and animated effects. Create a design of your own for computer art or a commercial. Try making your initials appear three-dimensional. Create a storyboard to describe them rotating and moving through space.

12–40 Many times, artists combine several media to arrive at a single image. Betye Saar, *Wizard*, 1972. Assemblage box and mixed media, 13 ½″ x 11″ x 1″ (34 x 28 x 2.5 cm). Collection of the artist.

12–41 One specific category of mixed media is collage. Pablo Picasso was one of the first artists to make collage a popular medium in which to work. Pablo Picasso, *Still Life with Chair Caning*, 1911. Oil and pasted oilcloth simulating chair caning, oval 10 ⅝″ x 13 ¾″ (27 x 35 cm). ©1993 ARS, New York/SPADEM, Paris.

Mixed Media

So far, we have covered everything from mosaics to computer art in this chapter. Since the nineteenth century, new media like acrylics, silk screen, photography, film, video, and computer art have been developed. No doubt the list of two-dimensional art will continue to grow in the twenty-first century.

Many artists no longer adopt the pure approach of keeping the media separate. Some artists mix two or more together, or add "foreign" materials. Recall, for example, the stuffed goat attached to a painting in Chapter 1 (fig. 1–11). The artist of that work, Robert Rauschenberg, has made a career out of what he calls "combine paintings." Some of these works often are not paintings at all. Betye Saar combined assorted fabrics, brass hardware, jewelry, knickknacks, and pictorial elements in *Wizard* (fig. 12–40). Like Rauschenberg's goat, Saar's mixed media work is difficult to interpret. Because it tends to mix two-dimensional and three-dimensional approaches, Saar's work is also difficult to classify.

Collage

A *collage* consists of fragments of things that are pasted on a flat surface. The artist may use photographs, colored paper, pieces of material, news clippings, and other odds and ends. In addition, strokes of paint, charcoal smears, or anything, as long as it is basically flat, may be combined with the collage materials. This type of two-dimensional art was invented around 1912 by Pablo Picasso and Georges Braque. Collages have become very popular in recent years.

Still Life with Chair Caning (fig. 12–41) is an early collage by Picasso. Picasso combined painting with a piece of oilcloth that looks like the woven material of a chair. What was Picasso trying to express? Probably

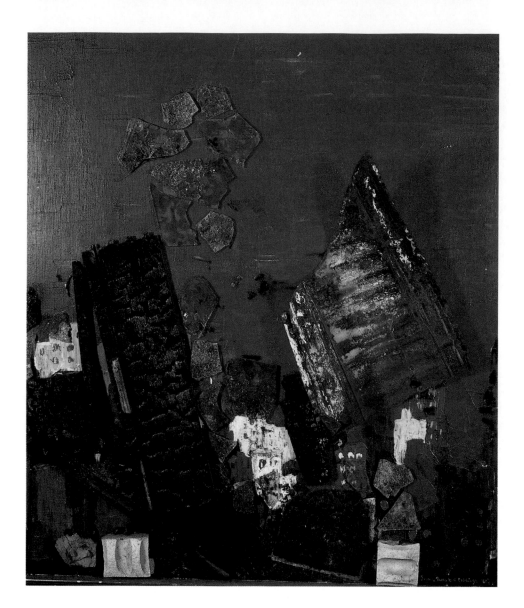

12–42 What do the materials used in this collage seem to be suggesting? Yvonne Parks Catchings, *The Detroit Riot*, 1967. Collage, 28″ x 36″ (66 x 91 cm). Collection of the artist.

nothing. More likely he simply wanted to experiment, to pioneer a new kind of medium that others could use for expressive purposes. A half century after Picasso's experiment, Yvonne Parks Catchings expressed the pain of social crisis in a collage titled *The Detroit Riot* (fig. 12–42). The red symbolizes the heat and violence of the riot itself. The scraps of wood and broken glass symbolize the destruction.

Documented Art

During the late 1960s and early 1970s some artists began to create a new kind of art that mixed art with the life around it. Their works engaged the viewer in ways very different from that of traditional media. Examples of this new art include the wrapped coastline and the performance piece with a coyote you learned about in Chapter 1. (You will learn more about this art form, called "environmental art," in the next chapter.)

Studio Experience 12.6

A Unified Collage

Make a collage with a combination of found materials and drawn or painted elements. Select materials that have special meaning for you.

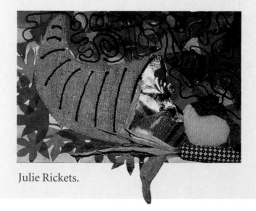

Julie Rickets.

> "One of several proposals to rid my life of accumulated art. With this project I will have all of my accumulated paintings cremated by a mortuary. The container of ashes will be interred inside a wall of the Jewish Museum. For the length of the show, there will be a commemorative plaque on the wall behind which the ashes are located. It is a reductive, recycling piece. I consider all these paintings a body of work in the real sense of the word. Will I save my life by losing it? Will a Phoenix arise from the ashes? Will the paintings having become dust become art materials again? I don't know, but I feel better."

12–43 Conceptual art pieces are usually temporary events. Therefore, many of these events were documented either by filming, photographing or writing in order to keep a record of the actions that took place. John Baldessari, *Cremation Piece*, 1969. As shown at The Jewish Museum in the exhibition *Software*, 1970.

Other artists began a trend going in the opposite direction. They reduced their art to just its idea or concept. Some of these artists have argued that it is possible to create art without objects. This type of art is sometimes called *concept* art.

One thing that both developments had in common was the use of *documentation*. Because the works were temporary, a record of them had to be made. Works were documented in the form of writing, photocopies, photographs, film, audiotape, or videotape. The wrapped coast and the performance piece were documented with photographs (figures 1–10 and 1–12). John Baldessari's *Cremation Piece* is documented in a printed statement (fig. 12–43). The statement describes the idea, as well as some of the actions that Baldessari took to carry out his idea back in 1969.

Try it Yourself

Recall the comparisons made between Dürer's traditional approach to printmaking and Catlett's modern approach.

Examples of concept art, like the one by Baldessari (fig. 12–43), could be described as *post-modern*. Do you think this post-modern approach may lead to new possibilities in the future? Explain.

Summary

This chapter on two-dimensional media has indeed been complex. It organized two-dimensional media under the topics of drawing, painting, mosaic, printmaking, photography and film, video art, computer art, and mixed media.

Charcoal, pencil, and ink are examples of drawing media. They are monochromatic. They involve only the color of a single tool mixed with that of the paper. Colored chalks and pastels are multicolored, and resemble painting. However, like other drawing media, they have a fragile surface.

Painting includes watercolor, tempera, oil, acrylic, and fresco. Most painting media have ancient origins. Oil on canvas was not fully developed until the sixteenth century, however, and acrylic was developed in this century.

Mosaic is created from pieces of stone or glass that are set in walls, floors, or ceilings. Because of its unique materials and working process, mosaic differs from fresco and all the painting media.

Printmaking includes relief, intaglio, and planographic processes. The oldest of these media is the woodcut, a relief process. Engraving and etching, both intaglio methods, date back to around 1500 when they replaced the woodcut. The planographic methods are relatively new. Lithography was developed in the 1800s. Silk screen was developed in this century.

Photography and film involve photochemical processes. Video art and computer art, which involve electronic processes, use even more modern technologies.

Mixed media reflects new ideas about art. Many twentieth-century artists have experimented with using media, both new and old, in novel ways. They have mixed the media, as in collages. They have combined media with life itself. Other artists have attempted to eliminate the medium altogether and keep just the idea.

Chapter 13
Three-Dimensional Media

13–1 Auguste Rodin, *The Thinker,* 1880. Bronze, 28 ⅛″ x 14 ⅜″ x 23 ½″ (72 x 36 x 60 cm). ©1993 National Gallery of Art, Washington. Gift of Mrs. John W. Simpson.

In Chapter 12, you learned about the media that artists use for two-dimensional art. Artists use many other media to create three-dimensional art. In fact, there are few materials that are not used in the creation of art. If you were asked to list some examples of media used for sculptures, you would probably think of wood, stone, and metal, or pottery made from clay. You might also think of media you have used in school such as papier-mâché and plaster. Would you be surprised to learn that three-dimensional forms can be produced with crocheted fiber (fig. 13–2)?

Sculpture

We will begin this chapter with a discussion of four categories of sculpture: carving, casting, modeling, and construction. Each type of sculpture uses different media. Sculpture that is part of, or attached to, a surface is called *relief.* In a *low relief,* the shapes project slightly. The section of a carved sandstone wall made in the twelfth century for the Bayon Temple at Angkor Thom, Cambodia (fig. 13–3) is an example of low relief sculpture. *High relief* figures project a great deal, as in the cast bronze panel by Lorenzo Ghiberti (fig. 13–4). Sculpture that is created to be walked around and seen from all sides, like *The Thinker* by Auguste Rodin (fig. 13–1), is called sculpture in the round. Both reliefs and sculptures in the round can be cast, carved, or constructed in a variety of materials.

13–2   Norma Minkowitz, *Passage to Nowhere,* 1985. Fiber, acrylic, pencil, shellac, 7 ½″ x 9 ¾″ (19 x 25 cm) diameter. Bellas Artes, Santa Fe.

13–3   Processional Scene from the Bayon Temple, Angkor Thom, late twelfth century, Cambodia. Sandstone.

13–4   Lorenzo Ghiberti, *The Story of Jacob and Esau,* detail from *The Gates of Paradise,* ca. 1435. Gilt bronze, 31 ¼″ (79 cm) square. Formella dell Porta del Paradiso. The Baptistry, Florence. Scala/Art Resource, NY.

Try it Yourself

Look for relief sculptures in your community. What kind are they? What are they made of? Where are they located? Do the reliefs record or symbolize events or beliefs? Is their purpose simply decorative?

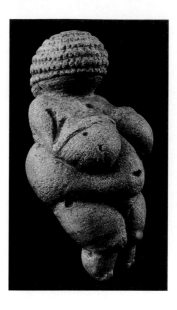

13-5 *Venus of Willendorf,* original ca. 15,000–10,000 BC. Stone, 4 ³/₈″ (11 cm) high. Naturhistorisches Museum, Vienna, Austria. Erich Lessing/Art Resource, NY.

13-6 *Pair Statue of King Mycerinus and Queen Kah-merer,* Fourth Dynasty. Greywacke, 54 ½″ (138 cm) high. Museum Expeditions. Courtesy, Museum of Fine Arts, Boston.

Carving

We know that humans have carved forms since the Stone Age. They used materials such as bones, horn, antlers, wood, and stone. Approximately 15,000 years ago, an Ice Age carver created the little figure known as the *Venus of Willendorf* (fig. 13-5). Imagine carving this statuette from stone with crude and clumsy tools made of stone. Over 4,500 years ago, Egyptian artists produced life-size figures in both wood and stone, using tools made of bronze (fig. 13-6).

The basic tools for sculpture in stone include metal hammers and a variety of chisels and files. The sculptor also uses sanding, grinding, and polishing equipment. Basic tools for wood include wooden mallets, gouges with different shaped cutting edges, rasps, scrapers, and sanding and polishing materials. Power sanders, band saws and chain saws are also used by some wood sculptors.

Stone sculptures can be small enough to hold in the hand, like the *Venus of Willendorf,* or large enough to fill a mountainside, like the portraits of four presidents on Mount Rushmore (fig. 13-7). This gigantic relief carving required the use of pneumatic hammers and chisels driven by compressed air. The size of carved wood sculpture is limited to the size of wood pieces that can be obtained from the largest trees.

Sculpting in stone or wood is very demanding. The sculptor usually makes drawings and small clay models to show what the sculpture will look like from all sides. In the first phase of carving, the sculptor chisels or gouges out the general forms on the surfaces of the wood or stone. The sculptor is interested in making all the forms on the surface interrelate. The viewer's eye should move from one part to the other.

As the carving continues, the forms are refined. The sculptor decides where to place positive and negative areas. Positive areas may be solid and/or **convex** (curving outward). Negative areas may be openings and/or **concave** (curving inward). These forms provide contrasts. They also contribute to eye movement around and across the sculpture. Positive turns to negative as the eye moves smoothly from solid forms to openings in Henry Moore's *Reclining Figure* (fig. 13-8). Ernst Barlach created contrasting convex and concave areas that direct eye movement around the forms of *The Vision* (fig. 13-9).

13-7 George Borglum and Son, *The Presidents,* 1927–1941. Carved granite. Mount Rushmore National Monument. Courtesy United States Department of the Interior, National Park Service.

13–8 Henry Moore, *Reclining Figure*, 1939. Elm wood, 37″ x 6′ 7″ x 30″ (94 x 183 x 76 cm). ©The Detroit Institute of Arts, Gift of Dexter M. Ferry, Jr. Trustee Corporation.

The finished stone or wood sculpture can be highly polished or textured. The sculpture may have both polished and textured surfaces. Moore sanded the surface of *Reclining Figure* to emphasize the wood grain. The smooth surface contributes to the flow of the sculptural forms. Barlach blended the characteristic marks of the gouge and the wood grain in *The Vision*. Do the textures add meaning to the two sculptures? How do the textures affect the feelings that you get from each sculpture?

13–9 Ernst Barlach, *The Vision*, 1912. Relief (oak). Staatliche Museen zu Berlin, PreuBischer Kulturbesitz, Nationalgalerie.

Studio Experience 13.1

A Sculpture with Movement

Carve an abstract or nonrepresentational sculpture from plaster. Create forms that cause the viewer's eye to move from one part to another.

Student works.

Casting

So far we have discussed sculpting in wood and stone. The sculptor works directly on these materials. Sculptors use a method called *casting* when they work with metals, plastic, or plaster. The liquid material is poured into a hollow shape called a *mold.* The material hardens into the sculpture itself. This is the simplest casting procedure. For example, you can press your hand in wet sand to make a mold, and fill it with plaster to make a cast. The most complex casting procedure is the lost-wax process.

Lost-Wax Bronze Casting. The first *lost-wax castings* were of small solid objects like the statuette in figure 13–10. Obviously, solid metal figures could not be made very large because of the weight and expense of the metal. In order to make large figures, ancient cultures developed the method of hollow bronze casting. The cast metal figures of horse and rider you often see in parks, plazas, and around state buildings are made with this process.

Today, the procedure for casting a metal sculpture is called lost-wax (from the French term *cire-perdue*). Keith Knoblock used this procedure to create a bronze sculpture of Abraham Lincoln (fig. 13–11). First, he used a nonhardening, oil-based clay to model a life-sized figure. The clay was modeled over an *armature.* An armature is a framework of metal rods and plaster. Next, he made a mold by applying plaster to the clay model in sections. Thin metal shims were placed between mold sections so they could be easily separated later (fig. 13–12). When the plaster was hard, he removed the mold in sections from the clay model.

The sculptor now had a mold of Lincoln made of plaster. His next step was to line each section of the mold with wax to make a wax casting. Knoblock brushed a 3/16-inch coating of melted wax onto each piece of the plaster mold (fig. 13–13). He removed the

13–10 Tell al-Judaidah female statuette, Phase G, about 3000–2700 BC. Copper-base alloy with sufficient tin content to be called bronze, overall height, 5 ¾″ (14.6 cm). Courtesy of The Oriental Institute of the University of Chicago.

13–11 Keith Knoblock, *Lincoln,* 1977. Cast bronze, 6′ 4 ¾″ (195 cm). McLean County Law and Justice Center, Bloomington, Illinois.

wax castings from the plaster molds and reassembled them into seven sections of the figure (fig. 13–14). Notice the wax rods and cup shapes attached to each wax cast. Long steel nails, which don't show here, were pushed through the wax so they protruded inside and outside of the wax cast. Each wax section was suspended in a cylinder made of black asphalt roofing felt with a wire mesh insert (shown raised here) that became part of, and reinforced, the mold (fig. 13–15). A liquid mixture of heat-resistant materials called the *investment* was poured outside and inside of the hollow wax casting to form the outer mold and the mold core. The tops of the cup shapes attached to the wax rods were left uncovered. When the mold material was hardened, the asphalt cylinders were removed. The wire mesh was now embedded in the outer mold. The molds were placed in a kiln (a high temperature oven) and baked at 1150°F for several days until the wax melted and ran out through the channels left by the

wax rods shown in figure 13–14. The nails, mentioned above, were now embedded in both the outer mold and the mold core. They held the core in place, preserving the empty space where the wax had been. Molten bronze was poured through the channels to fill the 3/16-inch voids that were the shape of the sculpture parts (fig. 13–16). When the metal cooled, the molds were chipped and dug away from the cast, and the sections were ground and cleaned with a variety of hand and power tools. The seven casts were welded together and the surface was treated chemically to give it a brownish color. The sculpture was completed by attaching it to a base of concrete in which the skatelike forms on the feet (fig. 13–14) were submerged to help steady the figure.

13–12 Applying plaster to the clay model.

13–13 Coating the sections of the plaster mold with melted wax.

13–14 The wax castings.

13–15 Reinforcing the mold with wire mesh and roofing felt.

13–16 Pouring bronze into the mold.

Plastic and Plaster Casting. Without the caption, you would think that figure 13–17 is a photograph of a football player. Yet the life-size football player is a sculpture. It was cast in a plastic reinforced with fiberglass. Duane Hanson applies plaster gauze strips directly to the body of a person to make a mold. The person's skin and hair is heavily greased so the plaster will not stick. Molds are made in sections and then painted with fleshcolored plastic. The plastic is coated, or laminated, with several layers of glass cloth. When assembled, the hardened sculptures are sometimes mistaken for real people.

George Segal forms molds of plaster gauze around living models who are fully clothed. The molds, which are made in sections for various parts of the body, are reassembled to become the sculpture (fig. 13–18). Segal does not smooth away the texture of the plaster. You can see and feel the rough surface of his sculptures.

13–17 Duane Hanson, *Football Player*, 1981. Polyvinyl, polychromed in oil with accessories, 43 ¼″ x 30″ x 31 ½″ (110 x 76 x 80 cm). The Lowe Art Museum, University of Miami, Museum purchase through funds from the Friends of Art and public subscription, 82.0024.

Studio Experience 13.2

Sculpture on the Wild Side

Use plaster gauze or papier-mâché over an armature of cardboard, tubes and small cartons to create a trophy or commemorative sculpture that's a bit bizarre. It might be for a sport, dancing, eating, a pet, a hobby, contest, etc.

Rod Lemke.

13–18 George Segal, *The Parking Garage*, 1968. Plaster, wood, metal, electrical parts and light bulbs, 10′ x 12′ 8″ x 4′ (3 x 4 x 1.3 cm). Collection of The Newark Museum. Purchase 1968 with funds from the National Council on the Arts and Trustee contributions.

Modeling

Modeling is a method that produces a sculpture made from a pliable material like clay, papier-mâché, wax, or plaster. In this section, we will consider *ceramic* sculpture made from clay and papier-mâché.

Clay is taken through four stages to produce either sculpture or pottery: preparation, shaping, decorating, and firing. *Preparation* involves mixing water with the clay. The clay is aged for several weeks until it becomes workable. Air bubbles must be forced out. *Shaping* the clay is done by hand-building methods or on a potter's wheel. *Decorating* the form can be done with techniques such as those shown in figure 13–19. *Firing* the clay form is done twice—once to harden it, and a second time to add a *glaze*, a transparent or colored glassy coating, to the work.

Solid Modeling. Perhaps you have made a solid sculpture from a lump of clay. Parts can be shaped from or added to the lump. Textures and patterns such as those shown in figure 13–19 can be added to the surface. Any parts of a solid clay sculpture that are thicker than one inch should be hollowed out to prevent the work from exploding when fired. When the clay is dry enough to support itself, but not completely dry, the form can be hollowed out from the bottom with a wire loop tool.

13–19   Texture pressed in clay.

13–20   Although this sculpture is bronze, it was first modeled in clay. It shows the expressive qualities of solid clay modeling. David Aronson, *Virtuoso*. Courtesy of Pucker Gallery, Boston, MA. ©1993 Photograph by David N. Israel.

Coiling. The coiling procedure was used by the Chinese over 2,000 years ago. The life-size figures of the warrior and horse shown in figure 13–21 were created from clay coils. (Thousands of figures like this were found during excavations at the tomb of the first emperor of Ch'in. No two of the ceramic warriors have the same face.) Coils are made by rolling ropes of clay to a desired thickness on a canvas-covered surface. The coils are placed on top of each other and pressed together. Coils can be made longer or shorter as needed. The artist smooths the inside and outside with vertical wiping movements. He or she finishes the surface by scraping or by beating it with a paddle.

Peter VandenBerge used coils to build his sculpture (fig. 13–22). Then he modeled clay on its surface to create three-dimensional features. The hat was made from slabs. The artist decorated the figure with colored clay *slips*, clay mixed with water to a creamy consistency, with coloring agents added.

13–21 *Cavalryman with Horse*, Qin dynasty (221–206 BC), terra cotta. Cavalryman is 5′ 10 ½″ (180 cm) high and saddle horse is 5′ 7 ½″ (172 cm) high and 6′ 7 ¾″ (203 cm) long. Courtesy of Cultural Relics Bureau, Beijing and The Metropolitan Museum of Art, New York.

13–22 Peter VandenBerge, *Zwartman*, 1986. Clay and slips, hand-built (coiled), 45″ x 14″ x 17″ (114 x 36 x 43 cm). Collection of the artist. Photograph courtesy George Erml.

13–23 Viola Frey, *Leaning Man III,* 1985. Clay and glazes, hand-built, 102 ½″ x 35″ x 18″ (260 x 89 x 46 cm). Rena Bransten Gallery, San Francisco.

13–24 Felipe Linares, Leonardo Linares-Vargas, David Linares-Vargas, *Alebrijes,* 1989. Papier-mâché. Photograph courtesy Musée national d'art moderne, Centre Georges Pompidou, Paris.

Slab Building. Slabs are sheets of clay that are beaten out with the hand or spread with a rolling pin. Sculptures made from slabs are supported by various materials until the clay dries. Materials such as crumpled newspaper, foam rubber, and dacron are used as supports. Slabs can be used to construct smaller sculpture. The slabs are rolled and folded. When they are dried but not completely hard, the slabs are joined together with clay slip.

Viola Frey makes very large ceramic sculptures with slabs and coils. She forms and fires them in sections. The sections are stacked upon each other when finished to complete the sculpture. Frey's *Leaning Man III* (fig. 13–23) is over eight feet (2.5 m) tall. Imagine having a sculpture that large in your home.

Papier-Mâché. Papier-mâché is an ancient modeling medium. Chinese soldiers used it to make armor before the Bronze Age. Papier-mâché, which is lightweight and strong, is made from wet paper and glue. The paper is soaked in water overnight. Then it is mashed in a strainer to remove the water. White glue is added as a binder.

This clay-like medium can be modeled into all kinds of shapes. It can be formed into molds or placed over armatures of wood, rods, and wires. When dry, forms made from papier-mâché can be carved, bored, sanded, and painted. The Linares family in Mexico create fantastic papier-mâché animal sculptures (fig. 13–24.)

Strips of newspaper that have been soaked in wheat paste can be placed over cardboard, tubes, and boxes. The form shown in figure 13–25 was created this way. This process requires several days for drying. The plaster gauze used by Duane Hanson and George Segal (figures 13–17 and 18) has replaced papier-mâché because it dries quickly. However, it does not have the smoothness and detail of papier-mâché.

13–25 Pierre Richard *Move Move Mann,* 1987. Papier-mâché, 27″ x 12″ (69 x 31 cm). Collection of Julian Davis Wade.

Construction

Constructions are sculptures that may be built from more than one material. They may be built from traditional materials, such as wood or metal, that are used in new ways. Constructions are a development of the twentieth century. They are a result of modern technology, as well as modern ideas about the nature of the art object.

George Sugarman glues together layers of wood that have been cut into shapes with a band saw. Then he paints the forms to hide the wood grain and to help direct visual movement over the surfaces (fig. 13–26).

Richard Lippold combines thin metal rods and wires to create constructions that radiate from a center as in *Number 7: Full Moon* (fig. 13–27). The central cluster of wires reflects light, and the metal rods create open three-dimensional forms. *Number 7: Full Moon* had to be carefully designed before it was constructed.

Assemblage. Sculptures constructed from a variety of found objects and materials are called *assemblages.* These materials, in their original states, were not necessarily meant to be used in art forms. The sculptor may select objects because of their similarities or their contrasts. The objects may suggest certain meanings. Assemblages may or may not meet the principles of composition, depending on the artist's intent. How an

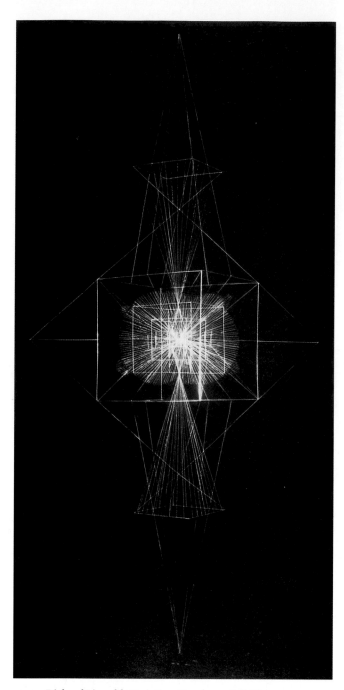

13–27   Richard Lippold, Variation *Number 7: Full Moon*, 1949–50. Brass rods, nickel-chromium and stainless steel wire, 10′ x 6′ x 6′ (305 x 183 x 183 cm). The Museum of Modern Art, New York. Simon Guggenheim Fund.

13–26   George Sugarman, *Freya*, 1964. Laminated, polychromed wood. 30 ¾″ (78 cm) high. Private collection.

13–28 Louise Nevelson, *Sky Cathedral*, 1958. Assemblage: wood construction painted black, 11´3 ½˝ x 10´ ¼˝ x 18˝ (344 x 305 x 46 cm). The Museum of Modern Art, New York. Gift of Mr. and Mrs. Ben Mildwoff.

assemblage is constructed depends on the materials used. Louise Nevelson nailed, glued, and pegged together discarded wood forms (fig. 13–28). Her assemblage is made up of dozens of boxes filled with carefully arranged wooden objects.

Assemblages allow artists great freedom in choosing materials that express their ideas. Marisol's life-size

Try it Yourself

List some materials to use in a construction that are more incongruous (not harmonious, not related) than those in Rauschenberg's stuffed goat assemblage (fig. 1-11).

13-29 Marisol, *Women and Dog*, 1964. Wood, plaster, synthetic polymer and miscellaneous items. 6′5″ x 7′7″ (196 x 231 cm). Collection of Whitney Museum of American Art. Purchase, with funds from the Friends of the Whitney Museum of American Art.

boxlike figures (fig. 13–29) may include wood, plaster life masks, paint, photographs, fabric, and more. Her constructions are caricatures. They are exaggerated descriptions of contemporary personalities, their manners and characteristics.

Assemblages and constructions include works that may be classified as reliefs, as well as those that are sculpture in the round. *Kastūra* (fig. 13–30) by Frank Stella is a construction that projects about two feet from the wall. Stella cut the parts out of sheet aluminum and painted them with a range of wild colors. The composition is given unity by repetition of shapes based on drafting tools.

13-30 Frank Stella, *Kastūra*, 1979. Oil and epoxy on aluminum and wire mesh. 9′7″ x 7′8″ x 30″ (292 x 234 x 76 cm). The Museum of Modern Art, New York. Acquired through the Mr. and Mrs. Victor Ganz, Mr. and Mrs. Donald H. Peters, and Mr. and Mrs. Charles Zadok Funds.

Marisol

1930–

Carved wooden boxes, plaster casts of faces and hands, and bits of fabric are uniquely combined and assembled to form a three-dimensional composition. "Found" objects, or discarded items collected and reused by the artist, are embellished with hand-crafted materials. Carefully drawn and painted details adorn the sides of figures sculpted from rough pieces of lumber. This arrangement of contrasting elements might be complemented with a background, creating a "tableau," or an arranged scene. The sculpted figures in these unusual works of art, known as assemblages, may wear three or more faces cast from plaster—all the single face of the artist, Marisol.

Born in 1930 in Paris, Marisol Escobar spent the early years of her life traveling from one glittering world capital to another with her wealthy Venezuelan parents. Her mother died when Marisol was eleven years old, and Marisol looked to her father for support. With his stability and encouragement, Marisol was able to become an adventurous artist and an independent and creative individual.

Her travels brought her from Europe to New York in 1950 where she studied art and developed friendships with other artists in Manhattan. At this time, Marisol explored a variety of different art media, searching for her own artistic style. During this quest for originality and independence, she discarded her last name; since that time she has been known simply as Marisol.

In New York, Marisol discovered a unique means of expression in sculpture, combining unusual materials in new ways. Using carpenter's tools—power saws, axes, electrical devices—in combination with traditional art supplies, she began creating the unique sculptures for which she is now famous.

A Wood Relief

Construct a relief of wood shapes, observing the principles of composition. Express an idea or theme in your construction.

Pete Belzer.

Metal Construction. There are many techniques for constructing metal sculpture. In general, metal can be cut with hand or power saws, hand or power shears, tin snips, and welding torches. Holes can be drilled in metal. Pieces can be joined with the use of metal screws, nuts and bolts, riveting, crimping edges together, soldering, and welding.

Richard Stankiewicz created a construction by welding industrial scrap and old machine parts (fig. 13–31). What do you think about the artist's comment on modern society's endless waste of objects and materials?

13–31 Richard Stankiewicz, *Our Lady of All Protections*, 1958. Iron and steel, 51″ x 31″ x 32″ (130 x 79 x 81 cm). Albright-Knox Art Gallery, Buffalo, New York. Gift of Seymour H. Knox, 1959.

13-32 David Smith, *Cubi XVII*, 1963. Stainless steel,
107 ¾″ x 64 ⅜″ (274 x 165 cm). Dallas Museum of Art. Eugene and
Margaret McDermott Fund.

Sheets of stainless steel are welded together by
David Smith to create combinations of cubes and
cylinders (fig. 13–32). These constructions of cubes
look like they should fall. Smith's sculptures are often
placed outdoors. The highly polished mirrorlike surfaces reflect everything around them.

Kinetic Sculpture. You were introduced to **kinetic**
sculpture in Chapter 8. These constructions move or
have moving parts, and may also use light and sound.
In previous centuries, machines and robotlike figures
had been designed for entertainment. But, like today's
cuckoo clocks, those automated constructions could
only repeat their actions. The movements of modern
kinetic sculptures are generally random. The sources
of energy for kinetic sculpture include wind and air
currents, falling water, temperature changes, springs,
motors of all kinds, air pumps, pull strings, thin rods
and wires that vibrate, pendulums, magnets, and
electromagnets.

Environmental Art

Environmental art began in the 1960s. Mixed media
and different procedures are used to create these
forms. The basic idea is to involve the spectator in the
artwork, or to make the work a part of the environment surrounding it. Environmental artists have taken
several different directions over the past twenty years,
as the following examples show.

Red Grooms constructs huge enclosed environments that people can walk through. *Ruckus Rodeo*
includes fourteen cowboys and cowgirls, a rodeo
queen on horseback, a sixteen-foot Brahma bull, and
more (fig. 13–33). The floor is covered with painted
burlap, and the rodeo audience is painted on canvas
that wraps around the walls. What would it be like
to enter the make-believe world of *Ruckus Rodeo*?
Imagine walking among Grooms's larger-than-life
figures frozen in a moment of action.

Another kind of environmental sculpture involves
making changes in a natural setting. These works are
called *land* or *earth art*. The artist may need the help of
construction crews and earth-moving equipment, as
in the case of *Spiral Jetty* (fig. 13–34). Robert Smithson
created a 1,500-foot-long earth and rock spiral that
extends into Utah's Great Salt Lake. According to a legend, the lake was once connected to the Pacific Ocean
by an underground waterway. The waterway supposedly caused whirlpools to form at the lake's center.
Perhaps Smithson's choice of the spiral form was
inspired by this legend.

Mary Miss takes another approach in her constructions. She combines wood, steel, and concrete
with earth and sometimes water in environmental
works like *Field Rotation* (fig. 13–35). Miss enclosed a
sunken area with a wall constructed of wood. She
mounded earth up against the outsides of the wall.
Eight rows of wooden posts extend from the central
construction out over a four-and-one-half-acre area
that makes up the whole artwork. Viewed from the
air, this environmental sculpture resembles a giant
pinwheel.

Many environmental works like those of Smithson
and Miss are placed in out-of-the-way locations where
you might not have a chance to see them. And, of
course, most of them are temporary. Photographs like
these are the only records of them.

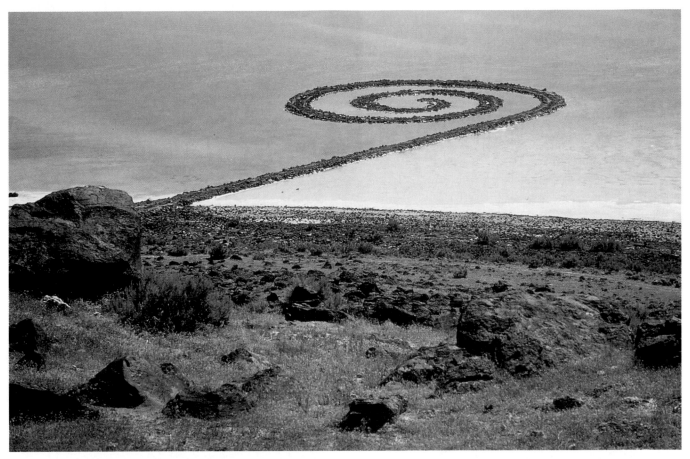

13-34 Robert Smithson, *Spiral Jetty,* 1970. Black rock, salt crystals, earth and red water (algae) composing a coil 1500´ x 15´ (457 x 5 m). Great Salt Lake, Utah. Photograph Gianfranco Gorgoni. Courtesy Contact Press Images Inc., New York.

13-33 Red Grooms, *Ruckus Rodeo,* 1975–1976. Sculpture wire, celastic, acrylic, canvas and burlap, 174″ x 606″ x 294″ (442 x 1539 x 747 cm). Commissioned by the Modern Art Museum of Fort Worth. Museum purchase with funds from the National Endowment for the Arts and the Benjamin J. Tillar Memorial Trust. See page 79.

13-35 Mary Miss, *Field Rotation,* 1981. Wood, gravel, concrete, steel, earth and water. Structure, 7´ x 56´ x 56´ (2 x 17 x 17 m), centered in 4 ½ acre site. Governors State University, Illinois.

And finally, there are the performance works like Joseph Beuys's *I Like America and America Likes Me* that was presented in Chapter 1 (fig. 1-12). These productions, sometimes called *happenings,* usually involve the artist in person and some props. Sometimes, the viewers are invited to participate.

Try it Yourself

If there is space in your classroom, construct an environmental artwork. Or, draw a plan for such a work. Choose a theme, an event, or an idea you wish to express about the environment.

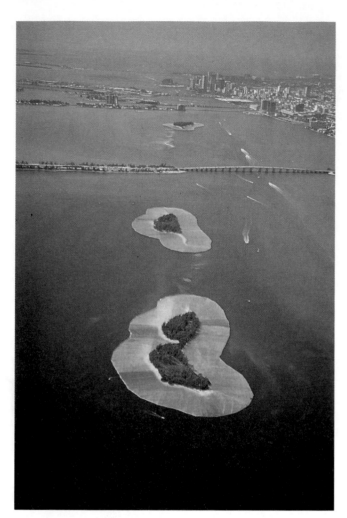

13–36 Christo, *Surrounded Islands, Biscayne Bay, Greater Miami, Florida,* 1980–1983. ©Christo 1983. Photograph: Wolfgang Volz.

The largest environmental projects have been created by Javacheff Christo. His *Wrapped Coast* is shown in Chapter 1. In 1983, he finished surrounding eleven islands in Biscayne Bay with 6,500,000 square feet of pink plastic that floated on the water. The plastic extended 200 feet from the shore of each island (fig. 13–36). Can you picture what the project looked like from an airplane? Picture eleven pink-skirted islands covered with lush vegetation, surrounded by blue-green water, and basking in a bright sun.

On a smaller scale, George Segal creates environments based on events from everyday life. They include life-size plaster figures and real objects. The counter, stools, coffee maker, and other objects in *The Diner* came from a real restaurant (fig. 13–37). You can become a part of this little environment by moving around and viewing it from different angles. Perhaps you can imagine what the two lonely figures are thinking about.

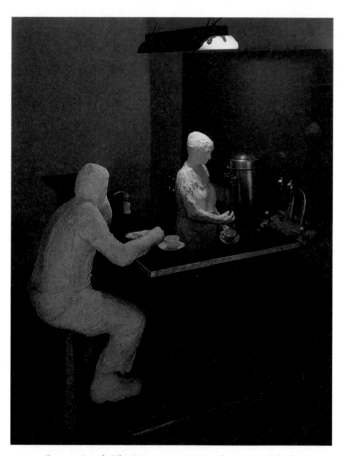

13–37 George Segal, *The Diner,* 1964–1966. Plaster, wood, chrome, laminated plastic, Masonite, fluorescent lamp, 93 ¾″ x 144 ¼″ x 96″ (238 x 366 x 244 cm). Collection Walker Art Center, Minneapolis. Gift of the T. B. Walker Foundation, 1966.

Ceramic Pottery, Jewelry, Fibers, and Glass

Before the Industrial Revolution in the 1800s brought the mass production of goods, items such as dishes, metalware, and clothing were hand-crafted. Today, artists who work with ceramics, jewelry, fibers, and glass sometimes provide designs for industrial mass production. However, mainly they make one-of-a-kind creations that are expressive, personal, and valued for their unique qualities.

Ceramic Pottery

Imagine life without containers to eat and drink from or to store things in. Prehistoric people used animal skins, shells, gourds, and woven baskets as containers. The baskets were sometimes coated on the inside with clay to seal them. Pottery making may have been discovered by the accidental burning of such a basket, which resulted in hardening the clay lining. The first pots and clay figures were fired in shallow pits lined and covered with twigs and dry wood.

> ### Try it Yourself
>
> Every early culture developed its own style of pottery. Research a culture and write a short report on its pottery. How was it made, decorated, and fired? What was the pottery used for?

Hand-Building Procedures. It is easy to make pottery by hand. Clay is easy to handle. The methods for making pottery by hand are similar to those used for ceramic sculpture. The methods of *pinch, coil,* and *slab* building can be used to hand build pottery.

Pinch pots are made by pushing the thumb down in the center of a fist-sized ball of clay, leaving enough clay for the bottom. The walls are formed by squeezing the clay up and out between the thumb on the inside and the fingers on the outside, while rotating the pot in the other hand. The procedure is repeated until the wall of the pot is as thin as desired. A coil may be added to the bottom for stability, and designs can be incised or pressed on the surface (fig. 13–38).

A *coil pot* can be made in almost any shape. The first coil is attached to a base made from a slab of clay. The form can be curved outward by making the coils progressively wider in circumference. The process is reversed to make the form curve inward.

The jar shown in figure 13–39 was made by people who lived on the island of Crete over 3,000 years ago. It is four feet high. Its thick coils were thinned and shaped by beating the outside with a paddle while a rounded form was held inside.

13–38 *Left:* Pinch pot with foot. *Right:* Coil built pot with some coils partially exposed as part of the surface decoration. Earthenware.

13–39 Pithos, Knossos, Crete, ca. 1450–1400 BC. Earthenware storage jar with applied rope decoration, height 4′ (122 cm). Reproduced by Courtesy of the Trustees of the British Museum, London.

Slabs, or sheets, of clay are rolled out with a rolling pin or pounded out with a paddle. Containers may be formed by draping slabs over convex forms like a volleyball. Slabs can also be pressed into concave forms such as a dish. The edges of slabs can be joined with slip to build geometric containers (fig. 13–41). The surfaces can be decorated with textures.

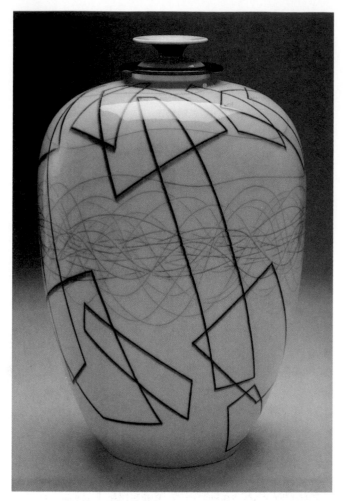

13–40 Michael Remsen, *M. S. 2*, 1991. High-fired porcelain with transparent Chun glaze, 24″ (61 cm) high.

13–41 Joining edges.

13–42 Slab-built sculpture.

Studio Experience 13.4

A Hand-Built Coil Pot

Build a coil pot inside a mold to emphasize the coils as a decorative element.

Bethany Weeks.

Throwing on the Wheel. *Throwing* is the term used to describe forming clay on the potter's wheel. The production of small wheel-thrown pots began about 3000 BC. The wheel lets a person make rounded symmetrical forms in much less time than by coiling.

The potter centers a ball of clay on a rapidly turning wheel. He or she raises the clay into a cylinder or rounded form. It takes great technical skill and a keen sensitivity for good form to create a beautiful jar. Michael Remsen made the vessel shown (fig. 13–40) of porcelain clay. He threw the jar and the lid separately. He decorated the ceramic ware by slicing the surface and filling the depressions with colored slip. This method is known as *mishima*, a decorative art that originated in Korea. To finish the piece, the artist covered the jar and lid with a transparent glaze.

Jewelry

Prehistoric people made jewelry from materials such as bone, wood, seeds, stones, shells, and hair. Once metalworking procedures were developed, metal became the most common material for jewelry and ceremonial objects. For over 6,000 years, gold has been the most sought after metal. Gold is not only beautiful, but it also never tarnishes. It is easy to stretch. One ounce of gold can be hammered into a sheet of one hundred square feet! This ability of gold (or any metal) to be extended or shaped by hammering is called malleability. Because gold is so malleable, ancient metalworkers used it to create paper-thin objects. They used a process called *repoussé.* The sheet metal is hammered on one side to create shapes and patterns on the other side. The features of the mask (fig. 13–43) were raised in relief by pushing the lines and shapes out from the inside with modeling tools.

In addition to repoussé, other metalworking procedures developed over 2,500 years ago. These procedures include casting, annealing (heating metal to make it easier to form), soldering, bending metal over

13–43 Funeral mask, about 1500 BC. Beaten gold, about 12˝ (30 cm) high. Royal tombs, Mycenae. National Archeological Museum, Athens.

13-45 Colette, *Pectoral #6*, 1985. Sterling silver, fine silver, 24k and 14k gold, bronze, cloisonné, enameled, fabricated. 9 ¼″ x 3 ⅛″ x ¼″ (24 x 8 x .6 cm). ©American Craft Museum. Photograph: George Erml.

13-44 Mary Ann Scherr, *Waist Watcher Monitor Belt Buckle*. This buckle buzzes if the wearer's posture sags. Sterling silver and NU-Gold (bronze), electronics and leather. Courtesy of the artist.

13-47 Earl Krentzin, *Truck*. Silver, 18k gold, semiprecious stones. Courtesy of the artist.

steel stakes or into depressions, cutting, piercing, and engraving. Look closely at the belt buckle (fig. 13–44). Notice how the metal was pierced. Some parts were cut with a saw and soldered on the larger silver form. The metal was bent slightly, and the line designs were engraved in the recessed areas.

Enamels are made from ground glass and metal oxides for color. They can be fused to metal by heating them to about 1,450°F in a kiln. Over the centuries, several different methods have been developed to make enameled jewelry. One of these is **cloisonné.** The pendant shown in figure 13–45 is an example.

Today, some artists use the materials, tools, and procedures needed to make jewelry to produce small sculptures (fig 13–47). Can you tell which parts were sawed, pierced, bent and shaped by hammering and cast, before being soldered together? Krentzin may be a jeweler, a sculptor, or both. He produces carefully crafted art forms that challenge your imagination.

Woven Fiber Forms

Weaving is the most common method of working with fibers. Weaving can be done on a complex loom or a simple wooden frame (fig. 13–48). In plain weaving, one thread, called the *weft*, crosses alternately over and under *warp* threads. The warp threads are stretched on the loom. Weaving was once just a two-dimensional art. Today, it is used in three-dimensional pieces. In figure 13–49, layers of fibers were woven together. Then the layers were gathered to create depth. Other woven works may be stuffed with materials such as dacron or foam rubber to make them three-dimensional.

13–48 Simple frame.

13–49 Barbara Bohnett, *Joy Inside My Tears,* 1978. Woven fiber, 42″ x 22″ (107 x 56 cm). Collection, The Universtiy Museum, Illinois State University, Normal, Illinois.

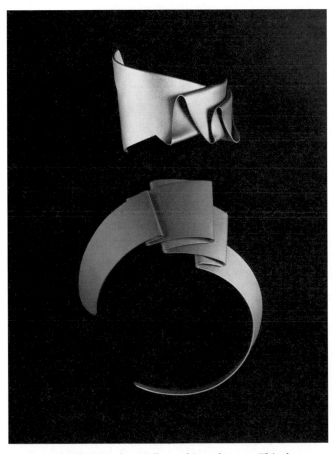

13–46 Gerhardt C. Herbst, *Collar and Bracelet,* 1985. This aluminum collar and bracelet was colored by anodizing, a process of depositing an oxide film electronically on the metal's surface so it will absorb dye colors. Aluminum, sandblasted, anodized. Collar: 6″ diam. x 1″ (15 x 3 cm). Bracelet: 3″ x 2 ½″ x ¾″ (8 x 6 x 2 cm). ©American Craft Museum. Photograph: George Erml.

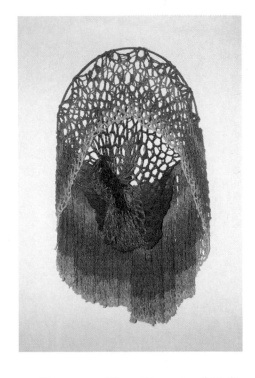

Nonwoven Fiber Forms

Three-dimensional forms can be made from fibers with nonweaving procedures. *Macramé* is done by tying fibers in a series of knots such as the square knot and the clove hitch. Sometimes knots are combined with weaving to give the work more support. The three forms that make up *Implications* (fig 13–50) by Jane Sauer have knotted inner cores. Strands of the fiber were pulled from the cores to give the forms a hairy texture.

Claire Zeistler constructed *Tri-Color Arch* (fig 13–51) by wrapping one fiber around a core of other fibers. For tall pieces like this one (about six feet), the artist may wrap the fiber around a wire armature.

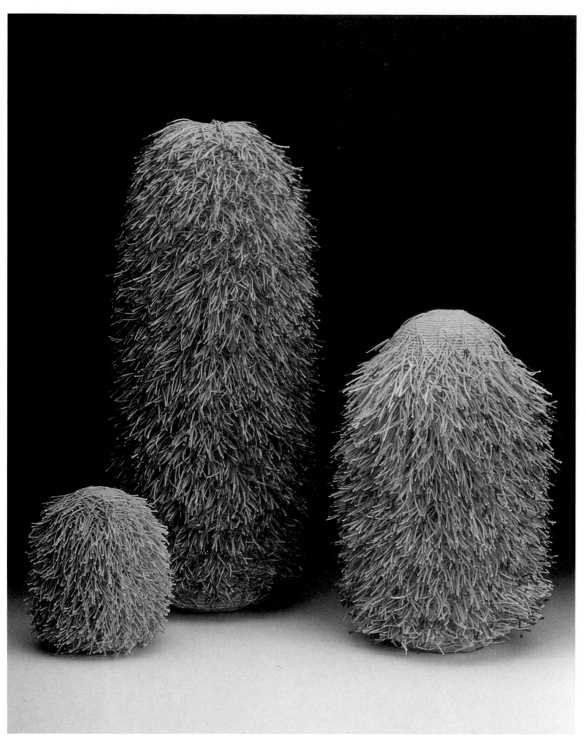

13–50 Jane Sauer, *Implications*, 1985. Waxed linen, paint, knotted, 14″ x 6″ (36 x 15 cm) diam.; 8 ½″ x 5″ (22 x 13 cm) diam.; 3 ½″ x 3 ½″ (9 x 9 cm) diam. Courtesy of the artist.

13-51 Claire Zeistler, *Tri-Color Arch*, 1983–1984. Hemp, synthetic fiber knotted, wrapped, 74″ x 11″ (188 x 28 cm); spill 66″ x 44″ (168 x 112 cm). Courtesy Rhona Hoffman Gallery, Chicago.

13–52 Claes Oldenburg, *Shoestring Potatoes Spilling from a Bag,* 1966. Canvas, kapok, glue, acrylic, 108″ x 46″ x 42″ (274 x 117 x 107 cm). Collection Walker Art Center, Minneapolis. Gift of the T. B. Walker Foundation, 1966.

13–54 Glass bottle shaped like a fish, ca. 1370 BC Egyptian, from el Amarna. Glass, 5 ½″ (14 cm). Reproduced by Courtesy of the Trustees of the British Museum.

13–53 Jo Ellen Trilling, *Portrait.* Fabric, wire, fur and paint, 27″ x 20″ (69 x 51 cm).

Soft Sculpture

Claes Oldenburg was one of the first persons to create soft sculpture out of stuffed fabrics (fig. 13–52). His innovative use of fabrics inspired other artists. Soft sculpture artists began to experiment with a combination of materials to create three-dimensional forms. Jo Ellen Trilling combined fabric, wire, fur, and paint in *Portrait* (fig. 13–53).

If you look at commercial stuffed animals, you can get some ideas about how soft sculpture is constructed. However, the artist must adapt construction procedures to the individual project and to the materials being used. Almost any fabric, whether printed or plain, textured, furry, coarse, or shiny, can be used for soft sculpture.

Glass

Glass is also a beautiful art medium with a very long history. The Egyptians discovered how to make glass about 3000 BC. The first glass objects were beads and solid shapes. Sometime between 1500 and 1350 BC, the Egyptians produced glass vessels, such as the fish-shaped bottle in figure 13–54.

13-55 Rolling the gather on the marver.

13-56 Indenting a groove using jacks.

13-57 Using wet newspaper to form the hot glass.

13-58 Blowing the glass form.

13-59 Reheating the form in the glory hole.

13-60 Shaping the glass attached to a pontil.

13-61 Steve Ramsey, freeblown glass vessels.

The invention of the blowpipe between 200 and 100 BC was to glassmaking what the potter's wheel was to ceramics. The blowpipe made it possible to produce hollow glass forms rapidly. Glass can be cast flat or into a mold. It can be *freeblown,* or formed on the blowpipe in the open air. It can also be blown into a mold. While hot, glass can be bent, twisted, and pulled into shapes. Glass can even be welded to glass.

When glass is freeblown, the heated tip of a blowpipe is barely dipped in molten glass. Then the blowpipe is rotated to wind the glass into a *gather* on the end of the pipe. The artist rolls the gather on a flat metal surface called the *marver.* This allows the glass to chill. The artist is also able to center the gather on the blowpipe (fig. 13-55). Next, the artist aims the blowpipe toward the floor and blows a small bubble.

Working at the glassblower's bench, the artist rolls the pipe back and forth on the bench arms. Spring steel legs connected at the bend, called *jacks,* are used to indent a shallow groove on the glass just in front of the blowpipe (fig. 13-56). While constantly rotating the pipe on the bench arms, the artist forms the hot glass. The artist may use tools such as concave wooden

blocks, paddles, the jacks, cutting shears, and even a wet pad of newspaper to form the glass (fig. 13-57).

Each time it is blown in this forming stage, the vessel increases in size (fig. 13-58). To keep the glass in a workable stage, the artist periodically reheats it. The artist inserts the vessel into the furnace opening, called the *glory hole* (fig. 13-59). The vessel is transferred from the blowpipe to a *pontil.* A pontil is an iron pipe to which the glass is attached for final shaping. The hot glass may be opened up by using a paddle on the inside of the rotating form (fig. 13-60). Eventually, the vessel is removed from the pontil and cooled slowly in an oven.

The artist may etch or engrave the glass form. Further enhancing can be done by sandblasting, cutting, grinding, and polishing the glass. Steve Ramsey used colored transparent glass to create these freeblown vessels (fig. 13-61). In these pieces, glass interacts with the light that passes through it.

Stained Glass. Windows of stained glass cause a special excitement when the light in a room is transformed by the colors of the glass. In the window shown in figure 13–63, the artist carefully selected colors so that they relate to the theme of the work and balance one another. He also planned the organization of the lead lines that run through the panel. The lines not only hold the glass together and provide structural strength. They also create an attractive composition of lines and shapes. When a panel is completely made up of colorless glass, (fig. 13–64), the composition of the lead lines is an important factor in your enjoyment of the panel.

Before constructing a stained glass form, the artist makes a full-size drawing of a design on pattern paper. The pattern shapes are cut out and used to guide the cutting of each glass shape. Individual pieces of glass can be held in place with channeled lead strips called *came.* These strips are soldered together at joints where they meet.

A work may include many intricate and curved shapes, or be three-dimensional like a container or lamp. The edges of each piece of glass can be wrapped with copper foil tape, leaving about $1/32$ inch overlap on both sides. The pieces of glass are soldered together along the foiled edges. The foil technique was used to construct the Baroque style lamp in figure 13–62. The glass contains streaks and swirls that give it movement when lit from behind, softening and diffusing the bulb light.

13–63 Terry Garby.

13–62 Terry Garby.

13–64 Terry Garby.

Studio Experience 13.5

A Harmonious Stained Glass Panel

Use stained glass pieces to construct a panel. Arrange the pieces to create harmonious colors and shapes. **Warning: Use extreme caution when you handle pieces with jagged edges.**

Lila Marks.

Studio Experience 13.6

A Window Panel with Paper

Use tissue paper or cellophane shapes sandwiched between two sheets of construction paper to make a window panel. Openings in the construction paper will reveal the colored tissue.

Myra Schwartz.

Summary

Three-dimensional art forms can be created with almost anything. As you have seen, artists are not limited to traditional materials such as wood, stone, or metal for sculpture. If a material is safe to work with, it may be used to create artworks.

Some three-dimensional forms are made to be seen from all sides. These works may be freestanding, located indoors or outside, or suspended from ceilings. Other three-dimensional works, called reliefs, project out from a surface. Reliefs are viewed mainly from the front.

Sculpture can be divided into categories based on the kinds of materials and procedures used to make it. *Carving,* most commonly done in wood or stone, requires the artist to cut material away to produce a form. *Casting* may be done in metal, plastic, or plaster. Casting involves making a mold from a model. *Modeling* is a building-up process, usually done with clay to produce sculpture. The sculpture is made permanent by firing it in a kiln. *Construction* is a twentieth-century development. Constructions can be reliefs or sculpture in the round. Anything that can be glued, nailed, crimped, welded, bolted, wired, melted, soldered, or otherwise joined may be used for constructions.

In the 1960s some artists began creating environmental artworks that capture and transform space. They frequently involve the spectator. There are several categories of environmental art. Some works may be an area enclosed with some material such as canvas, and filled with constructed forms, special lighting, and sound effects. Other works may be outdoor projects that involve the real environment of land, sky, and water.

Other three-dimensional art include pottery, jewelry, fibers, and glass. All of these arts have histories of development extending over several thousand years. Every early culture developed pottery and methods of decorating and firing it. There are many materials used to make jewelry. The procedures were developed by ancient cultures; some have been borrowed from modern industrial technology. Even fibers, originally used for weaving and the production of fabrics, are now used to create three-dimensional art. Glass can be blown, cast, molded, and laminated to produce three-dimensional art. Stained glass, once reserved mainly for church windows, is now used to create both two- and three-dimensional artworks such as windows, lamps, containers, and constructions.

The growth of modern technology has lead to discoveries of new art media. Given the artist's exploratory nature, the list of art media will continue to grow. The forms that art may take will probably become even more diverse.

Chapter 14
Careers in Art

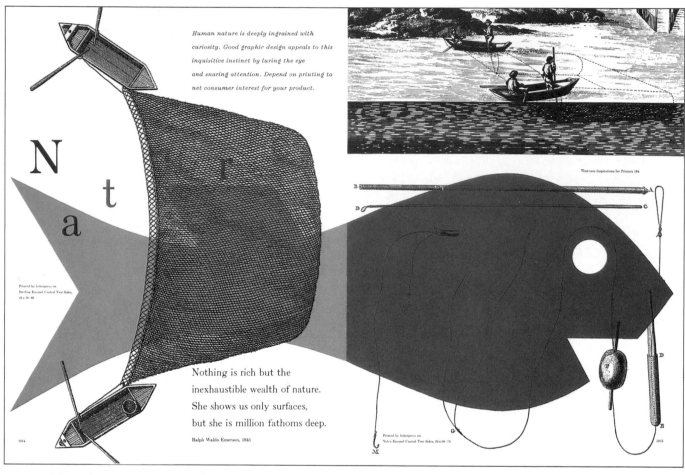

Human nature is deeply ingrained with curiosity. Good graphic design appeals to this inquisitive instinct by luring the eye and snaring attention. Depend on printing to net consumer interest for your product.

N
t
a
r

Printed by letterpress on
Sterling Enamel Coated Two Sides,
62 x 38 - 80

Nothing is rich but the
inexhaustible wealth of nature.
She shows us only surfaces,
but she is million fathoms deep.

Ralph Waldo Emerson, 1841

Printed by letterpress on
Velva Enamel Coated Two Sides, 62 x 38 - 70

14–1 An eighteenth century engraving printed over a fish becomes modern graphic design, perhaps influenced by an earlier design. Bradbury Thompson, *Nature*, 1953. Courtesy Westvaco.

Throughout this book, you are invited to look at and read about the work of fine artists. They have produced an incredible variety of two- and three-dimensional art. However, their work makes up only a small percentage of the art we experience every day. Did you know that this book was made by artists? A designer selected the type style and decided on the size of the pages and the page layouts. A designer created the cover, and graphic artists provided drawings and charts.

Whenever you open a book, magazine or newspaper, turn on the TV, or go to a movie or a play, you encounter the work of artists. An artist's work is visible when you walk through a shopping center or grocery store, drive down a highway or a city street, or select some item of wearing apparel. Artists' designs determine the appearance of things all around us—advertisements, furniture, automobiles, toys, and your school building, to name a few. Some of the hundreds of art careers will be described in this chapter.

Architecture

Architects design buildings from private homes to manufacturing plants and skyscrapers that meet specific functions and satisfy a client's needs. Architecture is often referred to as the art of space. The architect must use space wisely and without waste to provide beauty and comfort in functional and flexible environments.

Architects estimate costs, follow local building codes, and provide detailed construction plans. He or she plans for everything that goes into a building, including construction materials, heating and plumbing, ventilation, stairways, and lighting to name a few. Construction methods for the foundation and supporting structure must be explained. The exterior appearance of a building is also the architect's responsibility. New structures should fit into their surroundings. They should be made with materials and in a style compatible with what is already there.

Architects must be able to draw, build models (fig. 14–2), have a good background in mathematics, know construction materials and procedures, and be knowledgeable of the history of architecture. They need a good sense of design and plenty of imagination.

Architectural Renderers. An architectural renderer creates drawings and paintings of the proposed building so that everyone involved can see what it will look like. The drawings may include trees, automobiles, people and surrounding structures. These elements suggest scale and show how the building will look in the selected environment (fig. 14–3). Construction materials such as brick, wood, aluminum, and stone must be easily identified. Architectural renderers can be employed by architectural firms or work free-lance. Architectural renderers need skill and imagination in working with watercolor, acrylics, pen and ink, and pencil.

14–3 Rendering of proposed new office towers for downtown Houston. Courtesy Houston Chamber of Commerce.

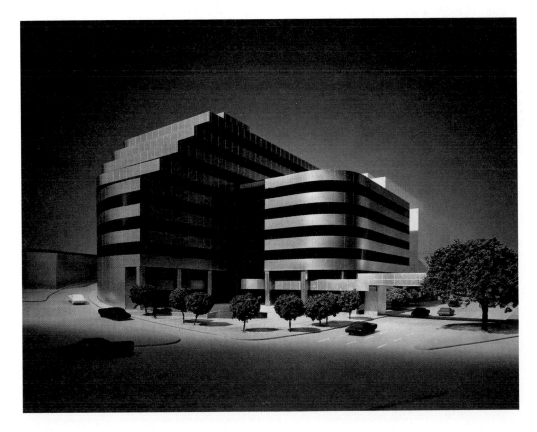

14–2 Model of Selegie Road Commercial Center, Singapore, 1986. Emery, Roth and Sons.

Landscape Architects. Some architects specialize in planning outdoor areas. They design usable and visually pleasing grounds around buildings and residences. They plan for drainage, land contours, and the planting of trees, flowers and shrubs. Landscape architects advise architects on how best to relate buildings to the land on which they are located. Landscape architects plan outdoor areas for private homes, commercial sites, school grounds, housing projects, highway beautification, and recreational grounds. They are knowledgeable about art, architecture, mechanical drawing, botany, and ecology. They generally have attended architectural schools that have an emphasis in landscape architecture.

Interior and Display Design

Interior designers plan and design interior space for everything from homes to giant industrial plants, from automobiles to airplanes (fig. 14–4). They advise on color schemes, furniture, fabrics, floor coverings, and lighting fixtures. They make drawings, paintings, and models of interiors. Plans may be drawn for the interior of one room or an entire department store. They are trained in art schools that specialize in interior design. Interior designers are skilled in architectural drawing, color, and design. They are employed by manufacturers of furniture, automobiles, airplanes, and buses. Interior designers plan the environments in which people live, work, study and play. Any company with interior space that is used by people, such as restaurant chains and hotels, uses the services of interior designers.

Exhibit and display designers work for agencies that sell some item or service such as department stores, museums, and art galleries. Manufacturers that exhibit products at convention centers employ these designers to plan and construct exhibits and displays. Exhibit and display designers design and build display cases and lighted boxes, organize props, and arrange lighting for the displays. They often make sketches and scale

14-5 Milton Glaser, Grand Union Supermarket.

14–4 Skylit Solar Court, Albany County Airport, Colonie, N.Y. Norman McGrath, photographer. Photograph: courtesy Einhorn Yaffee Prescott, P.C.

models for clients. They need a knowledge of graphic design, type, color, display, theatrical lighting, and carpentry. In addition, they need skill in drawing and model building.

Department store display designers specialize in interior and window displays for department stores. Large department stores may employ display designers, but these designers frequently freelance for several different stores and shops. Individuals who specialize in department store displays need skills in design, color, lighting, lettering, illustration, and carpentry.

Graphic Design

You see the work of graphic designers every day. Advertisements on TV and in magazines and newspapers, signs and billboards, posters, brochures, record jackets, clothing logos, package design, and much more are done by graphic designers. Graphic designers

translate the ideas of clients into visual images that the public will find appealing and difficult to ignore.

Corporate art directors supervise people in art or design departments. The art staff create visual materials that project a positive image of the company and the product. They produce magazine and newspaper advertisements, promotional packages, audio-visual materials, TV ads, brochures, and public relations materials. Corporate art directors are knowledgeable in all areas of graphic design. They must be good administrators since they work with sales people, production workers, and management personnel, as well as the staff in the art department.

Advertising agency art directors also head teams of artists who produce all kinds of advertising materials for clients. Agency art directors consult with clients to determine how to best promote a product. The agency team studies the market that will buy the product, then

14-6 Courtesy Input-Output Computer Imaging Center, Normal, Illinois.

14-7 Logo design for T-shirts. Design by Erika Wade. Courtesy Chandler Magnet School.

develops a marketing plan. The plan includes ideas for advertising and promotional displays. The director prepares sketches and layouts of each piece of advertising. The layouts show text and typeface, color, illustrations, and photographs. If the client approves the plan, specialists on the agency team prepare newspaper and magazine advertisements, radio and television commercials, posters, and brochures. Agency directors must know advertising, have a good design background, and be able to visualize and develop ideas.

Graphic designers plan visual presentations for such things as record jackets, advertisements, brochures, package designs, magazine covers, filmstrips, posters, and billboards. Graphic designers work out sketches called roughs. The roughs offer clients and art directors alternatives to choose from. Approved roughs are then worked up in detailed drawings called comprehensives (in color if required). Everything is arranged to exact size, including blocks of text, the type of lettering, sketches of all artwork, and photos. When the comprehensives are approved, the designer works with computer artists, illustrators, typographers, and photographers to make finished pieces. These pieces are turned over to paste-up artists who prepare the materials for photocopying.

Computer graphic designers. Instead of pens, brushes and rulers, the computer graphic designer uses a digitizing pad or a mouse. Using special software and color printers, the computer graphic designer can put together text, type, images, and layout to create full-color or black-and-white graphics. Images can also be put on videotapes or slides. Three-dimensional images can be put into the computer and rotated in any direction to see all sides. The computer graphic designer must have a good sense of composition and a good foundation in graphic design.

Screen printers use their skills to reproduce images on T-shirts, uniforms, sports clothes, jackets, hats, posters, signs, greeting cards, calendars, and illuminated panels on pinball machines and mirrors (fig. 14–7). Screen prints can be produced on almost any surface including paper, fabric, glass, plastic, metal, rubber, wood, leather, and fur. The screen printer must know about different screen procedures and inks and paints that are suitable for various surfaces.

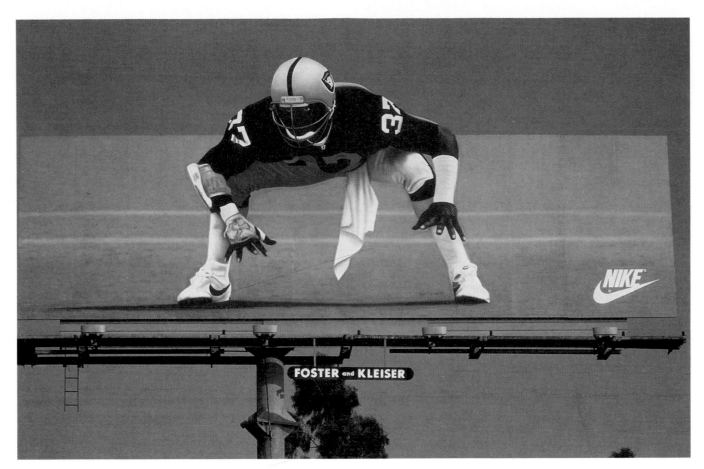

14-8 Courtesy NIKE, Inc.

Record jacket designers. On an album or CD cover, a designer tries to produce an image that communicates the mood or message of the music, the performance style of the recording artist, or the personalities of the group. The designer sketches several ideas for a cover. A comprehensive drawing of the accepted sketch is made to show color, images, and lettering. Photographers, illustrators, typographers, and printers produce a finished jacket.

Signage. Effective signs result from careful attention to design, lettering, and color. Commercial artists and graphic designers create both illuminated and non-illuminated signs. Examples include carved and sandblasted signs, truck lettering, wall murals, banners, and show cards. Signage also includes signs that are developed according to a "systems" approach. For example, all of the signs in a hospital or a corporate office building have a similar design format. This type of signage is called architectural sign systems or environmental graphics.

Outdoor advertising. Outdoor advertising is another form of commercial advertising. Poster panels or an eight-sheet poster for a billboard are often part of a multimedia campaign. In preparing outdoor advertising media, the designer must consider cost, size, method of reproduction, and location. Billboards have become a popular art form offering creative compositions of shapes and colors. They sometimes involve three-dimensional form, moving parts, and lighting effects (fig. 14-8). Outdoor advertising designers need skills in photography, painting, illustration, and type design. A knowledge of advertising psychology also helps.

Industrial Design

Industrial designers work to improve the appearance and quality of products. Products can be as simple as a soft drink can or as complex as a space shuttle. Designers are responsible for the form and appearance of all the objects that are part of your daily life, from automobiles and calculators to your skateboard and bicycle. Industrial designers must understand production processes, the characteristics of the materials used in those processes, and the function of every product they work on.

Product designers are employed by manufacturers that make consumer products. They must have a keen sense of design, understand consumer needs, and know style trends. The product must perform well, be attractive to consumers, and economical to manufacture. When planning a product such as a new vacuum

14-9   Preliminary prototypes of paper, clay and wood. Courtesy Eureka Vacuum Company.

14-10   Marco Ferrari and Sam Hohulin, *Step Saver Vacuum.* Courtesy Eureka Vacuum Company.

cleaner, the designer works from sketches to develop a model, called a prototype. The model may be made from paper, clay, or wood (fig. 14-9). Once a design is approved, the designer makes detailed drawings and works with engineers to produce a full-scale working model (fig. 14-10). If the working model is approved, detailed working drawings are developed for the engineers to use in producing the new product.

Package designers design containers that will attract consumers, inform them about the product, and make them feel confident about the product's quality. Once sketches for a new package are approved, a prototype box is made. Designers may use a foam core, colored paper, transfer letters, and marker and pencil illustrations (fig. 14-11).

Furniture designers create all kinds of new furnishings that are constructed from wood, metal, plastic, and fabric. They work closely with manufacturing engineers to design furniture that is durable, attractive, and that can be produced cost-effectively with available technology. Suppose a furniture manufacturer asks a designer to create a plastic table. The designer works up ideas in drawings. If the manufacturer likes one, the designer builds a model. If the model is approved, the designer makes precise drawings, which are used to make a production model.

Toy designers are employed by manufacturers of games and toys. Most toy designers have backgrounds in industrial design. They know what kinds of materials are safe, durable, and easy to maintain. They must like to work in miniature. Like other industrial designers, they take the development of a toy or game

14-11   (left) Prototype box, and (right) final production box. Courtesy Eureka Vacuum Company.

through the steps of research, sketching, designing, model building, and production. A knowledge of children's interests and development is necessary.

Fashion Design

Fashion designers create clothing for every kind of activity, from athletic events to formal occasions. Fashion designers must be creative with colors, textures, and fabrics. They must be able to sketch their ideas with flair and style in various media. Because their drawings are used for the production of new garments, they must understand how garments are assembled. A knowledge of the history of clothing design and contemporary trends is necessary.

Fashion illustrators draw clothing and models for newspapers, magazines, department store catalogs, and brochures. They must be able to illustrate the texture and special qualities of the fabrics. For example, some fabrics cling to the body, others fall straight or in folds. They also have to illustrate jewelry and hair styles. Along with a knowledge of painting media, a knowledge of the history of fashion and contemporary fashion is helpful.

Illustration

Editorial illustrators are employed by magazines, newspapers, television stations, and book publishers. Editorial illustrators need to make drawings and paintings that complement the written text. The style of an artist usually determines the type of illustrations he or she creates. Some illustrators specialize in certain media such as pen and ink, watercolor, or collage. An art director may hire them for jobs which require that specialty. Illustrators may also specialize in subjects, such as sports activities, automobiles, animals, or landscapes.

Medical illustrators create extremely accurate pictures, transparencies, and overlays for medical schools, medical supply companies, publishers of medical journals and books, and advertising agencies. In addition to drawings for the public and medical profession, they also prepare charts, graphs, and diagrams for medical researchers. Their work requires patience, attention to detail, a knowledge of anatomy, and excellent drawing skills.

14–12 Diane Bigda created this watercolor and pen and ink illustration for a magazine article about a meeting of computer software producers that was to be held in Holland, 1993.

Cartoonists produce drawings for advertisements and stories, comic strips and comic books, editorial cartoons, greeting cards, and animated cartoons for TV or movies. Comic strips are meant to entertain. Editorial cartoons aim to influence public opinion, and advertising cartoons are meant to sell products. Most cartoonists do their work with brush, pen and ink, wash, and Zip-a-Tone (commercially printed stick-down patterns of dots or lines). They may be employed by newspaper chains and magazines. Some cartoonists work on a free-lance basis and sell their work to publishers. Cartoonists must have rich imaginations and be able to generate ideas continually. The ability to draw well and rapidly in a distinctive style that people recognize is essential for success. Comic strip cartoonists must be able to write stories or one-liners to accompany their work.

Technical illustrators produce drawings for assembly of everything from bicycles to the installation of instrument panels in airplanes. For a good example of their work, look at an automobile repair manual. Technical illustrators are employed by every kind of industry. Their drawings aid in the construction and maintenance of complex machinery and industrial products.

Film and Television

Art directors coordinate the efforts of artists, graphic and costume designers, and scene builders involved in making a film or television production. They work with film directors and producers to develop appropriate environments for their production. Art directors are responsible for the authenticity of sets, costumes, props, and locations. The director must be able to create set constructions for a scene that establish a mood. An art director must understand the production from beginning to end.

Storyboard illustrators are employed by advertising agencies and the film and television industries. They develop storyboards based on a story for a film or the action for a TV commercial. A storyboard may contain fifty or sixty sequenced sketches that illustrate the progress of action. The dialogue is printed under each drawing. The number of storyboards needed depends on the length of the production and may range from three to thirty. The comic-strip-like boards are used by the film director as an outline of the characters' actions in a film or the progress of an animated commercial. Storyboard artists must be able to produce descriptive drawings very rapidly.

Television graphic artists are employed by television studios to produce advertising and promotional materials. They create visuals for newscasts, art for commercials, and sets for shows. They also design logos for the station. They must quickly provide finished products that will be impressive on the screen.

Animation artists also use storyboards to draw and develop the characters for animated films. They listen to recordings of the voices for the characters as they develop them in drawings. It takes twenty-four drawings for each second of film. The animation artist must be able to draw well and rapidly, and have the patience to work on a project for a long time. Some feature length films take several years to complete.

Art Education

Elementary and secondary art teachers work with children and adolescents from kindergarten through high school. They are certified to teach art and hold degrees from colleges and universities. School art teachers need a background in art history, critical aesthetic analysis, and a working knowledge of many different art media. They must be able to help students use these media to express their ideas and feelings. The art experiences can give children and adolescents a lifelong enjoyment of the visual arts. Art teachers plan programs that give students basic art skills and knowledge. Secondary art teachers must provide experiences for students who wish to specialize in one area of art production. They can also advise talented individuals who might pursue an art career.

College and university art teachers are often *studio art instructors* who majored in a studio area during their college training. They instruct courses in their area of specialization (drawing, painting, printmaking, ceramics, etc.). They generally have a Master of Fine Arts degree. In addition to teaching, most university art teachers produce art for exhibition and sale. Some achieve regional and national recognition for their artwork. Participation in selective and competitive exhibitions is expected of studio art instructors.

Art historians are employed by colleges and universities to teach art history. They must have completed graduate programs with emphasis in an area of art history, such as Modern Art, Greek and Roman Art, or Baroque and Rococo. Art historians conduct research, write papers and books, and sometimes give lectures to community groups.

Art educators are employed by colleges and universities that have teacher education programs. They usually have a Master's or Doctoral degree and experience as public school art teachers. They instruct courses to prepare people to teach art in elementary and secondary schools, or at the university level. They may also prepare people to work in art administration or as city art supervisors.

14–13 Courtesy Wave Inc., Worcester, Massachusetts. Photographer: Jonathan Kannair.

14–14 John Joiner. Photograph courtesy The Arizona Bank.

Crafts

Crafts can be defined as works in wood, clay, fiber, metal, glass, and plastic that have some use or are related in form to useful objects. For example, wheel-thrown pottery is a craft, although not all wheel-thrown pots can be used to hold food or liquid.

Like fine artists, craftspeople often find it difficult to make a comfortable living from the sale of their works. Many teach their craft or supplement their income with a second job. Some craft studios specialize in one medium such as ceramics or stained glass. They employ craftspeople to produce work from the designs of others, rather than original works of their own.

In recent years, the differences between crafted objects and fine art have become less obvious. Wooden chairs have taken on the look of fine sculpture. Woven clothing is often hung on walls as decoration. The distinctive styles of a few craftspeople have even placed them on a par with fine artists. There is great demand for their work.

Fine Art

Fine artists create two- and three-dimensional works of art to sell. A fine artist must have the self-discipline to work several hours a day to produce his or her art. Most fine artists work alone, motivating themselves to start and finish their projects. In order to become known by the art-buying public, fine artists must establish a connection with a gallery. The gallery "represents" artists. The gallery agrees to show, advertise, and sell their work. It charges each artist a percentage of the final selling price in exchange for its services.

Because it may take years for an artist to establish a reputation, find a suitable gallery and produce enough artwork to sell, many must hold a second job to supplement their income. Most artists need a studio or workshop to work in. And while some are self-taught, many artists have university or art school degrees. The life of a fine artist may seem attractive and simple, yet it is a life of constant challenge.

Photography

Photojournalists take the pictures you see in magazines and newspapers. They make pictorial stories with their cameras. Photojournalists must be expert in the use of many different cameras and lenses. They must be able to handle them with speed and accuracy under all kinds of conditions. They also know darkroom and printing procedures. They travel to many different locations to photograph people and events, such as scenes of human tragedy, war, celebrations, and affairs of state. Because it takes so many years to develop a reputation as a photojournalist, many of them start out as freelancers. They may take pictures on assignment from editors or try to sell their work to a publisher.

Fashion photographers create pictures for newspapers, department store catalogs, and magazines. They work with models in a studio or on location at such places as a beach, a shopping mall, or an airport. They are skilled in creating special lighting effects on location and in the studio. Photographing models in action at fashion shows requires planned lighting and rapid camera work during the presentation. Fashion photographers create moods in pictures. They direct the movements of the models, from natural to dramatic poses to flamboyant action.

Illustration photographers provide photos for books and magazines, record jackets, travel brochures, corporation annual reports, and advertisements. Photographs are frequently used in place of drawings and paintings for commercial publications. Illustration photographers work closely with agency and corporate art directors. They use models, props, backgrounds, and sets to make an idea come alive. An illustration photographer must be able to produce photos that are vital and stimulating.

Advertising photographers specialize in taking pictures of products for advertisements. The photographer may work with an ad agency art director to fulfill the needs of an ad layout. They take pictures of products ranging from jewelry to refrigerators. The finished photos must attract the public's attention, make the product appealing, and hold the viewer's attention long enough for communication about the product. Ad photographers take photos of many different surfaces (foods, fabrics, fur, glass, diamonds, wood, plastic, metal, and so on). They must have skill and experience in arranging backgrounds and lighting effects.

Portrait photographers make photo studies of their subjects. They generally have a studio, but will go to locations for special events such as graduations, weddings, birthdays, and award ceremonies. Portrait photographers are expert at posing subjects and arranging complementary lighting for children, men, and women of all ages. They know how to use a variety of cameras, film, and development processes. They can produce photographs that resemble painted portraits.

There are many other art-related careers that were not discussed in this chapter. For more information about careers in art, you may want to consult your art teacher or school guidance counselor. You can also write to college and university art departments and professional art schools.

14-15 Courtesy The Worcester Telegram and Gazette.

Research Experience 14.1

Exploring a Career in Art

Research a career in art that interests you. Consider the training, responsibilities, and rewards of the job. Write down reasons why you feel you would like this job.

Part V
What Is It Saying?

Henri Matisse, *The Red Room*, (detail) 1908–1909. Oil on canvas, 71″ x 97″ (180 x 246 cm). The Hermitage Museum, Leningrad.

Chapter 15

Interpretation: There Is More to It Than Meets the Eye

In Chapter 5, you learned how to describe an artwork. In Chapter 9, you learned how to analyze an artwork. You have been introduced in other chapters to the visual elements, principles of design, and the major two-dimensional and three-dimensional media. At the same time, you discovered a new vocabulary to help you describe and analyze art.

Interpretation and Meaning

Now that you are able to describe and analyze, you are ready to *interpret*. To interpret an artwork is to explain the *meaning* of it. What does it express? What is its content? You have already had some experience in interpretation. For example, you have seen how lines can be nervous or relaxed, how colors can be warm or cool. Shapes can be closed or open. Positive and negative areas of a carved sculpture can flow into one another. Those qualities expressed certain feelings or ideas that you, the viewer, could interpret. The focus of this chapter is on the interpretation and meaning of artworks.

An Example of Interpretation

Imagine being asked to interpret *The Toll Collectors* (fig. 15–1) by Charles M. Russell. First of all, you would describe and analyze it.

As you can see, the subject is a landscape containing people and animals. In the foreground are a cowboy and a Crow Indian. Both are mounted on horses, both are carrying weapons, and both look serious. In the middle ground are cattle, a cowboy on the left, and more Crow Indians on the right. In the distance are more cattle. A large herd seems to be headed this way. In the far distance are the faint outlines of a mountain

range. You might have guessed from the title and the gesture of the Crow Indian that a *toll*, or payment, is involved. (Indeed, the Crow Indian warrior is demanding payment before he will allow the cattle and cowboys to cross tribal land. His raised finger indicates a toll of $1.00 per head.) With just the information provided so far, you may be ready to offer an interpretation.

However, your observations would not stop at just the subject matter and the title. You would also note the visual elements, the principles of composition, and the oil medium. You would note that Russell's style is basically realistic. Animals, men, and land are quite natural looking; the sense of open land is especially convincing. The artist skillfully used colors and values to suggest that the time is early morning (or late afternoon) and that the atmosphere is hazy. (Note the effective use of aerial perspective.) Russell used the oil medium much as Renoir did in *Luncheon of the Boating Party* (fig. 3–1). He used short brushstrokes, which you can see clearly in the distant herd. Several lines of continuation unite the scene horizontally. Look at the broad sweep of the hill in the foreground as well as the mountains on the horizon. The cowboy and Crow Indian are painted in warm colors. They overlap the bluish shapes of the mountains and unite foreground and background.

Of course, much more could be said about Russell's painting. For this example, only the main features have been noted. Now you are ready to interpret the work. Like the description and analysis, the interpretation that follows is not intended to be complete.

You might begin by saying that *The Toll Collectors* is about a meeting between a cowboy and a Crow Indian. However, because the Crow Indian is demanding a toll, this meeting could mean a challenge, even

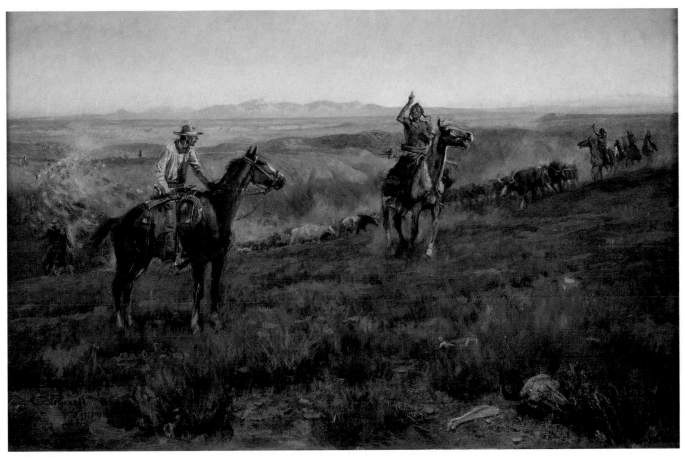

15–1 Charles M. Russell, *The Toll Collectors*, 1913. Oil on canvas, 24″ x 36″ (61 x 91 cm). The Mackay Collection, Montana Historical Society.

danger. Perhaps the meeting should be called a *confrontation*. The confrontation itself, however, is not overly dramatic. The men seem ordinary in appearance. Russell's earthy realism tends to downplay a sense of drama or heroics. Except for the presence of weapons, there is no indication of violence. Except for the cattle in the background pushing ever closer, there is very little movement.

But there is more to consider than the men, their weapons, and the cattle, important as these are. The setting is a vast wilderness—the "Old West." This wilderness stands for more than just the land used for cattle drives. It adds a sense of scale that enlarges its meaning. The scene becomes a symbol of a much greater confrontation. It expresses a territorial struggle between two cultures with extremely different lifestyles and histories.

Sources of Meaning

The meaning we have discussed so far is based on things you see in the picture and information in the title. The tasks of describing, analyzing, and interpreting helped you to bring out the most from these seen things.

But the meaning of Russell's picture is also based on things you do *not* see. For example, you do not actually see a "territorial struggle between two cultures." This part of the interpretation is based on what you *know*. You have learned in school about conflicts between American Indians and the white settlers. Cowboys, cattle drives, sagebrush, and the semi-arid landscape of the western territories are all a part of your knowledge of the Old West, an American legend.

You also probably learned about cowboys, American Indians, and outlaws through movies and TV. Most of those stories were exaggerated and very misleading about the true conditions of the western territories. However, they did make you familiar with the facts and legends of the Old West. Without this knowledge, Russell's painting would have had little meaning. Indeed, you probably would not even have

15–2 Charles M. Russell, *Wild Meat for Wild Men*, 1890. Oil, 20 ¼″ x 36 ⅛″ (51 x 92 cm). Amon Carter Museum, Fort Worth, Texas.

15–3 *Fowling the Marshes*, wall painting, ca. 1400 BC. Reproduced by Courtesy of the Trustees of the British Museum.

recognized the two people as being a cowboy and an American Indian!

Russell based *The Toll Collectors* on memories of his own experiences in the Montana Territory in the 1880s. (This was about the time that Renoir painted *Luncheon of the Boating Party* in France.) Russell spent a winter with the Blackfoot Indian tribe. He developed an admiration for the American Indian that lasted the rest of his life. Russell paid tribute to his "red brothers" by painting their exploits (fig. 15–2). If you knew more about the artist and had seen many of his paintings, you no doubt would have discovered even deeper meanings in this work.

Unfamiliar Art from Unfamiliar Places

Now, imagine being asked to interpret a mural (fig. 15–3) painted on a limestone wall of a 1400 BC Egyptian tomb.

Some things you can identify right away: A man is standing, legs spread, on what appears to be a boat. With one hand he is grabbing two birds by their feet, in the other he holds an odd staff. Also in the boat are two females, both much smaller than he. In front of the man are swarms of birds and a cat gripping one bird in its teeth and clinging to another with its front claws. Directly in front of the boat are what appears to be strange plants. Directly below the boat are some fish.

Sokari Douglas Camp

1958–

Strips of steel are bound together to form the structure of a bed. The metal frame sags with the weight of a body which is not there. Only the spirit of a person remains behind. Surrounding the bed are huddled figures drawn in ribbons of steel. *Church Ede* is a memorial to the father of Sokari Douglas Camp, the artist who created this unusual sculpture. It reconstructs the Nigerian funerary ceremony which honored her father's death. Turn on the electric motor that operates this moving work of art, and the grieving figures begin to move. As they fan the missing body with fly whisks, the bed begins to shake, symbolizing the continuing vitality of the afterlife. The sound of the whirring motors, the shaking fans held by the mourners, the rattling metal strips which form the bed, and the partially complete figures compel your imagination to complete this scene. At once, the viewer captures a glimpse of the Kalabari culture in which this ceremony originated.

Sokari uses the materials and techniques of contemporary Western art to create sculptures that tell of the Kalabari people among whom she was raised. Though Sokari's early life was spent in the Niger Valley of southern Nigeria, she moved to England as a child to live with her sister.

Sokari's experiences in Africa and in the Western world have had unique influences on her

Sokari Douglas Camp, *Church Ede (Decorated Bed for Christian Wake)*, 1984. Steel, cloth, H. 8″. Collection of the artist, courtesy the National Museum of African Art, Smithsonian Institution, Washington, DC. Photograph: Jeffrey Ploskonka, Eliot Elisofon Archives.

life and art. Her early exposure to the ceremonies and festivals associated with Kalabari culture were significant to Sokari. Her schooling in England and later in the United States influenced the methods and materials she uses to express these early memories of Nigeria. Sokari Douglas Camp combines Western art with the traditional culture of the Kalabari people to express ideas and communicate stories in an art which is uniquely her own.

(We might be able to see more fish if that part of the mural were not damaged.)

The images of the people are flat and relatively stiff. Compared to them, the birds, cat, and fish are very lifelike and active. There is even some overlapping among the birds. You can almost hear them screeching and flapping their wings as they are being attacked by the man and the cat.

Other than the overlapping, the mural is almost completely lacking in depth. Notice that the boat is *on* the water and not *in* the water.

Beyond these few impressions, there is little else that you can get out of this work, leaving you with little to say about it by way of interpretation. Indeed, the more you study the mural, the more questions it raises. Among the many questions you may have are: What is the purpose of the mural? Who are the people? Why is the man so much bigger than the women? Why is the picture located in a tomb? Who was the artist? Why are the people so flat, and the whole picture lacking in depth?

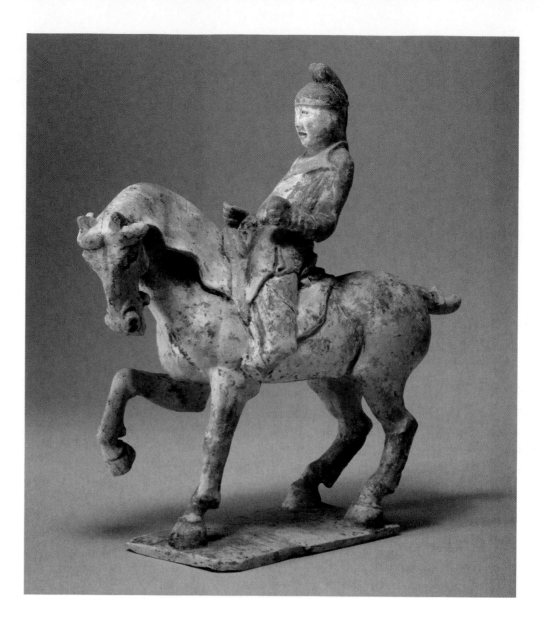

15–4 Terra cotta grave figure, T'ang dynasty. Museum of Far Eastern Antiquities, Stockholm.

Unlike your interpretation of *The Toll Collectors,* your interpretation of the Egyptian mural depends almost entirely on what you *see.* What you *know* about ancient Egypt and its art, compared to what you know about the Old West and its legends, is obviously limited.

Now, look at the small statue in figure 15–4. You recognize this as a man on a horse. In a captured moment, the rider is restraining the horse with his reins (now missing). The posture of the horse, which seems to have come to a sudden stop, is in rhythm with the posture of the man, who is leaning back sharply. You may have recognized that the sculpture is ceramic. Its rough textures are suited to the forms of the stocky horse and rider.

You can get meaning from this sculpture from the forms. But without additional knowledge, that meaning is rather limited. The sculpture was made in China during the T'ang dynasty (600s AD). This bit of information helps you to locate it in time and place. Perhaps it helps you understand the costume of the man. But think how much richer the meaning would be if you knew something of the history and culture of China, especially during the T'ang dynasty.

As stated earlier, meaning is based on things you see, but also on things you do not see, that is, things you know. The images, colors, and shapes in a work are not always enough to help you understand its meaning. If the images do not "connect" with your own experiences, background and education, you may be unable to discover sufficient meaning. This is especially true for a work from an unfamiliar time and place, such as ancient Egypt or T'ang dynasty China. This would even be true for a work like *The Toll Collectors* if a viewer had little knowledge of American history.

Art History

Art history is the study of art within a *social* and *historical context*. That means studying the art of a particular time by also studying the history and social customs of the time. Art history provides information about periods of history, periods of art, and changing styles. Knowing about the period in which an artwork was created can help you understand the work.

Like an archeologist, an art historian sifts through the evidence. He or she looks at other artworks, books, and records of the period. Like a storyteller, he or she attempts to "re-create" an artwork in the context of its original time and place. How did people who were living at that time experience the art? As writer Gerald Brommer explains, "Art history adds personality to works of art."

Knowledge like this can bring an ancient mural and a Chinese sculpture back to life. Of course, you can never experience the mural exactly as the citizens in Thebes, Egypt, did in 1400 BC, or experience the statue the way people in Hsian, China, did in the 600s AD. But by using art history, you can reconstruct some of those experiences, and thus better understand the meaning of these works.

The next four chapters, which discuss non-Western and Western art history, will provide an overview of China and Egypt, among other cultures.

Criticism Experience 15.1

Interpreting *American Gothic*

Interpret *American Gothic* by Grant Wood. Use your earlier description (Criticism Experience 3.1: Describing an Artwork) and your analysis (Criticism Experience 9.1: Analyzing *American Gothic*). In addition, you can rely on what you have already learned in your own experiences. Use the following guidelines (or those provided by your teacher) for interpretation.

Grant Wood, *American Gothic*, 1930. Oil on beaver board, 30″ x 25″ (76 x 63 cm). Friends of American Art, The Art Institute of Chicago.

1. Organize information from your description and analysis to help you identify what the artwork expresses or means. If you did not do a description or analysis, complete them now. The guidelines for Criticism Experiences 3.1 and 9.1 will be helpful.

2. To identify what the artwork means, add what you already know about the subject matter, the elements such as form, shapes and colors, and the theme of the work.
   a) Does the work remind you of anything?
   b) Have you seen, read, or studied about situations or things like those you see in the artwork?

3. Form a *hypothesis* about what the work means. A hypothesis is an assumption, or an informed guess based on evidence you have collected.
   a) Do your description and analysis support your hypothesis?
   b) Does the information you bring to this work support your hypothesis? Consider knowledge you have picked up from personal experiences, studies, travels, and reading.

4. If your evidence does not support your hypothesis, try another one.

Chapter 16
Non-Western Art I

Introduction

The great *civilizations* of India, the Orient, Islam, and pre-Columbian America, and the tribal societies of Africa and North America are among the many non-Western cultures. Any culture that is not related to Western civilization (the people of North America and western Europe) is referred to as **non-Western.**

As a collection, non-Western cultures represent an incredible variety of geography, peoples, history, beliefs, and art. Indeed, they have little in common with one another—beyond the fact that they all pro-duce (or did produce) art. But some generalizations about them can be made by contrasting them as a group with Western culture.

Consider the theme of *individualism,* for example. Individualism has been a tradition in Western culture for centuries. This tradition is perhaps emphasized more today than it was in the past. Among other things, individualism is responsible for our concepts of free speech, free thinking, and free enterprise. Individualism has no doubt been a source for the creative energy and inventiveness that have distinguished our culture through time. But individualism has also contributed to people leading lives of egotism and greed, and placing self-interest above the common good.

By contrast, people of non-Western societies, especially Asians, believe the opposite. They believe that it is better to place the common good above one's own interests. Such an attitude obviously affects the ways people relate to their jobs, families, nation, and even to nature. This attitude, along with other values, beliefs and themes, also is reflected in a culture's symbols and art.

Another difference between Western and non-Western cultures involves the concept of art itself. In the twentieth-century West, the purpose of art is primarily for aesthetic enjoyment (Chapter 2). In non-Western societies, art has many purposes, including magic, worship, ritual, sacrifice, propaganda, status, and even politics.

16-0   Ranganathaswanny Temple, Tamilnadi, South India. At 236 feet (78 m) this is the tallest temple tower in Asia. Photograph courtesy James Ellison Thomas.

India

India can trace its roots to recently discovered settlements near Mohenjo-Daro on the Indus River in what is now Pakistan (fig. 16–1). Excavations there revealed that these settlements go back in time more than 5,000 years. They consisted of cities with hundreds of houses, shops, streets, wells, and drainage systems. There is even evidence that the people of those ancient cities wrote contracts and signed legal documents.

16–2 Four Seals with a bull, a rhinoceros, an elephant, and a horned tiger. Karachi Museum, Karachi, Pakistan. Borromeo/Art Resource, NY.

Among the smaller finds were *seals* carved in stone (fig. 16–2). Officials used the seals to stamp (or "sign") documents written on tablets of damp clay.

The Mohenjo-Daro civilization appeared in the fertile valley of the Indus River between 4000 and 3000 BC. Around this same time, other civilizations also emerged in river valleys in different parts of the world. Egypt developed along the Nile River. China developed along the Yellow River. Sumeria, which is now Iraq, developed between the Tigris and Euphrates Rivers.

Modern India has more people than North and South America combined in a space that is not quite half the size of the United States. India can claim to be one of the oldest continuing civilizations. It is a nation of fourteen languages. Although Hinduism is the main religion, there are many others and several ethnic groups. Like its geography of extreme contrasts—from snow-covered mountains to steamy jungles—India has a rich mixture of cultures.

Around 2000 BC a tribal people invaded India from the north. The newcomers not only conquered the native Indians, they introduced their own hymns called the *Vedas.* (These are like the poems of the Jewish Old Testament or the myths of the ancient Greeks.) These hymns marked the beginning of **Hinduism,** the world's most ancient religion.

16–1 India.

16–3 The Great Stupa, Sanchi, India, second century BC–first century AD. Solid masonry. Scala/Art Resource, NY.

Unlike Christianity, Hinduism is *polytheistic.* Hindus believe in many gods rather than just one god. But perhaps the most unique feature of this religion is its belief in *reincarnation.* Reincarnation is the belief that life can be an endless cycle. The stages of birth, life, and death are repeated again and again. A person's soul never dies but is continually reborn (or reincarnated) in a new body, either human or animal. The type of body that a soul occupies in any given life depends on its *karma.* Karma is a kind of reward or punishment based on the soul's behavior in its previous life. If the soul was good, it might be given the body of a prince or princess. If the soul was bad, it might be given the body of a rat or snake.

Hinduism was the dominant religion for about 1,500 years. Then Buddha was born, about five hundred years before the birth of Christ. During his youth, Buddha (the "enlightened" one) experienced a vision while sitting under a shade tree. He saw the endless succession of birth and death in the stream of life.

From this experience he determined that all evil and suffering were caused by desire, and that human desire started with birth. After seven years of meditation, he proceeded to the city of Sarnath. Here he preached about his insight and founded the new faith of *Buddhism.*

At first, Buddhism was considered just a splinter denomination of Hinduism. However, Buddhism became stronger than Hinduism in India (at least for a while), and then spread to other countries. It became one of the largest religions of the world. The goal of all Buddhists is to achieve *nirvana,* the final state of eternal bliss. To do so, one must conquer not only desire, but the self, and lead a life of perfect justice, patience, and kindness. Only then can the soul break the endless cycle of birth.

A fitting symbol of the Buddhist faith is the *stupa,* a dome-shaped form that evolved out of a burial mound. The best example of this form is the Great Stupa at Sanchi (fig. 16–3). Except for a small burial chamber in the center, the Great Stupa is almost solid

16-4 *Seated Buddha,* Gandhara, first–third century AD. Black schist, 2´4¾˝ x 22½˝ (73 x 57 cm). Yale University Art Gallery (Anonymous gift through Alfred R. Bellinger).

16-5 Seated Buddha Preaching the First Sermon, Sarnath, fifth century AD. Stele, sandstone, 63˝ (160 cm) high. Archaeological Museum, Sarnath.

masonry (built of stone, brick or concrete; in this case the material is brick). It was intended to represent the dome of heaven or the world mountain. The little balcony on its top was meant to stand for the home of thirty-three gods. Four ornamental gates were built to face north, south, east, and west. Because the stupa is circular, it is a perfect metaphor for the cycle of life. The simplicity of the dome symbolizes the serenity of nirvana.

There is no image of Buddha himself on the Great Stupa. However, his throne, his shade tree, and even his footprints appear on the gates. Human images of Buddha did not appear until about 100 AD in Gandhara. Gandhara, a northwest region that is now Afghanistan and Pakistan, had once been occupied by the Greeks. Therefore, the style of the early images of Buddha (fig. 16-4) resembled Greek or Roman styles. However, the sculptures express the Buddhist qualities of inward peace and release from desire. Buddha is shown quietly meditating. He is seated with legs crossed in the *yoga* position. The Gandhara sculptors

gave Buddha long ear lobes, a bulge on his head, and a dot between his eyes. These were all meant as signs of Buddha's superhuman perfection.

Later, in areas south of Gandhara, sculptors began to create statues of Buddha in a different style. The new style was more like that of the carvings on the gates of the Great Stupa. The Buddha from Sarnath (fig. 16-5) is wearing a thin gown. The body is curved and feminine. This style became typical of later statues of Buddha. In addition to the signs of perfection found in the Gandhara statue, this one shows Buddha with spoked wheels on the soles of his feet. Buddha is practicing stylized hand gestures called *mudras.*

Buddhism had started out as a reform of Hinduism. As time went on, Buddhism drifted farther away from the humble teachings of Buddha himself. At the same time, Hinduism was experiencing a revival. Buddhism was soon overtaken by its rival religion. Hinduism became stronger in India, although Buddhism was becoming stronger in the rest of Asia.

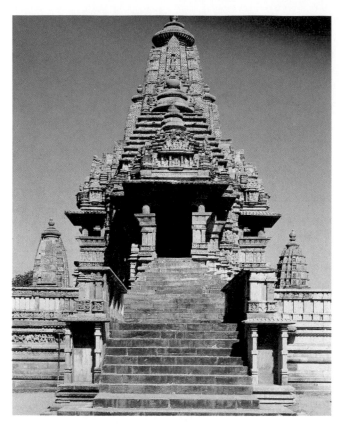

16–6 Temple of Laksmana, frontal view. Khajuraho, India, tenth–eleventh centuries. Scala/Art Resource, NY.

16–7 Post and lintel.

Perhaps as a tribute to Buddhism, Hinduism accepted Buddha as one of its gods. Hinduism's main gods were *Brahma* the creator, *Vishnu* the preserver, and *Siva* the destroyer. To this day, Hindus worship cows as representatives of the divine. They have a strict division of social classes, called a *caste* system. "Brahmans" are at the top and "untouchables" are at the bottom.

Buddhism and Hinduism existed together for many years. Therefore, they often shared the same styles of architecture. In Khajuraho, India, a sacred neighborhood of temples was built around the eleventh century. Some temples are Hindu and some are Buddhist. Yet all are similar. One of the most impressive temples is a Hindu temple dedicated to Siva as Mahadeva, Lord of Lords (fig. 16–6). Because of the cone-shaped domes, the Mahadeva shrine looks like a cluster of beehives. The surfaces are richly carved. Unlike the Great Stupa, this shrine is heavily decorated.

Also unlike the Great Stupa, the Mahadeva shrine is not solid. Inside, there are sanctuaries, aisles, and assembly halls surrounded by porches. But none of these is large. This temple, like most ancient temples, has a post-and-lintel construction. In a **post-and-lintel** building, the walls, posts, or columns support a masonry ceiling (fig. 16–7). Because a masonry ceiling is so heavy, the inside of any post-and-lintel building is very small compared to the mass of material used to build it.

Hindu gods tended to be exotic. Brahma had four faces. Siva had three eyes, and another god had one thousand. Almost all gods had four arms. These extraordinary features were signs of extraordinary knowledge, activity, or power.

The bronze sculpture of Siva (fig. 16–8) shows the god's extraordinary grace. Like Buddha, the god has a feminine body. However, unlike Buddha, the god is not sitting. Within a flaming arch, the god is performing a dance. He is balancing on one foot while performing delicate *mudras* (hand movements) with each of his four hands. This sculpture portrays Siva as Lord of the Dance, one of his many reincarnations. It was made to be placed in a shrine or carried in a procession.

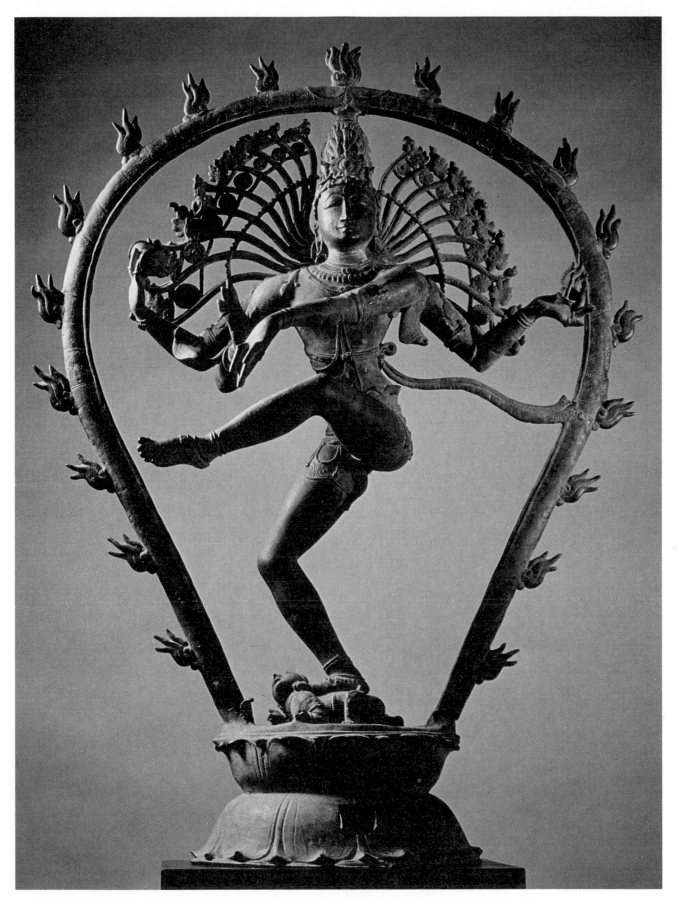

16–8 Tamilnadu, *Siva, King of the Dancers Performing the Nataraja*, Chola dynasty, India, tenth century, bronze, 30˝ x 22 ½˝ x 7˝ (76 x 57 x 18 cm). The Los Angeles County Museum of Art (Anonymous Gift).

Southeast Asia

Indian culture spread to Burma, Thailand, Kampuchea (Cambodia), Sumatra, and Java (fig. 16–9). Buddhism had spread to Tibet, Mongolia, China, and Japan. Buddhism also took root in Southeast Asia. Southeast Asian art has a rich complexity of styles and symbolism. This art reflects the influences of not only Buddhism, but also Hinduism.

Rising on a plain in Java is one of Buddhism's greatest monuments: the stupa at Borobudor (fig. 16–10). The shrine is actually a rounded hill that has been terraced with masonry. Therefore, it effectively embodies the Indian concept of the sky as a bowl covering the world mountain. It consists of ten levels. Of these, the base (which is mostly underground) and first five levels are rectangular. The next three are circular, and the top level consists of a single stupa.

On the base are relief sculptures that show people caught in the grip of desire. They are trapped in the endless hell of birth, death, and rebirth that Buddha warned about. The next five rectangular levels illustrate a variety of Buddha's teachings. The three circular levels contain seventy-two miniature bell-shaped stupas. Each stupa contains a seated Buddha.

Thus, the stages of enlightenment are unfolded as one progresses from the bottom level to the large stupa at the top, the climax of the shrine. The symbolism is Buddhist, but the tropical profusion of architecture and carving is more like Hindu art. Imagine the experience of intrepid pilgrims as they climb the stairs, walk through the corridors, and view this virtual encyclopedia of Buddhist culture.

16–9 Southeast Asia.

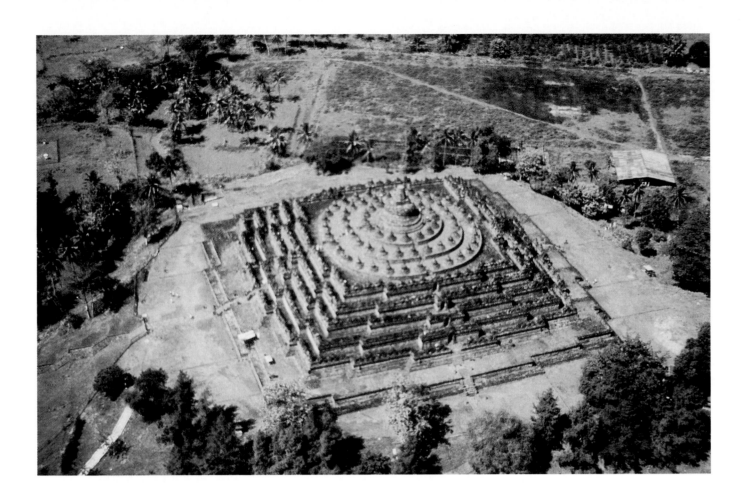

16-10 Stupa, Borobudor, Java, ca. 800 AD. Borromeo/Art Resource, NY.

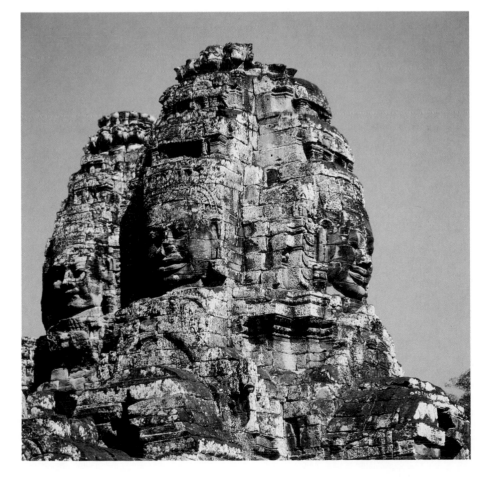

16-10A Rulers in ancient Cambodia were seen as gods. To make their divinity visible, they constructed huge temples influenced by the Hindu religion. This temple, Angkor Thom, shows the sculptured faces of Jayavarmin VII. It was built about 1190 AD. Giraudon/Art Resource, NY.

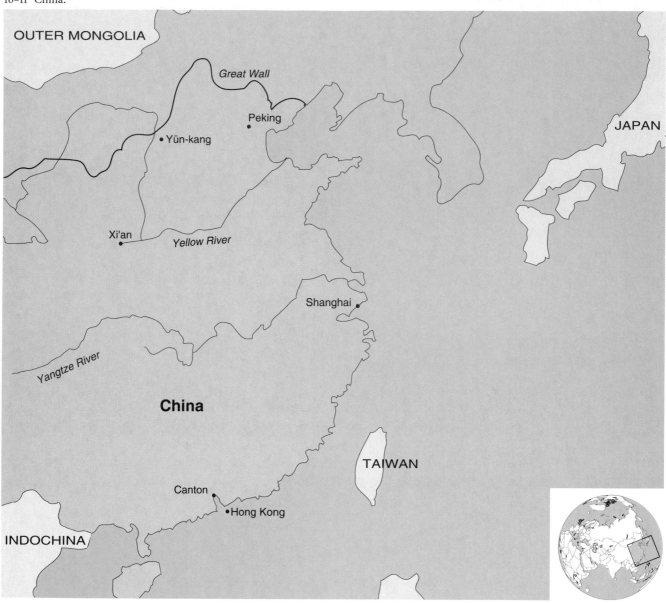

OUTER MONGOLIA

Great Wall

Peking

• Yün-kang

JAPAN

Xi'an

Yellow River

Shanghai

Yangtze River

China

TAIWAN

Canton

• Hong Kong

INDOCHINA

China

Modern China (fig. 16–11) is a country endowed with great rivers, fertile valleys, windswept plains, majestic mountains, and natural harbors. It is remarkably similar to the United States in size and geography, but its population is four times as large. In history, China is twenty times older.

Any country this large is bound to have regional diversity among its people. Nine-tenths of the population is crowded into the eastern sixth of the nation. The spoken language is so varied as to be unrecognizable in different areas. However, the Chinese have a common racial heritage and a culture as old as India's. The written language is understood by everyone. China is hemmed in by the Pacific Ocean on the east,

by high mountains in the south and southwest, and by desert in the west and north. It was splendidly isolated through much of its history. Thus it was able to develop its cultural traditions in relative security.

The earliest art of China that we know about is from the Shang dynasty. **Dynasty** refers to a succession of rulers who are members of the same family. The Shang dynasty thrived from the eighteenth to twelfth centuries BC in the northern part of the country. Remarkable bronze objects were discovered in graves in 1928. The objects were cast by means of piece molds rather than the lost-wax process (Chapter 13). Scholars were so impressed by their craftsmanship that they believed the Shang must have practiced this technique for centuries.

Most of the objects are ritual vessels for holding wine or food used in sacrificial rites (fig. 16–12). Their forms, unlike those of most vessels, tend to be rather angular. The low-relief decorations consist of animal symbols along with spirals, ovals, and zig-zags. These designs are compact and vigorous. In many ways these vessels resemble suits of armor. Perhaps they reflect a militaristic and barbaric society.

The Zhou dynasty saw the flowering of Chinese philosophy and writing. The sixth century BC, the century Buddha was born, was the golden age of Chinese philosophers. (Half a world away in Greece, another age of philosophy was dawning at about the same time.)

Lao-tzu, one of the sages, recommended withdrawal from the hurly-burly of society to become one with nature. A quiet person who distrusted intellectuals, Lao-tzu taught mostly by example. He followed a

16–13 Portrait of Confucius based on Ancient Traditions. Relief from the Stele in the Pei Lin of Sigan-Fou. The Bettmann Archive, New York.

philosophy called **Taoism.** According to Taoism, the secret of wisdom and lasting happiness was to follow a life of simplicity, modesty, patience, and obedience to the laws of nature. To this day, the principle of submitting to nature is deeply ingrained in the minds of the Chinese. By contrast, Westerners tend to believe that nature should submit to the will of people. (This attitude is fostered by the Old Testament teachings of Genesis 1:26 and Psalm 8:6.)

China's greatest thinker was Confucius (fig. 16–13). Like Lao-tzu, Confucius preached humility, patience, and respect for nature. But unlike Lao-tzu, he recommended taking an active role in society rather than withdrawing from it. He came up with the familiar maxim, "Do not do unto others as you would not wish done unto yourself," five hundred years before Christ. Like Christ, he taught by word of mouth rather than by writing. Fortunately his words were recorded by his disciples, and kept alive by scholars down through the

16–12 An example of a vessel used in sacrificial rites. Ceremonial vessel of the type Chia, twelfth century BC, Shang dynasty, China. Bronze, 21″ x 12″ (53 x 30.5 cm). Courtesy of the Freer Gallery of Art, Smithsonian Institution, Washington, DC.

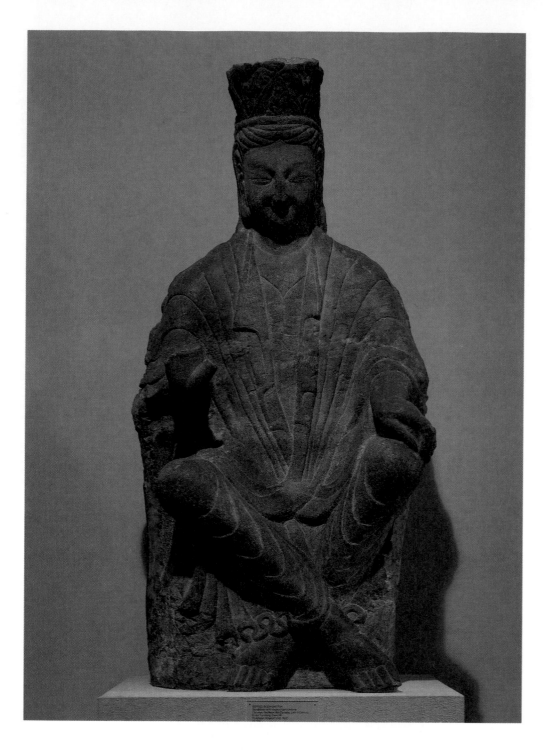

16–14 Bodhisattva from the Yun K'ang temple grotto. Northern Wei Period, late fifth century, Sandstone, 57 ½″ x 29″ (146 x 74 cm). The Metropolitan Museum of Art (Rogers Fund, 1922).

ages. His teachings and sayings, like the Gospels of the New Testament, influenced a whole culture. This culture spread to Korea, Japan, and parts of Southeast Asia.

The Han dynasty took control of China in 206 BC. The Roman Empire in the West existed at the same time. Just as Rome extended its boundaries all over Europe and northern Africa, China, under the Han emperors, extended its boundaries. China included Korea in the north, Vietnam in the south, and Afghanistan in the west. Silk production increased

dramatically, and trade routes penetrated as far as the eastern parts of the Roman Empire. Confucianism was the official policy of the state. Also like Rome, the Han empire experienced chaos and barbaric invasions during its final years. During this time Buddhism was introduced into China. The new religion seemed to answer the needs of the Chinese people during their times of trouble.

The new religion also provided some ready-made subject matter and styles for art. A fifth-century sculpture of a bodhisattva, a type of saint in Buddhism (fig. 16–14), reflects many of the qualities of the Indian statues of Buddha. Its gown is similar to the gown of the Gandhara Buddha (fig. 16–4). Its soft features and gentle mudras are similar to those of the Buddha from Sarnath (fig. 16–5). The bodhisattva's passive face and body capture the spirit of serenity preached by Buddha himself. And yet it was made during the period of unrest after the Han dynasty.

The T'ang dynasty (618–907 AD) ruled during one of China's greatest periods. An enlightened emperor named Tang Tai Zong brought order to the northern borders and led his armies to the ends of the deserts in the west. He reestablished old trade routes. He built libraries and universities, and encouraged the arts and the development of printing. Students from Tibet, central Asia, Korea, and Japan flocked to China's capital.

The non-Buddhist art made at this time, like the ceramic sculpture discussed in Chapter 15 (fig. 16–15), reflected the vigor of the T'ang dynasty. Mounted warriors were important for keeping order and protecting trade routes. The ceramic horse and rider are strong, taut and determined. You can easily imagine the two escorting a caravan of silk merchants across the Gobi desert, a place similar to Russell's desert in the American West (fig. 15–1).

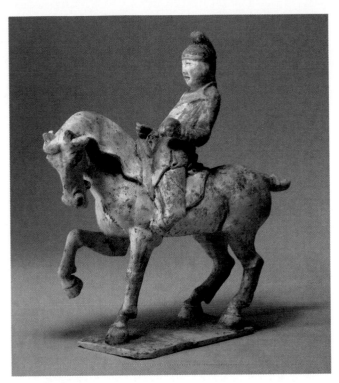

16–15 Terra cotta grave figure, T'ang dynasty. Museum of Far Eastern Antiquities, Stockholm.

The T'ang dynasty, after three centuries of successful rule, ended in a series of civil wars. During this troublesome period, the Chinese turned to a source of hope, just as their ancestors had turned to Buddhism at the end of the Han dynasty. Only this time, the source was nature. The image of this source was a landscape instead of a statue of Buddha or a bodhisattva.

Chinese artists may have painted landscapes even before the T'ang dynasty. However, the finest examples of this art were created during the Sung dynasty (960–1279 AD). Sung artists expressed all three elements of China's spiritual heritage: Taoism, Confucianism and Buddhism. They combined a reverence for nature, Confucian philosophy and the serenity of Buddha. Ma Yuan's *Bare Willows and Distant Mountains* (fig. 16–16) is a good example of this combination. The same work was discussed in Chapter 7 as an example of aerial perspective (fig. 7–26).

16–16 *Bare Willows and Distant Mountains,* attributed to Ma Yuan, Sung dynasty, twelfth–thirteenth century. Round album leaf, ink and colors on silk, 9″ x 8″ (24 x 21 cm). Chinese and Japanese Special Fund. Courtesy, Museum of Fine Arts, Boston.

16–17 Underglaze porcelain jar, Chiangning, Kiangsu.

Ma Yuan used the technique of ink wash on silk to create the effects of mist and endless space. This medium requires the respect of the artist, just as nature demands respect. A wash cannot be forced; the artist must literally "go with the flow" as the watery ink glides across the surface and sinks into the fabric. In addition to washes, Ma Yuan used darker lines for detail and to provide focus. A sense of mystical infinity is expressed in the airy landscape.

Western paintings were meant to be hung on walls. Chinese paintings, however, were often stored in scrolls. They were meant to be viewed in private—like reading a book of poems.

Sung landscape paintings expressed the deepest spiritual values of China. They are an excellent example of Chinese civilization. Fine landscapes, and nature studies, like the one shown in figure 4–12, continued to be produced during later dynasties.

But no review of Chinese art would be complete without discussing ceramic art. This art goes back to prehistoric China. Discoveries of excellent pottery at sites in Honan have been dated to 3000 BC or earlier. As we saw in Chapter 13, the Chinese of the Ch'in dynasty (just prior to the Han dynasty) made life-size ceramic sculptures using slab and coil methods (fig. 13–21). Under the T'ang emperors, the Chinese began to produce bowls, plates, jars, vases, bottles, flasks, and pitchers that were both functional and graceful.

Porcelain is a white ceramic that is hard, non-porous and translucent. It may have been invented during the T'ang dynasty. (To a Westerner, the test of porcelain was translucency; to the Chinese, it was the musical note a vessel made when struck.) At any rate, porcelain was produced in quantity by Sung potters. It was not until eight centuries later, in the eighteenth century, that Europeans learned to produce porcelain. Europeans made porcelain in such places as Meissen, Germany and Sèvres, France.

To the Chinese, Sung artisans produced the most "classical" examples of all ceramic wares. But to Westerners, Ming pottery (1358–1644), which tends to be more lavishly decorated, was the most popular. The stately porcelain jar in figure 16–17 is a good example. European potters tried to imitate Ming pottery—mostly without success—in the sixteenth and seventeenth centuries.

A Watercolor Wash Landscape

Create a mystical landscape with a Sung dynasty style. Use gradations of wash to show foreground, middle ground, and background with an aerial perspective effect.

16–18 Japan.

Japan

In many ways, Japanese art was influenced by Chinese art. Buddhism was introduced to Japan in the mid-sixth century; with it came aspects of Chinese culture. But Japan had its own culture even before Buddhism was introduced. Over the centuries, Japan (fig. 16–18) alternated between isolation and interchange with foreign governments. The Japanese had their own independent creativity and imitated the creativity of other cultures. Japan basically has two religions: *Shintoism,* the native religion, and Buddhism.

The facts of early Japanese history are clouded in myth. We do know that Japan was originally settled by a loose collection of tribes and clans. (A clan is a family that claims descent from a common ancestor.) Shintoism, the oldest and still largest religion of Japan, developed out of a form of ancestor worship. Shinto means "the way of the gods." This religion emphasizes reverence for family, race and, above all, the ruling family as a direct descendant of the gods.

Shintoism is also responsible for an early form of Japanese architecture: the Shinto shrine. The main building of the Ise Shrine (fig. 16–19) was originally constructed in the third century. It was, and continues to be, destroyed and rebuilt every twenty years. The structure we see today is a faithful copy of the methods and styles of third-century Japan. The construction is post and lintel. In this case, thick wooden columns (cut from the trunks of cypress trees) support a thatched

16–19 Shoden, main building of the Ise Shrine. Rebuilt in 1973, reproducing third century type. Art Resource, NY.

roof. Cylindrical weights run the length of the ridge-pole, the horizontal timber at the top of the roof. They provide a distinct rhythmical accent as well as help to stabilize the structure.

Sometime in the 500s, Buddhism was introduced to Japan by a Korean king. After some opposition, the new religion became firmly established. Chinese influence, mostly through Korea, rose dramatically. In 710 the Japanese established a capital at Nara for the imperial family. They began to model their political, economic, and social life on that of the T'ang dynasty in China. The extent of this influence can be seen in the Horyu-ji temple complex at Nara. Some of these temples are among the oldest in the world. They follow closely the temples built in China during the T'ang dynasty. Even fourteenth-century buildings, such as the Gold Pavilion in Kyoto (fig. 16–20), provide a glimpse of seventh-century Chinese architecture. Consisting of massive, slightly curved, tiled roofs supported by wooden columns, these structures are basically post and lintel. Yet their openness and complicated system of bracing foreshadow modern frame construction (Chapter 19).

In 784 the capital was moved to Heian (modern Kyoto). Japanese culture entered its golden age. The emperor became the leader in name only. The real power was held by certain clans. The Fujiwara family became the dominant clan. They surrounded themselves and the court with art. Their artists created their own styles of art that were different from the Chinese styles. They produced lacquered wooden carvings and painted scrolls of the finest quality. Scrolls of Buddhist subjects were richly colored and gilded.

Artists also produced inked scrolls that used humor. In one humorous scroll Buddha, in the form of a frog, is being honored by a whimsical collection of monkeys, a cat, a rabbit, and a fox (fig. 16–21). The Japanese used satire, animal caricature, and cartoon styles six centuries before the appearance of American comics. Note that the line of the frog's bench, the altar, and the scroll table go back in space but do not converge. This is sometimes referred to as "isometric perspective."

The leadership of the Fujiwaras was ended by a clique of warriors who created a *shogunate* (military dictatorship). They moved the center of power to the

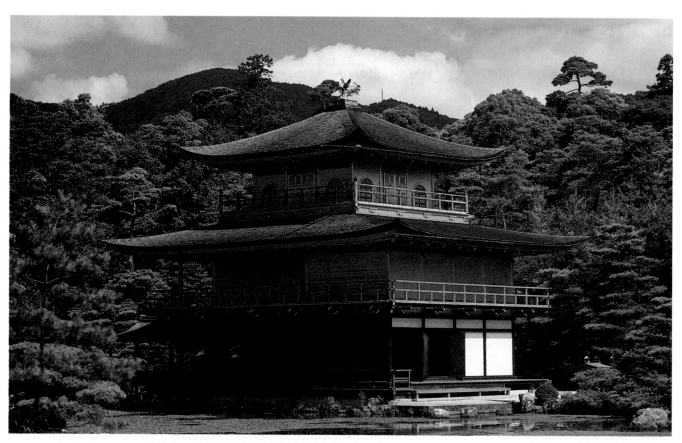

16–20 Japanese Gold Pavilion. Kyoto, Japan. Cooper/Art Resource, NY.

16-21 Animal caricatures, detail of a horizontal scroll attributed to Toba Sojo, later Heian period, ca. late twelfth century. Ink on paper, approx. 12″ (30. 5 cm) high. Kozan-ji.

16-22 Temple Guardian, Kamakura period, ca. 1300. Wood, fully painted. Toshogu Shrine, Kyoto.

city of Kamakura. Among other things, the new leaders smashed an invading armada mounted by Kublai Khan in 1274 and 1281.

As a reaction against the refined art of the Kyoto court, Kamakura art was more realistic. Sculpted figures were lifelike and colorful. Sculptors used glass to enliven the eyes. The temple guardian in figure 16–22 was made to ward off demons and evil spirits. With his vivid realism, he could frighten almost anyone—real or imagined.

The Ashikaga shoguns of Kyoto took control in 1392, but were unable to maintain a permanent peace. Therefore, their reign of nearly 200 years is referred to as a "dark age." But the arts thrived during this time. Once again, China was the source. Chan Buddhism, the sect that inspired Sung artists, was known as Zen Buddhism in Japan. Zen Buddhism became an important cultural force. The cult of Zen appealed especially to the aristocracy and a Japanese warrior class called *samurai*. Japanese painters imitated the landscapes of the Sung and Ming masters, but with a personal flourish.

Sesshu was the most celebrated of the Zen painters. He could capture the essence of a landscape (fig. 16–23) with just a few bold strokes. Sesshu applied his brush with the same finesse as a samurai might handle a sword. Do you recall the principle of closure

16–23 Sesshu, *Landscape*,
Ashikaga period, 1495.
Detail of a hanging scroll,
ink on paper. Tokyo
National Museum
(Photograph courtesy of
the International Society
for Educational
Information, Inc.).

(Chapter 4)? To fully see a Sesshu scene, the viewer must supply the details and contours.

The cult of Zen gave rise to the tea ceremony. The tea ceremony was a major social custom of the aristocracy. It featured many rules and was performed with calculated grace. Supplying tea ceremony needs dominated the art of potters. Their bowls, water jars, and tea-powder jars, like Sesshu's art, attempted to strike a delicate balance between refinement and informality.

Despite its sophisticated art, the Ashikaga shogunate was a political failure. The Tokugawa, an upstart family of shoguns, moved the seat of government to Edo (modern Tokyo) in 1617. To impose order, the new shogunate undertook drastic measures. Christianity, introduced by St. Francis Xavier in 1549, was banned, less for religious reasons than for political reasons. Tokugawa leaders sought to close Japan to all outside influence. Except for a handful of Chinese and Korean traders, no foreigners were allowed on Japanese soil.

The shogunate also tried to freeze Japanese society into separate classes. The samurai were the highest class, followed by farmers, artisans, and merchants. Employees were bound to their employers for life. Because the lines between the social classes could not be broken, each social class developed its own culture.

Zen landscapes, such as the one by Tohaku shown in figure 5–33, continued to be preferred by the aristocracy. But a new kind of picture, known as **ukiyo-e** ("the art of the floating world") became popular with the merchant class. Ukiyo-e art drew its subject matter from popular entertainment, popular fiction, and sight-seeing.

Because of its whimsy, some of ukiyo-e art can be compared to the humorous Heian scrolls (fig. 16–21). The favorite medium was the woodcut. The woodcut was invented by the Chinese during the T'ang dynasty and introduced to Japan during the eighth century. With this method, ukiyo-e artists could make dozens of inexpensive replications.

Scenes such as Hiroshige's *Ohashi, Sudden Shower at Atake* (fig. 16–24) provide vivid glimpses of Japanese life during the Ashikaga period. But they came to be valued in the West during the late 1800s for their aesthetic qualities. European artists of that era, as you will learn in Chapter 19, were influenced by the Japanese aptitude for flat pattern and bold composition.

Art History Experience 16.2

Report on a Non-Western Art Form

Prepare a report on one art form you feel most represents one of the non-Western cultures discussed in Chapter 16. The art form may be architecture, sculpture, metal work, ceramics, painting or printmaking. Ask your teacher for guidelines.

16–24 Ichiryusai Hiroshige, *Ohashi, Sudden Shower at Atake (Storm on the Great Bridge)*. Japanese, Tokugawa period, date of print: 1857. 13″ x 8 ¹¹⁄₁₆″ (33 x 22 cm) The Toledo Museum of Art, Toledo, Ohio (Carrie L. Brown Bequest Fund).

Chapter 17
Non-Western Art II

This second chapter on non-Western art looks at the art of Islam, tribal Africa, pre-Columbian America, and North America.

Islam

Islam is the religion of the Moslems. Islam also refers to the nations that practice the Islamic religion. Islam is one of the five major living religions. (The others are Hinduism, Buddhism, Judaism, and Christianity.) It is also the newest.

The Prophet Mohammed was born in Mecca (on the west coast of Arabia) 570 years after Christ, and over 1,100 years after Buddha. Like Buddha, Moham-

med had a vision. He was told by the angel Gabriel that he was the messenger of Allah (God). The people of Mecca did not believe him, and even threatened his life. In 622 he was forced to flee from Mecca to Medina.

Eight years later Mohammed returned to his hometown of Mecca in triumph, and most of Arabia was converted. Not long after his death, his followers converted the peoples of the Middle East, North Africa, and Spain in a lightning series of conquests (fig. 17–1).

The teachings of Mohammed were collected in the *Koran,* the Moslem's sacred book. The content of the Koran is closely related to the Christian Bible. It teaches **monotheism,** or the belief in one god. Stories about the Jewish prophets of the Old Testament are included in the Koran. Jesus, however, is identified as

17–1 Islam.

17–0 Artist Unknown, *Layla and Majnun at School*, sixteenth century, Safavid Period. Ink, colors, and gold on paper, 4 ¾″ x 7 ½″ (12 x 19 cm).
Khamseh (Quintet) of Nizami, style of Shaykh Kadeh. The Metropolitan Museum of Art, Gift of Alexander Smith Cochran, 1913.

17-2 Mosque of Mutawakkil (view from the north), 848–852 AD, Samarra, Iraq.

17-3 Interior of the Sanctuary (view from the east), Mosque, Cordova.

17-4 Arch.

one of the prophets rather than as the Son of God. Moslems believe that Mohammed is the last of the prophets. Moslems must pray in the direction of Mecca five times a day. There are no priests. The only public worship is Friday noon.

The Moslem place of worship is called a **mosque.** Early mosques were very simple. The one at Samarra, Iraq (fig. 17–2), was simply a walled rectangle. It covered ten acres and was large enough to contain all the worshippers of Samarra. It faces south, the direction of Mecca. The *qibla,* or wall on the Mecca side, has a small prayer niche called a *mihrab* in the center. Opposite the qibla is the **minaret,** or prayer tower. A *muezzin* (myoo EZ in), or crier, called the faithful to prayer from the minaret. Later minarets were slender and resembled a medium-range ballistic missile. Today, little is left of the mosque at Samarra. Nothing remains of the roof and the 464 pillars that supported it.

Fortunately, the mosque at Cordova, Spain, is still standing (fig. 17–3). Its interior, with its many arches and pillars, is very dramatic. The pillars are spaced to create multiple aisles. Notice how the pillars and arches draw the eye to the qibla wall.

Arches support the ceiling above the pillars. An arch (fig. 17–4) is a masonry curve made of stones or bricks. The wedge-shaped blocks press against one another instead of falling. The arches in the Cordova mosque are made with stones of contrasting colors.

Arches are placed one on top of the other. These double-tiered arches add complexity and drama.

Like the mosque at Cordova, the Court of Lions of the Alhambra, a palace in Granada, Spain (fig. 17–5), is an outstanding example of Islamic arch construction. An Alhambra arch is richly decorated with stucco and tile reliefs. These reliefs are delicate and create an airy effect. The arches themselves seem almost to hang from, rather than support, the ceiling.

Granada was the last Islamic city on the European continent to fall to the Christians. In 1492 it surrendered to the armies of Spain's Ferdinand and Isabella.

But the splendor of its Islamic heritage, especially its architecture, left a lasting impression on the European imagination.

Mohammed was very opposed to *idolatry*, the worship of idols. He smashed all of Mecca's sculptures of gods and goddesses. Indeed, he did not allow the use of religious images of any kind. To this day, the walls of mosques, unlike those of Buddhist temples or Christian cathedrals, have no statues or pictures of human or animal figures.

17–5 Court of Lions, The Alhambra, 1354–1391, Granada.
© Joe Viesti/Viesti Associates, Inc.

17–7 *Two Warriors Fighting in a Landscape,* from a Persian manuscript, 1396. Reproduced by Courtesy of the Trustees of the British Museum.

intricate design must have been a moving experience.

The absence of human or animal figures in the carpet is due in part to the Islamic aversion to idolatry, mentioned earlier. Another reason is that Arabian culture tended to specialize in craft objects instead of sculptures and painting. Islamic artists did not specialize in pictorial art. Even in Islamic provinces that were not Arab, pictorial skills were never developed.

Book illustration was an exception, however. Islamic artists, especially in Persia, illustrated poems and books with miniature paintings. Persia, which is now Iran, had a highly developed culture. It was also a crossroads for traders and invaders from east and west. In the 1200s Persia was invaded by the Mongols under the notorious Genghis Khan (the grandfather of Kublai Khan). The Persian illustration *Two Warriors Fighting in a Landscape* (fig. 17–7) shows how Persian painting was influenced by the Mongols. Like Sung painters, the artist chose a landscape setting. The rocks and mountains are somewhat Chinese in style. But the delicate details and two-dimensional design are definitely Islamic.

For centuries Islam led Christian Europe in government, philosophy, literature, science, mathematics, and medicine, in addition to architecture and crafts. Many Islamic contributions entered European culture during the Crusades (Chapter 18). The extent of the Islamic legacy is reflected in our language. Many Arabic words have entered our vocabulary: alcohol, bazaar, caravan, check, chemistry, nadir, satin, tariff, and zenith, among others. Arabic numerals (1, 2, 3, 4, etc.), together with the concept of zero and algebra, replaced Roman numerals. (Imagine trying to divide XLV by IX!)

European builders enriched their cathedrals by borrowing the pointed arch, stained glass, and arabesque designs from the Moslems. And European craftspersons learned the secrets of porcelain and silk—which came from China through the Moslems.

However, abstract decorations were allowed. Moslem artists covered the insides of Islamic buildings with inventive designs. The term **arabesque,** meaning "in the Arab style," was coined to describe the complex designs. The designs featured patterns of intertwined lines and shapes.

The kind of lacework arabesques seen in the Alhambra are also found in Islamic crafts. Objects of ceramic, bronze, silver, and glass were all richly covered with arabesque decoration. These objects were used to furnish mosques and palaces.

But the most highly valued Islamic craft was textiles, especially the weaving of carpets. The Ardabil Carpet (fig. 17–6) may have as many as three hundred knots to the square inch. The carpet was probably made by a group of weavers and intended to cover a floor or hang on a wall of a mosque. The medallion design in the center is surrounded by stylized and interlaced leaves and flowers. Even to study such an

Art History Experience 17.1

Connecting Art and Culture

Prepare a report on the meanings, functions, social and religious values of art in one of the non-Western cultures discussed in this chapter.

17–6 Maqsud of Kashan, *The Ardabil Carpet*, 1540, Safavid dynasty, Persia, Tabriz. Silk and wool, 23′ 11″ x 13′ 5″ (729 x 409 cm). The Los Angeles County Museum of Art, Gift of J. Paul Getty.

Africa

Africa is a checkerboard of religions and belief systems. The African continent has deserts, highlands, grassy savannas, and river forests. The African population is divided among nomadic tribes, farming villages, and great kingdoms—each with its own language.

There is no such thing as a single style of African art. The style of an object depends on the culture, its purpose, or sometimes the individual artist. African art can be realistic or abstract. It can be highly structured or relatively formless. African art does not always fall into the typical categories of sculpture or craft. For example, a footstool can look like a human figure. A jar handle can be shaped like a crocodile, and a hat can look like a pair of antlers.

Africans did not (and still do not) make sharp distinctions between art and life, as Westerners do. Some of their art, like Western art, was intended to be permanent. But much of it was made to be used for a special occasion and then thrown away. Its functions are as varied as Africa's different beliefs. The art may be intended to appease spirits, to honor ancestors, to ensure fertility, to symbolize authority, to frighten enemies, or simply to celebrate. (Recall the memorial sculpture of Sokari Douglas Camp in Chapter 15.) For these reasons, African art is difficult to analyze. Yet this art, as a class of objects, has captured the imagination of modern artists and collectors. With this in mind, we

will look at a sampling from those regions of Africa (fig. 17–8) that are especially noted for their art.

The Dogon are a peasant-village people in Mali. They are well known for their imaginative wood sculptures. Dogon carvers whittled bowls, jars, stools, masks, granary doors, and figurines in human and animal form. They sometimes even combined both forms.

Although Dogon styles vary, their human figures exhibit a sensitive blend of organic and geometric forms. The ancestral couple in figure 17-9 have long bodies and egg-shaped heads. Their surfaces are engraved with complex geometrical designs. This sculpture expresses a tender, almost wistful, relationship between a man and woman. The abstractness of its style appealed to early twentieth-century artists and collectors. We must remember, however, that Dogon images were made for ritual purposes and not to be admired as art objects.

The Dogon are also known for their architecture. The houses and granaries of the Dogon village in figure 17–10 are organically related to the natural contours of the hillside. They provide an interesting variety of levels and spaces. The buildings themselves, which were built by hand, have the qualities of sculptures.

However, it is the plan of the houses and layout of the village that interests twentieth-century sociologists and city planners. Each house is intended to symbolize a human body. The kitchen area is the head. On a larger scale, the arrangement of houses and granaries in a village is also intended to represent a human body. The symbolic connection between the houses and the village reflects a sense of community that is a part of the Dogon culture. In the Dogon society, families are linked both by marriage and by collective ownership. Each Dogon citizen is connected socially and symbolically to the village.

Unlike the village culture of the Dogon, the Ife society in Nigeria was aristocratic. This society flourished between the 1100s and the 1300s. Its art is lifelike, not abstract, as shown by the bronze head of a king in figure 17–11. The facial features are correct and realistic. The details of his royal headgear are faithfully drawn. Even the tattoos, which follow the contours of his face, seem accurate.

Ife bronzes were made by the lost-wax method of casting (Chapter 13). Some experts have speculated that Ife artists learned this technique from Egyptian

17–8 Africa.

17–10 Dogon village, Mali, West Africa. Courtesy Woodfin Camp
& Associates, Inc. New York.

17–9 *Seated Man and Woman,*
Dogon origin, Mali. Wood,
30″ (76 cm) high. Photograph
©1989 by The Barnes
Foundation.

Studio Experience 17.2

A Role Mask

Create a mask with features in relief. Produce
relief effects by shaping plaster gauze over a
balloon or large plastic jug. The role you create
for the mask may come from your own time
and experience, or from a play, movie, story
or legend.

sculptures. Because the bronze portrait of the king has a classical air, others have speculated that the Greeks may have influenced the Ife artists. Today, however, most experts agree that Ife art was not influenced by other cultures. Still, the superb craftsmanship and aesthetic qualities of Ife art call to mind the art of ancient Egypt, classical Greece, and Renaissance Italy (Chapter 18).

A little to the south of Ife was the Benin kingdom, which flourished between the 1400s and 1700s. Possibly, the Ife and Benin kingdoms had historical ties. At any rate, Benin sculptors shared with their Ife neighbors the method of lost-wax. They created bronze castings of a high technical level.

The body of the little flute player in figure 17–12 neatly combines realism with caricature. His propor-

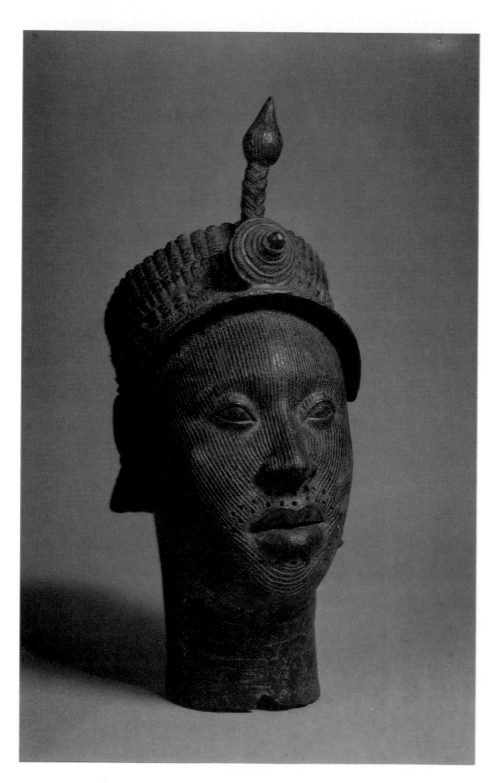

17–11 Oni (King) of Ife, twelfth–fourteenth centuries. Bronze, 14 ½″ (37 cm) high (life-size). Reproduced by Courtesy of the Trustees of the British Museum.

real judge who could try and convict people. (Imagine, for example, being issued a parking ticket by a person wearing the mask of a meter maid.) Each Dan mask expressed the personality of a particular role. Roles could vary from teachers to executioners. Thus, mask carvers were challenged to come up with a range of forms and styles. Some masks were smooth, highly polished, and with delicate features. Perhaps these were intended to express pleasant roles. Some, like the one in figure 17–13, were coarse with enlarged features. With its large nose, staring eyes, gaping mouth, and fur, the mask is very striking. Was it intended to represent a shaman, a witch doctor, a philosopher, a hermit, a cranky old man, or all of the above?

In Africa, art is not separated from life, as it often is in the West. It is an essential part of the way of life of a tribe. It expresses the social and spiritual values of each culture. Daily living, the natural, and the supernatural are all mingled in African art.

17–12 Flute player, fifteenth–sixteenth centuries. Benin culture, Nigeria. Engraved bronze, 24 ½″ (62 cm) high. Reproduced by Courtesy of the Trustees of the British Museum.

tions (the relationship of a part to a whole) are obviously exaggerated. His overall height is about three times the height of his head. An average man's height is about seven times. The proportions in his face, compared to those in the Ife bronze, are also exaggerated. Nevertheless, there is something very lifelike about him. Look at his large almond-shaped eyes, the folds of his kilt, his stubby legs, and, especially, the way his little arms support the flute. His body and clothes, like the Ife king's, are heavily decorated with engraved designs.

Masks are found in tribal societies all over the world. Perhaps wearing a mask satisfies a universal urge to change identity, be anonymous, or assume the power of another person or animal. This may explain the thrill of wearing masks on Halloween. In tribal societies, masks were usually used in dances and rituals. The purpose of a ritual could vary from a sacrificial offering to entertainment.

Masks were used differently among the Dan-Ngere people of the Ivory Coast. Masks were emblems of authority, much like a police uniform. A person wearing the mask of a judge was not pretending, but being a

17–13 Mask, Dan-Ngere people, Ivory Coast. Wood, animal hair, copper and pigment, 11″ x 6 ½″ x 8″ (28 x 16.5 x 20 cm). Collection, The University Museum, Illinois State University, Normal, Illinois.

17–14 Meso-America and South America.

17–15 Portrait jar, Moche, Peru, fifth–sixth centuries. Ceramic, 11 ½″ (29 cm) high. Neg./Trans. No. 121197. Photo by T. L. Bierwerx. Courtesy Department Library Services. American Museum of Natural History.

Pre-Columbian

Around 4000 BC, people of Asian stock began migrating to the New World. They came from Asia to Alaska by crossing the Aleutian Islands. They began to settle in both North and South America. **Pre-Columbian,** as the name implies, refers to the history of those people up to the time of Columbus. However, the term is most often used to mean the Indian civilizations that flourished in Mexico, Central America, and South America (fig. 17–14) before the arrival of the Spanish conquistadors in the 1500s.

South America

The civilizations of South America developed mostly in the central Andes Mountains. The earliest civilization was fully developed by 700 BC (around the time of China's Chou dynasty). This civilization was known for its irrigation canals. The Moche culture arrived on the scene somewhat later. Thriving from AD 1 to 800, the Moche people were known for their metallurgy and sun-dried brick pyramids. They were also known for their remarkable ceramics.

No pre-Columbian culture used a potter's wheel, so all pottery was hand-built or cast from molds (Chapter 13). Glaze also was unknown, so their pots were decorated only with slip (Chapter 13). However, Moche potters were so skilled that their round vessels appear wheel-thrown. The surfaces of their pots resemble those of glazed ware. The portrait jar in figure 17–15 is obviously not wheel-thrown. However, it is an example of their superb craftsmanship. The dual function of portrait and storage vessel is in itself a skillful achievement. As a portrait, it is as solemn and dignified as the Ife bronze. As a vessel, it is both functional and lightweight. Note especially the slenderness of the stirrup spout, one of the unique features of Moche pottery.

Around 800, the Moche kingdom, along with other groups in the highlands and along the coast of modern Peru and Bolivia, came to an end. They may have been conquered by a people known as the Tiahuanacons, but this is not certain. It is certain, however, that around 1400, another ambitious group started from Cuzco (Peru), and rapidly overran all the Peruvian kingdoms. Named for the title of their leader, Inca, these people proceeded to establish an empire that stretched over 2,000 miles from northern Ecuador to Chile.

The main regions of their empire were scattered along the most rugged mountains of the world. To connect Cuzco to these regions, the Incas strung hanging bridges across rivers, and built solid roads. To grow crops, they learned to terrace and irrigate. They also domesticated the llama and the alpaca. To record their business transactions, they used a unique system of knotted cords for numerals. They worshiped gods of thunder, earth, sea, mountains, and rivers. Of these, the most important was the sun god, who they believed was their ancestor. Sun temples were built all over the empire, including one at Machu Picchu (fig. 17–16).

Located on top of a high mountain, Machu Picchu is an extraordinary place to locate a temple, let alone a whole settlement. Its construction must have been a severe challenge to Inca builders. The site has some two hundred buildings. Incan masonry is remarkable. Stones are fitted so closely that a knife blade cannot be run between them. This is even more remarkable because the stones were not cut to uniform sizes.

Today Machu Picchu is sometimes called the City in the Sky or the Lost City. Since it was rediscovered in 1911, it has raised more questions than answers. Was it primarily a religious sanctuary? Was it also a fortress? Why was it built there? And why was it suddenly abandoned? The answers died with the Inca civilization itself when Atahalpa, the last great Inca ruler, was executed by conquistador Pizarro.

Meso-America

Meso-America refers to the area of modern Mexico and the northern countries of Central America. The pre-Columbian civilizations that arose there differed from the Incas and the others of South America. They developed mainly in the central highlands of Mexico, the lowlands along the Gulf of Mexico, and the lowlands of the Yucatán Peninsula.

The oldest civilization was centered at Olmec around 600 BC. The culture of Olmec influenced later civilizations in Meso-America. The Olmecs settled in the swampy lowlands along the coast (in the Mexican states of Tabasco and Vera Cruz).

17–16 Machu Picchu, Peru. Art Resource, NY.

17–17 The Pyramid of the Sun, Teotihuacán, Mexico. Werner Forman/Art Resource, NY.

Another group, called the Teotihuacán, was just beginning to get organized in the central highlands north of modern Mexico City. They dominated the region from 300 BC to 800 AD. (This was roughly the same time as the Han and T'ang dynasties combined.) Like the Incas, they worshiped nature. Their worship centered around *Tlaloc*, god of rain, and *Quetzalcoatl*, a culture hero who was later deified as a feathered serpent. To feed their gods and produce unity between the gods and the people, the Teotihuacán practiced human sacrifice. These rituals occurred frequently at their capital, Teotihuacán, which meant "place of gods." It was perhaps the largest city in pre-Columbian America. Estimates of its peak population range from one hundred thousand to almost one million.

The ritual center of the city had many temples and palaces, and was planned around a broad avenue (fig. 17–17). The largest temple, dedicated to the sun, was a five-tiered pyramid with a broad stairway. A smaller temple was decorated with sculptures of the heads of Quetzalcoatl and Tlaloc. The name Quetzalcoatl comes from the word *quetzal*, meaning "a brilliantly plumed bird" and *coatl*, meaning "snake." Judging by the fierceness of his image (fig. 17–18), Quetzalcoatl clearly commanded respect.

17–18 Feathered Serpent on the Pyramid of Quetzalcoatl, ca. 500 AD. Art Resource, NY.

The downfall of the Teotihuacáns, around 800, coincided with the rise of the Toltecs. The Toltecs took over many aspects of Teotihuacán culture, though their language (Nahuatl) may have been different.

Around 1300, the Aztecs, another Nahuatl-speaking group, came to power. The Aztecs established Tenochtitlán (modern Mexico City) as their capital. A very warlike people, the Aztecs expanded their empire to include all of Mexico. However, despite their skills as warriors and empire builders, they fell to the Spaniards in 1520 when Cortez conquered Tenochtitlán.

While the Teotihuacáns were building their civilization in the highlands, the Mayas were building theirs in the lowlands of Guatemala and Honduras. Of all the pre-Columbian cultures, the Mayan culture was perhaps the finest. Between AD 300 and 900, they developed writing, a form of arithmetic, a calendar, and the corbeled arch. Mayan numerals—a dot (equal to the number 1), a bar (equal to five dots), and a crescent (equal to four bars)—have been compared to Arabic numerals for simplicity and effectiveness.

The Mayan year was divided into eighteen twenty-day months, with five extra days for special religious observations. This resembles a modern calendar in principle. The relief carving in figure 17–19 illustrates not only the Aztec version of the Mayan calendar, but also an example of Aztec carving. To the Mayas, the calendar and the related science of astronomy were so important that many of their priests were astronomers.

The **corbeled arch** allowed Mayan builders to make rooms and hallways within their stone buildings. Like a round arch, a corbeled arch uses short stones. However, the arch is created by projecting succeeding rows of stones inward until they reach the top. This kind of arch cannot span a wide area, and it requires a lot of masonry material for support. Therefore, the rooms in a Mayan temple were narrow (no more than fifteen feet wide) and dark.

Around 900, the Mayas abandoned their sites in Guatamala and Honduras and moved to the Yucatán Peninsula. We still do not know why. Was it due to drought, crop failure, foreign intervention, or perhaps a combination of these? While in Yucatán, the Mayas were invaded by peoples of Toltec affiliation. But this did not prevent them from building some of the finest architecture in pre-Columbian Mexico. Mayan temples were usually built on tiered pyramids, similar to those at Teotihuacán. They were richly decorated with relief carvings and covered with stucco. The major temple at Chichén Itzá (fig. 17–21), rises grandly from the Yucatán plain. It stands not only as an example of handsome Mayan architecture, but also as a reminder of a once-proud culture.

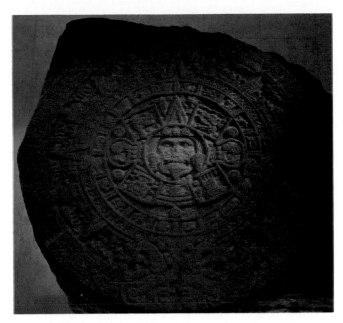

17–19 The Aztec Calendar Stone: Mask of Tonatiuh at Center. National Museum Anthropology. Werner Forman/Art Resource, NY.

17–20 Corbeled arch.

17–21 El Castillo, Mayan pyramid temple of the Toltec period, at Chichén Itzá, Yucatán, dedicated to the Feathered Serpent, patron deity of Chichén Itzá.

North America

The previous review of South American and Meso-American cultures looked at their history before Europeans came. The review of North American Indians in this section looks at their development after Europeans came. Little is known about the histories of North American Indians prior to the 1500s. Unlike the Mayas, they left behind no writing, and few monuments of architecture and sculpture. What we do know of their precontact days comes mostly from graves and burial mounds.

We do know a great deal about their histories since the 1500s, however. Unlike the Incas, Toltecs, Aztecs, and Mayas, their cultures were not immediately destroyed or absorbed by conquerors. Despite displacement and massacres by the white settlers, most of them managed to maintain their cultural identities through the 1800s. (Some held on to their culture through the 1900s.) Since the late 1800s, native North Americans have been the object of intense study by historians and anthropologists.

North American tribal groups (fig. 17–22) had very different customs and beliefs. One expert counted fifty-six different languages. But all groups, except perhaps the Plains Indians, lived near rivers and lakes. They raised corn (maize), beans, and squash. Although they had different religions, all practiced a form of nature worship. They honored such gods as the sun, morning star, south wind, water spirit, and rabbit.

Southwest

One early culture, the Anasazi, did leave a substantial record of their existence. Located in the plateau country of what is now New Mexico, northern Arizona, and southwestern Colorado, the Anasazi made pottery and weavings. They built masonry-walled structures as

17–22 North America.

17-23 Cliff Palace, Mesa Verde National Park, Colorado, ca. 1100 AD. Photograph courtesy Department of Interior, Bureau of Reclamation.

early as the first century AD. Chapels, called *kivas*, were built partially underground.

The Anasazi also built cliff dwellings at Mesa Verde (fig. 17–23). The Mesa Verde dwellings are similar to the Dogon village. They are multileveled and interconnected. The cliff dwellings are made of stone, timber, and some *adobe* (sun-dried bricks). The settlement at Mesa Verde has over two hundred rooms and twenty-three sacred kivas. At one time, at least twenty-three clans lived here. The cliff dwelling was like a modern condominium, with an excellent view of Mesa Verde National Park.

The Pueblo Indians were a farming culture made up of the Zuni and Hopi tribes. They came after the Anasazi people. The Pueblo lived in traditional adobe dwellings. Although the Pueblo still live in New Mexico and Arizona, they have lost many of their traditional skills. Some Native American artisans, however, are reviving some of the skills. They are using traditional skills to make pottery like the handmade Acoma vase in figure 17–24. The vase is symmetrical, smooth, and thin-walled. It is ornamented with stylized parrots enclosed by leaves, arches, and geometric

designs. The Pueblo used abstract designs and repetition in their decoration. This preference is typical of nearly all tribal cultures.

17-24 Acoma Pueblo Water Jar, ca. 1900, 13 ¾″ (35 cm) diameter. Each Pueblo potter develops characteristic shapes and designs. Courtesy of Sotheby´s, Inc.

Maria Martinez

ca.1900–1980

Some of the most refined pottery ever produced in the United States has been made without the use of high technology, machinery, or even the potter's wheel. A unique technique for creating "black-on-black" pottery was developed by Maria Montoya Martinez, a Native American artist.

This remarkable pottery is made by hand-pinching thick coils of clay together to create delicate forms. Simple tools made from vegetable gourds are used to smooth and shape the wet clay before the pots are placed in the sun to dry. The dried pots are then covered with a thin layer of liquified clay called "slip." Special river-smoothed stones are used to polish or "burnish" the surface to create a glossy shine. Good polishing stones are highly valued and are often passed on from one generation of potters to another. In the final step, the pots are fired in a fire fueled by wood and manure. To achieve their characteristic rich black coloring, the fire is smothered with manure and covered with wood ashes to prevent air from escaping. The smoke which is produced carbonizes the clay pots, darkening the vessels and leaving a silvery-black sheen.

Maria Martinez was born at San Ildefonso Pueblo in New Mexico. She lived and worked in this small Native American community for over eighty years. There, Maria ritually collected sacred

Maria and Julian Martinez, ca. 1920. Photograph: Pedro de Lemos.

clay from special sources in the surrounding mountains. Mixing these clays with proportions of water and volcanic ash, she produced a workable material appropriate for potting.

During her lifetime, Maria worked very closely with her husband, Julian, and her son, Popovi Da, to create these unique vessels. Both were responsible for decorating Maria's pots with carefully painted designs of a matte or dull finish, created before the pot was smoke-fired. Brushes made from pieces of yucca plant are dipped in the slip and used to paint this type of unique pattern on the polished surface of the pot. Once the vessel is heated and the smoke-firing process complete, the polished surface shines, while the painted surface remains matte.

Today, Maria is known worldwide for the highly skilled method of pottery production which established San Ildefonso as a leading pottery producing community. By developing a method for creating black-on-black pots, Maria Martinez was able to revive the art of pottery making in the Pueblo community of the Southwest. Her knowledge and expertise has been passed on to other generations of potters in her community, enlivening the economy and culture of the Pueblo people.

Maria bowl. Collection of Gilbert and Jean Davis.

17-25　Navajo rug, 1850–1880. Wool. The Indian Art Center of California, Studio City.

17-26　Haida totem pole. Tlingit Indians of Southeast Alaska.

Although the Navajo were originally a hunting tribe from a different language group, they became associated with the Pueblo in the 1600s. They learned many of their customs from the Pueblo, including the art of weaving. Navajo blankets and rugs are among the finest in the world. Compare the design of the Navajo rug in figure 17–25 with that of the Persian rug (fig. 17–6). The Persian design contains stylized leaves, flowers, and geometric shapes. And, because of its arabesque interlacing of figures, shapes, and lines, it is much more complicated than the Navajo example. On the other hand, the Navajo design is starkly abstract. It contains precisely outlined, flat shapes. The colors of the shapes are subtly related and keenly balanced between positive and negative.

Northwest Coast

The Northwest Coast is made up of the Indian tribes of the Tlingit, Haida, and Kwakiutl. These tribes lived along the Pacific coast from Alaska to California. They depended mainly on food from the ocean, but they also farmed and hunted. Unlike the Pueblo, who built boxy houses of adobe brick, the Northwest Indians built gable-roofed houses of cedar planks. Wood was their most important raw material. In addition to houses, wood was used to make canoes, totem poles, and boxes—all without the help of metal tools.

A *totem* is an animal believed to be related by blood to a family or clan. A totem animal also symbolizes a family or clan. A totem pole (fig. 17–26) is simply a tall post carved with the clan's symbols. Totem poles stood in front of houses as signs of prestige and to showcase the family's totems.

Other objects were often decorated with totems. Haida artists, for example, carved reliefs of clan symbols on the outside of the wooden chest in figure 17–27. There are two central figures, shown facing forward. The largest may be a bear, and the smaller seems to be a human. Beside them are profiles of the heads of other animals—perhaps birds or fish. Although their heads are in profile, their eyes are facing front. The design is perfectly symmetrical. One side is a mirror image of the other.

17-27 Haida Art, Chest for clothes and jewelry, nineteenth century. Wood inlaid with shells and animal rusks. Reproduced by Courtesy of the Trustees of the British Museum.

Studio Experience 17.3

A Personal Totem

Invent your own totem. Form clay around a newspaper-wrapped cardboard tube or milk carton. Symbolize your hobbies, interests and achievements, or those of your family.

In addition to totem poles and chests, Northwest carvers decorated their canoes and houses, and made masks, rattles, charms, and wooden dishes. Like the chest and the totem pole, all of these have exuberant designs of stylized animals and humans.

Plains

Such tribes as the Crow, Sioux, Comanche, Cheyenne, and Arapahoe roamed the great plains, which stretch from the Mississippi to the Rockies. Of all the North American peoples, the Plains Indians are the most legendary. It was they who hunted buffalo, fought the white man, and defeated General Custer. Paradoxically, there was no Plains culture before the arrival of the Europeans, who brought with them the horse and rifle. Without these, American Indians were unable to hunt buffalo efficiently. Once horses and rifles became available, the buffalo became their source of food, clothing, and shelter. They ate its flesh, and they fashioned shirts, leggings, robes, shields, thongs, and cone-shaped tents called tepees from its hide.

Buffalo hides were even the source of Plains art. Buffalo-skin robes, tepees, and tepee linings were painted with geometric designs. Leather shirts were decorated with feathers, beads, thongs, and hair. The shirt worn by a Plains Indian chief discussed in Chapter 1 (fig. 1–3) is an example. (However, that shirt was made from deer hide rather than buffalo hide.) Plains Indians assembled headgear out of pelts and feathers. They made necklaces out of beads, bones, claws, or horns, and vests out of fur and leather thongs. Add face painting to all of this, and the resulting costume is truly a mixed media work of art. The artist George Catlin visited some forty-eight tribes and persuaded warriors and chiefs to sit for portraits (fig. 17–28). His pictures provide us with a priceless record of this now-extinct Plains art.

Conclusion

As you have seen, non-Western cultures represent an incredible variety of geography, peoples, history, beliefs, and art. Why is it important to study non-Western art?

One reason is that it has influenced our own art and daily life. Chinese porcelain, Japanese woodcuts, Islamic arabesques, and African sculpture have enriched our lives as well as theirs. Non-Western art can continue to be a source of inspiration. Studying the works of others helps us to see our own culture from a different perspective. Finally, and perhaps most importantly, understanding the cultural products of other people helps us to understand the people themselves. By seeing the world through their eyes, we learn to accept other people and other points of view. All of which emphasizes that we belong to one race—the human race—riding through time on a single spaceship called Earth.

17–28 Although George Catlin, who painted this portrait, was not himself a Native American, his painting allows us to see for ourselves the decorated clothing and striking face paint of the Plains Indians. George Catlin, *The White Cloud, Head Chief of the Iowas,* 1844–45. Canvas, 28″ x 22 ⅞″ (71 x 58 cm). ©National Gallery of Art, Washington, Paul Mellon Collection.

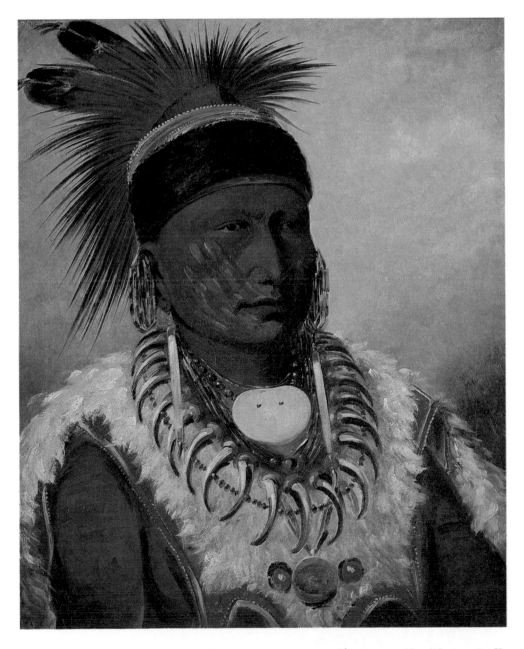

Chapter 18
Islands of Time I

The history of Western art begins with the earliest of cultures and ends with the present. This is such a big subject that only a few periods, or *islands of time,* will be reviewed. This chapter will review islands of time from the prehistoric era (12,000 BC) to the High Renaissance (1500s AD). Chapter 19 will survey the history of art from the 1600s to the present.

The discovery of the world's oldest painting marks our first island in time. In 1897 in northern Spain, Marcelino de Sautuola, an amateur archeologist, took his five-year-old daughter with him to explore a cave near their home. Because the cave was so full of rubbish accumulated over thousands of years, the ceiling was low, and the father had to stoop. His daughter, who did not have to stoop, was delightfully surprised to see pictures of animals on the ceiling. Sautuola was also surprised, for he believed they were, in fact, a very ancient art. But when he announced this amazing find to scientists, he was met with disbelief.

Later, other cave paintings were discovered in northern Spain and southern France. Some were partially covered by calcium deposits that scientists knew were thousands of years old. Eventually everyone realized that these paintings were the world's oldest known art. They probably had been made by people who lived at the end of the last glacial age.

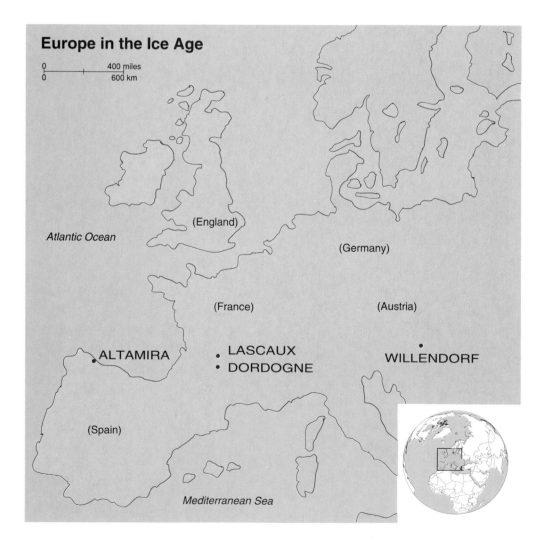

18–2 Europe during the Ice Age.

18–1 *Hall of Bulls*, left wall, Lascaux, ca. 15,000–13,000 BC. Dordogne, France. Courtesy of Scala/Art Resource, NY.

The Ice Age

What kind of place was Europe during the Ice Age (fig. 18–2)? England was still covered with ice. The rest of the continent was as cold as Siberia and forest-covered. Bison, wild horses, reindeer, elk, and wild goats, in addition to now-extinct beasts like woolly rhinos and woolly elephants, roamed the land. Europe was also populated with a race of people. These people hunted the animals, using spears made of shafts of wood tipped with animal bone, and knives made of chips of flint. Animals were a source not only of meat, but of hides for clothes and shelter, of bones, horns, and tusks for tools, and perhaps even of tails for paintbrushes.

These Ice Age people sculpted in clay, wood, bone, ivory, and stone. (Recall the little stone Venus of Willendorf, fig. 13–5.) However, they are best known for their animal paintings on the walls of limestone caves (fig. 18–1). They probably obtained pigments, such as gypsum (white) and iron oxide (brownish reds and yellows), from the ground and charcoal (black) from campsites. Then they mixed the pigments with animal fat or blood serum, and applied the mixture to the walls with animal tails or sticks frayed at one end.

Given their crude technology, along with the poor working conditions of a cave, it is a wonder that these hunter-artists were able to produce any art, let alone such vivid images. Ice Age animal pictures capture not only the forms of real beasts, but also their colorations,

18–4 *Standing Buffalo*, ca. 12,000 BC. Cave painting. Font-du-Gaume, France.

their details, and even their movements (fig. 18–3). In some caves, shading was used to suggest an animal's roundness (fig. 18–4). Thus, Ice Age art reached a level of quality close to that of modern cultures.

However, Ice Age art does have its limitations. Animals are shown in side view only. Little, if any, foreshortening was used to suggest an angle view of an animal. Rarely are two or more animals shown together in any purposeful way. An animal was painted on a wall regardless of the locations of other images on that same wall. Some animals are overlapped without any apparent reason. Apparently hunter-artists were not interested in organizing these images into a unified composition. Furthermore, they did not seem interested in depicting other subjects: trees, plants, ponds, rocks, even people.

What was the purpose of these paintings, many of which are located in cramped, inaccessible places? Scientists speculate that the purpose was magical. Painting an animal was equated with gaining power over that animal. The caves may have been temple-sanctuaries. Hunter-artists gathered there to paint animals and magically ensure their success in the hunt. But no one knows for sure.

Egypt

Much more is known about the art and beliefs of the ancient Egyptians. Many of their monuments are still standing (fig. 18–5). Their written language, a form of picture writing called *hieroglyphic* (fig. 18–6), was decoded by members of Napoleon's army in 1799.

By 2500 BC, Egypt had been a civilization for nearly 1000 years. Just as India's civilization began along the banks of the Indus (Chapter 16), Egypt's developed along the banks of the Nile (fig. 18–7). Nile farms became so successful that Egyptians were able to produce a surplus of food. People were freed to do other things besides farming or hunting. They gathered in large settlements that turned into cities. This development called for new jobs such as mayor, priest, judge, engineer, teacher, laborer, and, of course, artist.

Object Depicted	Egyptian vulture	Flowering reed	Flowering reeds	Forearm	Stool	Quail or chick	Foot	Horned viper	Owl	Water	Mouth	Reed sheltering field
Sign												
Translation	A	I	Y	A	P	W	B	F	M	N	R	H
Sound	A as in FAT	Y	Y as in Hebrew YODH	AH as in FATHER (guttural)	P	W	B	F	M	N	R	H as in ENGLISH

Object Depicted	Wick of twisted flax	Placenta	Animal's belly with teats	Bolt folded cloth	Pool	Hillslope	Basket with handle	Stand for jar	Loaf	Tethering rope	Hand	Snake
Sign												
Translation	H	CH	CH	S	SH	Q	K	G	T	CH	D	J
Sound	Emphatic H	CH as in Scottish LOCH	CH as in German ICH	S	SH	Q as in QUEEN	K	Hard G	T	CH as in CHEST	D	Emphatic S

18–6 Hieroglyphic writing with ink on papyrus, ca. 1025 BC. Courtesy of the Egyptian Tourist Authority.

18–5 South Temple, Ramses II. Abu Simbel. Courtesy of Art Resource, NY.

18-8 Pyramids of Gaza, Egypt. Courtesy of Goodfriend/Art Resource, NY.

18-7 Ancient Egypt.

Egypt's civilization was very organized with high levels of mathematics, engineering, and construction skills. These skills are evident in the scale of its surviving architecture and sculptures (figures 18-5 and 18-8).

The Egyptian religion was polytheistic. Egyptians also believed in *immortality,* or life after death, especially for such people as the pharaoh (king), priests, and noblemen. Egyptians took great care to make sure that the soul of an important man would live forever. The man's body was embalmed and mummified. He was buried in a solid tomb with all his earthly belongings and statues. (For an example, see the statue of Mycerinus and his queen, fig. 13-6.) Also included were painted images of the deceased, his wife, servants, maids, laborers, and even animals. It was believed that these images participated magically in his eternal happiness. The most impressive tombs are the pyramids for the pharaohs Khufu, Khafre, and Menkaure at Gizeh (fig. 18-8). But most of Egypt's surviving art is found in *mastabas* (fig. 18-9). Mastabas were relatively modest tombs for people below the rank of pharaoh.

In the mastaba of Nebamun (fig. 18–10) is a mural that was discussed briefly in Chapter 15. Nebamun, a nobleman from Thebes, is wearing the hairstyle, necklace, and kilt that signify his rank. He is also shown hunting on the River Nile. Because Egypt was a rich agricultural society, men like Nebamun hunted for pleasure not for survival. During his earthly life, he often went down to the river, at times accompanied by his wife (shown behind him) and his daughter or a maidservant (shown kneeling beneath him).

While Nebamun would catch birds, the women gathered lotuses. Papyrus plants, seen in front of the boat, grew abundantly along the banks of the Nile. These plants may have been harvested by Nebamun's workers and sold on the market to be used for writing material (paper was invented much later by the Chinese: chapter 16). Wildcats may have lurked among the papyrus stalks to challenge Nebamun in the hunt. Or, since Egyptians had domesticated cats, this one may have been trained by Nebamun to help in the hunt.

The Egyptians, as we saw, believed in immortality. They also believed that pictures played a magical role in the afterlife. Whatever was in a picture was believed to exist in the afterlife. Accordingly, this mural guaranteed that Nebamun would enjoy hunting with his family (and his cat) for eternity.

So, why is Egyptian art so flat, especially with regard to depictions of people? One reason had to do with the magical role of art. The figure of the nobleman, for example, follows a strict formula: his head, legs, and feet are shown from the side while one eye and his shoulders are shown frontally. This style was intended to convey the main features of the human body as clearly as possible. Over time, it became the "correct" way to show important people. To depart from this formula would have done magical harm to the soul of the dead man. The figures of the women also reflect this formula, but theirs show more variety. They are also much smaller. Is this because they were such small people in real life? No, it is because they were less important. Also, because they were less important, the artist was allowed some leeway in giving their bodies more variety of pose and movement.

Egyptian society, like Egyptian art, was very conservative. All of its cultural forms changed little over thousands of years. Egyptian art was almost as eternal in fact as it was in intent.

18–9 Mastabas, with plan and (at top) schematic section.

18–10 *Fowling the Marshes*, wall painting, ca. 1400. Reproduced by Courtesy of the Trustees of the British Museum.

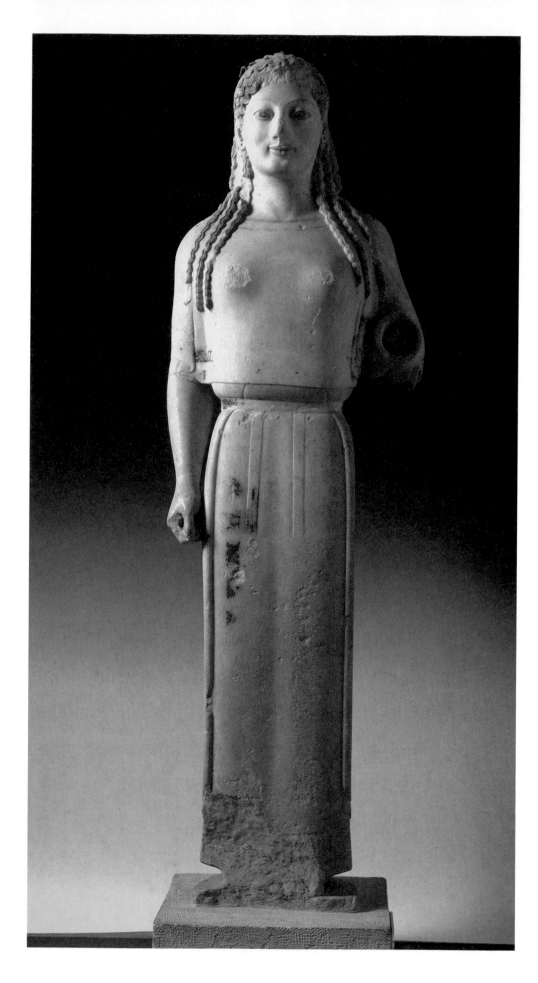

Classical Greece

Unlike Egyptian civilization and art, Greek civilization changed over time. Look at two statues separated by less than one hundred years. The sculpture of the young maiden sculpted in 530 BC (fig. 18–11) is simple and stiff. It contrasts vividly with the naturalness of the goddess Athena, a Roman copy of a statue sculpted by Myron in 450 BC (fig. 18–12).

The great era of Greek culture, known as the Classical Period, lasted from about 480 to 323 BC. Around 450 BC (the year of the *Athena* statue), the citizens of Athens began rebuilding a fortified hill called the *Acropolis* (fig. 18–15) and the temple of Athena called the *Parthenon* (fig. 18–16). Both had been destroyed by the Persians. This was not only the time of Myron, but also of philosophers Protagoras and Socrates; Sophocles and Euripides, the writers of famous Greek tragedies; and Pericles, the leader of Athens. Athens became the center of art and culture in the Greek world.

Myron's statue, like all Greek sculpture of this time, expresses two principles: humanism and idealism. **Humanism** is defined as a view of life based on the nature, dignity, and interests of people. Other societies in the ancient world, like Egypt and pre-Islamic Persia, were dominated by superstition. However, the Greeks were beginning to investigate the workings of the world and to question old ways of thinking. They believed the investigation should begin with humans. As Protagoras stated, "Man is the measure of all things."

The realism of Myron's statue reflects this humanistic tendency. In contrast to the puppetlike maiden of 530 BC, the *Athena* has the form and posture of a real woman. Her gown, which gathers at the waist and hangs in natural-looking folds, suggests the presence of a real body underneath. Her weight is placed more on her right foot than on her left. This causes a subtle movement throughout the body. The right hip is higher than the left. The upper body is bent so that the left shoulder is higher than the right (fig. 18–13). This movement, sometimes called "weight shift," was a real breakthrough in the art of representing the human figure.

The statue by Myron also reflects an idealistic tendency. **Idealism** has to do with a concept of perfection. *Athena* is obviously young, athletic, and beautifully proportioned. Greek philosophers reasoned that there was a perfect form for everything: a perfect woman,

18–12　Myron, *Statue of Athena*. Liebighaus Museum, Frankfurt am Main, Germany. Eric Lessing/Art Resource, NY.

18–13　"Weight shift" in *Athena Lemnia*.

18-14 Myron, *Discobolus*, Imperial Roman. Copy. Marble, 60˝ (152 cm) high. Museo Nazionale Romano, Rome. Scala/Art Resource, NY.

perfect man, perfect horse, perfect tree, and so forth. This statue is Myron's attempt to portray ideal womanhood as well as the goddess Athena.

Ideal manhood received equal attention from the Greeks. The *Discobolus* (fig. 18-14) is another copy of a bronze sculpture by Myron. A young athlete is poised to hurl a discus. The suggestion of movement was especially daring for the 400s. The statue must have seemed incredibly lifelike to the Greek public. Still, as with *Athena*, realism is tempered by idealism. Idealism is seen in the *Discobolus*'s proportions, its balanced posture, and its passive face.

Greek architecture of the time also expresses humanism and idealism. The Parthenon (figures 18–15 and 18–16), unlike an Egyptian pyramid or an American skyscraper, is built on a human scale. Although it is grand, it is not overwhelming. The method of its construction, as you can see, is post and lintel. Idealism is reflected in the proportional relationships between the columns and the rest of the temple. Column width and height, column height and the height of the temple, and even column width and the spaces between

18-16 The Parthenon, Athens, 448–432 BC. Northwest view. Scala/Art Resource, NY.

18–15 View of Acropolis, Athens. Scala/Art Resource, NY.

columns are proportional. These proportions represent a refinement of the **Doric** style of temple that took place over hundreds of years. The steps in this process (reading from left to right) are illustrated in figure 18–17.

The entire ancient world was in awe of Greek achievements, not only in sculpture and architecture, but in literature, philosophy, and human rights. Later generations of Europeans shared this awe. As we shall see in this chapter, much of European art bears the influence of Greek artistic styles.

18–17 Changes in Doric order proportions.

18–18 Wall painting transferred to panel, from a villa near Pompeii, 79 AD.

First and Second Century Rome

The Romans were the principal heirs of Greek culture. They copied Greek statues by the thousands. (Myron's *Athena* and *Discobolus* are known to us only through Roman copies.) Original Roman sculptures resemble Greek sculptures. Roman paintings were largely based on Greek paintings. As you can see, the pleasant scene in figure 18–18 creates pictorial depth by using several methods. The painting includes foreshortening, shading, placement, variations of scale, and aerial perspective. Notice, however, that the eye levels of the various walls, temples, and monuments are inconsistent. Linear perspective was not applied consistently. Neither the Greeks nor the Romans had developed a system of one- or two-point perspective. Finally, Roman temples, which were also made with post-and-lintel methods, resemble Greek temples (fig. 18–19). Most Roman temples, however, are in the *Corinthian* style rather than the Doric.

18–19 Maison Caree, Nîmes, France, first century BC. Giraudon/Art Resource, NY.

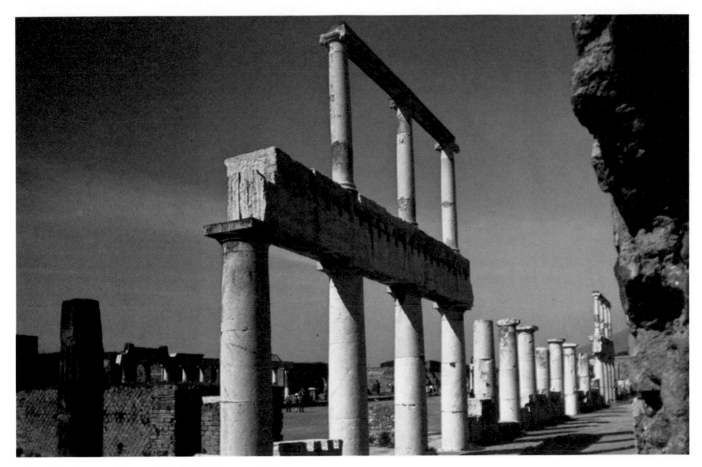

18-20 The Forum of Pompeii. Scala/Art Resource, NY.

In architecture, however, the Romans were original and unsurpassed in the ancient world. In the center of every major city was a ***forum,*** a combination of commercial district and civic center. A forum contained law courts, money exchanges, record offices, and assemblies. Today these forums are in ruins (fig. 18-20). Romans built harbors, bridges, sewers, and gigantic water conduits called ***aqueducts*** (fig. 18-21) that still line the landscape of Europe. They also built imposing gymnasiums, public baths, race tracks, and stadiums like the Roman *Colosseum* (fig. 18-27). Most of these structures employ one or both of two Roman technologies: the arch principle of construction, and concrete.

Just about all of the surviving architecture of the Egyptians, Greeks, and Romans were made of masonry materials. A masonry lintel, however, lacks *tensile* strength, the ability to withstand stress (fig. 18-22). A masonry lintel longer than twenty feet is apt to crack of its own weight. A temple with a masonry ceiling has to be supported by a forest of columns. A wooden lintel, which is lightweight and has tensile strength, needs less support. But wood is not a good material for public buildings because it rots or burns.

18-21 Pont du Gard. Roman arch, near Nîmes, France, first century BC. Giraudon/Art Resource, NY.

18–27 Colosseum, Rome ca. 70–82 AD. Scala/Art Resource, NY.

Cross section of the Colosseum.

A ***round arch*** (fig. 18–23), as opposed to either a post and lintel structure or a corbeled arch (see Chapter 17), solves the problem of masonry's tensile weakness. During construction, the stones of an arch are supported by a temporary wooden framework until the last stone (the keystone) is in place. Once it is finished, an arch is extremely strong and can span more than one hundred feet. A ***barrel vault*** (fig. 18–24) is an arch extended in depth. Like a ceiling, it can be used to cover a rectangular area. A ***cross vault*** (fig. 18–25), formed by two intersecting barrel vaults, can cover a rectangular area while remaining open on all four sides. A *dome* (fig. 18–26) is simply a radial form of the arch, and can be used to cover a circular area.

The Romans developed concrete as early as the second century BC. They used concrete as well as stones to make barrel vaults, cross vaults, and domes. Concrete resembles a thick sludge before it hardens. It can be poured into forms of almost any shape. Like stone, concrete is much stronger as an arch than as a horizontal lintel.

The legendary Colosseum (fig. 18–27) was begun under the emperor Vespasian and dedicated by his son Titus in 80 AD. It has every kind of arch except the dome. Three levels of repeated arches, called ***arcades,*** ring the outside. Barrel-vaulted ramps lead to the arena, and cross-vaulted corridors circle the entire stadium on all levels. In addition to covering the ramps and corridors, these vaults supported the stadium seats. The stadium could hold 50,000 spectators. Beneath the arena were cells for wild animals and locker rooms for the gladiators. At the dedication, more than 5,000 animals were killed. At one performance, the arena was flooded to stage a mock naval battle involving thousands of actors. Over 620 feet (189 meters) long, 513 feet (156 meters) wide, and 157 feet (47 meters) high, the Colosseum is ten times the size of the Parthenon.

18–22 Post and lintel.

18–23 Arch.

18–24 Barrel vault.

18–25 Cross vault.

18–26 Dome.

For thirteen centuries the solid concrete dome covering the Pantheon (fig. 18–28) held the record for being the largest in the world. (The view of the dome is obscured by the massive columned porch in the front.) Finished in 125 AD during the reign of Hadrian, the Pantheon was dedicated to the seven planetary gods— a legacy of the Greek religion. In the 600s it was converted to a Christian church. Because of this, the Pantheon was spared the dismantling that marred or ruined almost all other Roman buildings. Today it is a shrine for tourists. On clear days the sun streams through a round hole at the top. A bright disk of sunlight moves across the surface of the floor and walls with the speed of the rotation of the earth (fig. 18–29).

The architecture of Rome was a symbol of the power as well as the splendor of the ancient world until Rome's decline in the 300s and 400s. Christianity replaced the religious system of Greece and Rome. Almost all of the culture of the Roman Empire was rejected as pagan, if not immoral.

18–29 Pantheon, interior dome. Photograph: Jan Lukas. Scala/Art Resource, NY.

18–28 Pantheon, Rome, ca. 118–128 AD. Photograph: Nimatallah. Scala/Art Resource, NY.

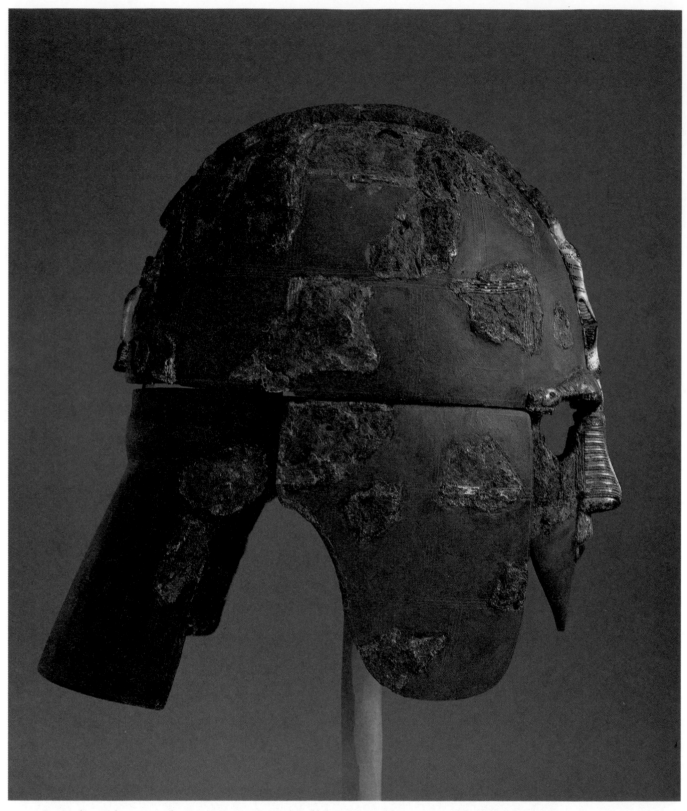

18–30 Sutton–hoo Helmet, seventh century, Saxon. Reproduced by Courtesy of the Trustees of the British Museum.

18–31 Frankish ornaments, (right) sixth century. Silver and paste, 1⅛″ (10 cm) each. Photograph by Bobby Hansson. (Gift of J. Pierpont Morgan, 1917.) (left) Langobardic ornament, seventh century. Silver-gilt and niello, 6 5/16″ x 3 ¾″ (16 x 10 cm). The Metropolitan Museum of Art, Purchase, 1955, Joseph Pulitzer Bequest.

18–32 Empire of Charlemagne.

Through the Dark Ages to Charlemagne

During the 400s, western Europe entered the **medieval** era, literally, the **Middle Ages.** This term applies to the long period of time between the Fall of Rome and the Renaissance (to be discussed). During the early part of this period, civilized life had all but disappeared. The people of Europe were illiterate and largely nomadic. They produced little painting, no large buildings, and no in-the-round sculptures. However, they did make such things as military helmets (fig. 18–30) and attractive ornaments for their weapons, their horses, and themselves. You may recognize the technique of cloisonné (Chapter 13) in the fancy pins (fig. 18–31) used to fasten their garments.

In the 800s, a Frankish king named Charlemagne united most of the continent into a Holy Roman Empire (fig. 18–32). Charlemagne was a patron of the

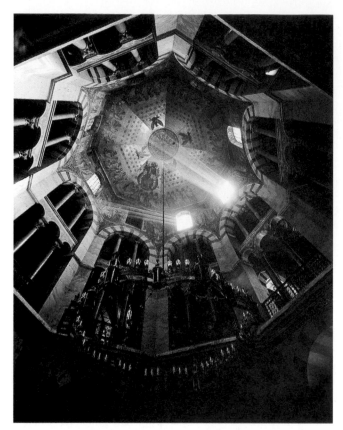

18–33 Aachen Cathedral, view into octagonal dome. Aachen, Germany, Europe. Erich Lessing/Art Resource, NY.

arts as well as a great military leader and statesman. He attempted to bring Europeans out of the Dark Ages by stimulating a rebirth of culture. He imported scholars, architects, and craftspersons from all over, but primarily from Constantinople. Constantinople was the headquarters of the Byzantine Empire. The forerunner of Eastern Christendom (modern Russia, Armenia, Greece, Serbia, and other parts of eastern Europe), the Byzantine Empire was much more civilized than western Europe. Charlemagne's private chapel (fig. 18–33) may have been modeled after a chapel in Constantinople. His chapel represents the beginning of medieval masonry architecture.

The hope of a united Europe and cultural growth was dashed with Charlemagne's death. But two political units grew out of his empire. The Holy Roman Empire, a cluster of German kingdoms in the east, and a French kingdom in the west continued to survive, though somewhat shakily. These, together with the states owned by the Catholic church in Italy and the Anglo-Saxon kingdoms across the English Channel, formed the power blocks of medieval Europe. Together they transformed the continent from a wasteland of peasant villages to a civilization of art and architecture. France was in the forefront of this transformation.

Medieval Crusades and Pilgrimages

By the 1000s and 1100s, large churches with vaulted ceilings were beginning to spring up all over Europe, particularly in France. This was the time of the *Crusades,* when knights and peasants traveled to Palestine to recapture Jerusalem from the Moslem Saracens. In 1189, Richard the Lion-Hearted, king of England, met the king of France in the church at Vézelay to begin the Third Crusade. They probably led their troops through Vézelay's doors under a relief carving of Christ and the apostles (fig. 18–34). Christ, in the center, is giving the apostles their spiritual assignments. The scenes in the eight side compartments show the apostles healing the sick. The scenes on the lintel below show them preaching the gospel to all nations. The knights who passed through the door and glanced up at this relief believed that they, like the apostles, had received a spiritual assignment.

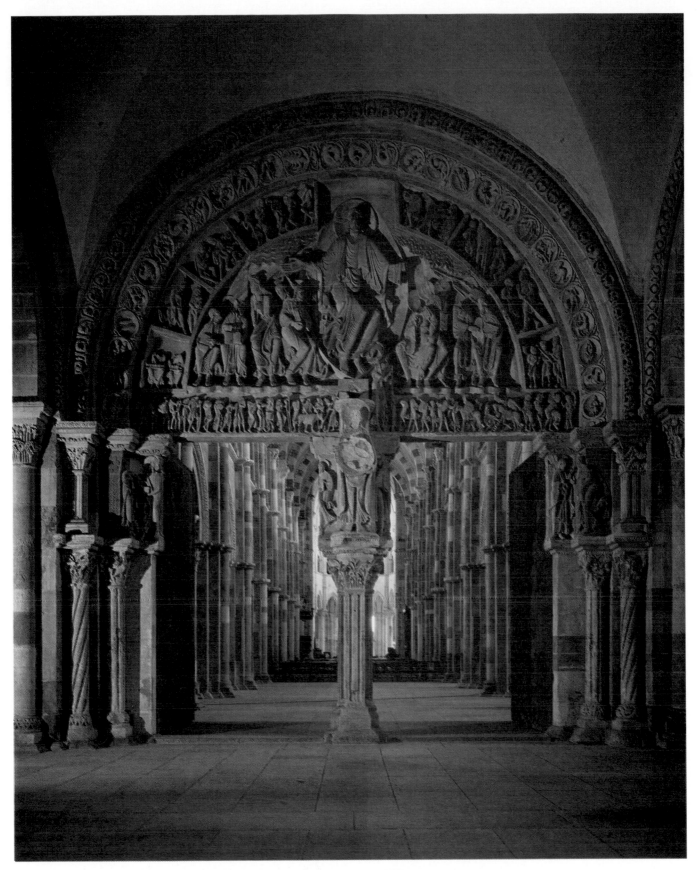

18–34   Central portal of La Madeleine, Vézelay, 1120–1132. Scala/Art Resource, NY.

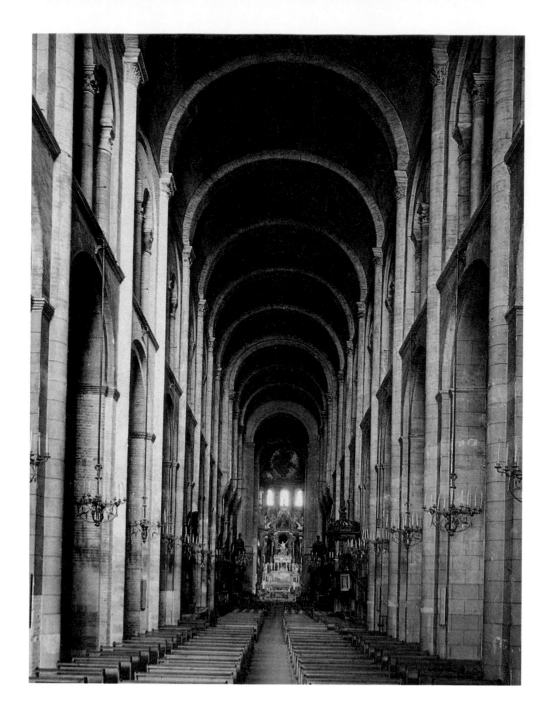

Compare the style of this relief to the classical examples reviewed earlier. Unlike the bodies of the Greek sculptures, these are stylized and unnaturally slender. The figures seem to be floating rather than standing firmly on the ground. The folds of their gowns are more decorative than natural-looking, though they do reveal their bodies to some extent. Unlike Roman murals, the scenes of this relief are completely lacking in three-dimensional space. Some of these characteristics are due to the limitations of relief carving, but most are due to a dramatic difference in point of view. The Greeks and Romans focused on humans and the natural world. The medieval Christians focused on God and the divine world.

The 1100s were also a time when pilgrims traveled to major shrines to see a *relic*. A relic is a remnant of a saint's clothing, hair, or even bones. People believed that a relic had the power to cure disease, forgive sins, and perform miracles. One of the churches on the pilgrimage route was St. Sernin in Toulouse (fig. 18–35). Imagine how pilgrims must have felt as they marched in a procession beneath the barrel vault of St. Sernin's main aisle, while listening to choirs of monks intoning chants. The vault is reinforced with ribs that form their own rhythmic procession as they lead the eye to the rear of the church. Notice also the heaviness of the supports and the relative darkness of the interior.

Gothic France

Although the Crusades were military failures, Europeans gained a great deal from their Moslem adversaries (Chapter 17). Among other things, they learned how to build pointed arches and make stained glass. These important lessons were applied to the *Gothic* style of church architecture. Gothic builders added three important features to Christian architecture: the pointed arch (fig. 18–36), pointed vaulting (fig. 18–37), and the flying buttress (fig. 18–38).

Ceilings based on the *pointed vault* are more stable than ceilings based on the round vault. Reinforcing the vaults with ribs makes them even more stable. Because vaulted ceilings are heavy, the walls holding them must be very thick so that they do not bow outward. *Flying buttresses,* or stone supports on the outside of the building, add support at those critical points where the ceiling joins the wall. Flying buttresses surround Chartres Cathedral (fig. 18–39), the first major church to use Gothic construction throughout.

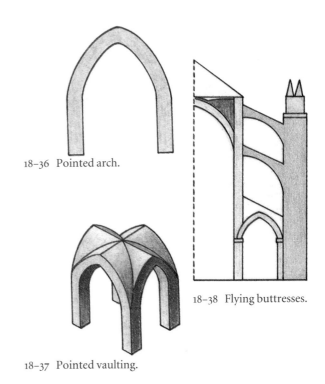

18–36 Pointed arch.

18–38 Flying buttresses.

18–37 Pointed vaulting.

18–39 Chartres Cathedral, France, twelfth–sixteenth centuries. Scala/Art Resource, NY.

18–40 Nave of Amiens Cathedral. Scala/Art Resource, NY.

With Gothic construction, churches could have very high ceilings. Amiens Cathedral is typical of a church of this type. Notice the pointed arches on the left and in the windows at the rear of the cathedral (fig. 18–40). The soaring vaults in figure 18–41 are based on the pointed arch. Notice in both figures the ribs outlining the contours of the vaults. In what ways do you think a Gothic cathedral expresses the Age of Faith?

Gothic construction produced more space per pound of material than any other kind of masonry construction. It allowed for large windows that could flood the interior with light. However, the brightness of this light was tempered by the used of stained glass. (Recall the methods of making stained glass windows in Chapter 13.) A window from Reims Cathedral (fig. 18–42) illustrates the splendor of this glass. The bodies of Christ and the saints are stylized. The space around them is abstracted into symbols and patterns of color. Some of these characteristics were due to the demands of the stained glass medium. However, this art also reflects the spirituality of medieval life. An abstract and symbolic art is often more appropriate than a realistic art to express the world of faith.

The Gothic style of architecture, which spread to other parts of Europe, flourished in the 1200s and 1300s. After that, it began to be challenged by architects working in Florence, Italy.

18–42 *Crucifixion*, detail of a window from St. Remi, Reims, ca. 1190. Stained glass, approx. 12′ (366 cm) high. Art Resource, NY.

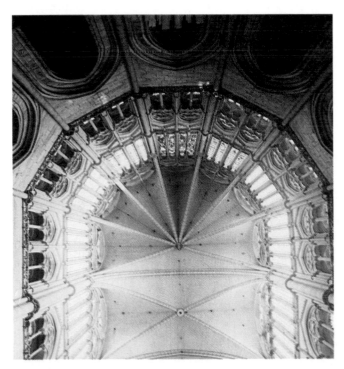

18–41 Choir vault, Amiens Cathedral. Scala/Art Resource, NY.

The Renaissance in the 1400s

Renaissance literally means *rebirth*. It refers to a period of time when attitudes changed dramatically, particularly in Florence, Italy. The spirit of humanism, which had ignited the achievements of the Greeks some 1900 years earlier, was being revived. Like the Greeks, Florentine thinkers focused on people and earthly life. Their questioning lead to major advances in science. At the end of the 1400s, Leonardo da Vinci began exploring the fields of optics, mechanics, and human anatomy, and Christopher Columbus began exploring the world. In the next century, Nicolaus Copernicus, a Polish astronomer, theorized that the earth revolved around the sun. For centuries people had believed that the sun revolved around the earth. These researchers, and others who followed, helped to create the scientific explosion that has affected all of our lives—intellectually, materially, and spiritually.

Renaissance scholars also revived an interest in the classical civilizations. In medieval times, the writings of people like Sophocles, Plato, and Virgil (Roman poet) gathered dust or were interpreted solely in light of Christian doctrine. Now these writings were studied for whatever universal truths they might contain. Earlier, Greek statues, Roman statues, and Roman copies of Greek statues were ignored or destroyed; now they were preserved and admired by artists. Earlier, Roman buildings had been robbed of their stones to construct churches; now they were studied by architects.

Florentine architect Filippo Brunelleschi admired the Pantheon (fig. 18–28), one of the few intact buildings. Brunelleschi's interest in Roman architecture is reflected in the small domed chapel (fig. 18–43) he designed for the wealthy Pazzi family. Notice that its spatial relationships, in contrast to those of a Gothic cathedral, are relatively simple. The use of the round arch, in addition to plain walls, is a change from the Gothic. The color accents were inspired by classical decorations.

18–43 Filippo Brunelleschi, interior of Pazzi Chapel, South Croce. Scala/Art Resource, NY.

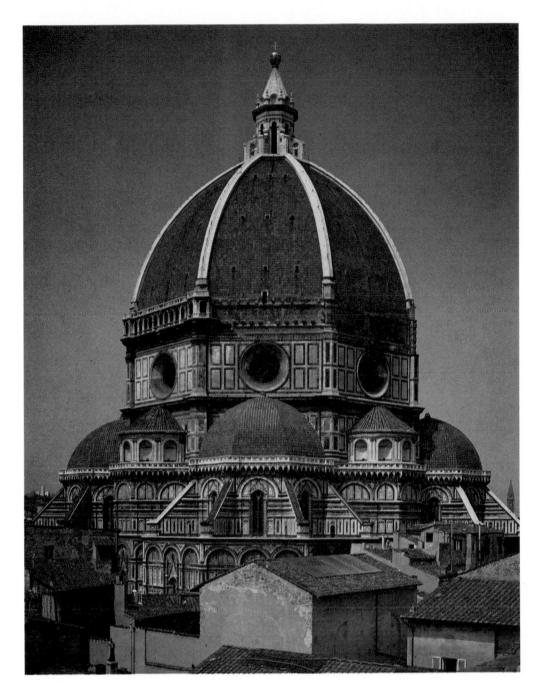

18-44 Filippo Brunelleschi, dome of Florence Cathedral, 1420–1436. Scala/Art Resource, NY.

18-45 Donatello, *St. Mark the Evangelist.* 1411–1413. Marble, approximately 7′ 9″ (236 cm) high. Or San Michele, Florence. Scala/Art Resource, NY.

Brunelleschi's most ambitious project was the dome of the Cathedral of Florence (fig. 18-44). The dome is very Renaissance in its boldness. Spanning a diameter of 140 feet (43 meters), it is 300 feet (93 meters) high (351 feet high including the decorative "lantern"). No dome this wide had been built since the Pantheon. No dome this high had even been built in the world. Despite its size and originality, however, this dome is Gothic in its construction. Unlike the dome on the Pantheon, Brunelleschi's is pointed and ribbed.

The change away from medieval styles is clearly reflected in Renaissance sculpture. Donatello shared Brunelleschi's interest in classicism. Donatello's *St.*

Mark (fig. 18-45) shows many similarities to Greek sculpture. The sculpture has human proportions and weight-shift posture. The clothing is natural-looking. Indeed, St. Mark's gown looks as though the apostle had slept in it. The principal difference between Myron's *Athena* and the *St. Mark*—aside from their gender—is in their faces. Athena's face expresses classical calm. St. Mark's face expresses the passion and seriousness of a Christian evangelist.

The men in *The Tribute Money* (fig. 18–46), a fresco by Masaccio (Tommaso Guidi), also look serious. They are as weighty and solid as sculptures, and they look as intense and serious as St. Mark. Here, Jesus and his disciples confront a tax collector in Capernaum (from St. Matthew 17:24–7). Jesus is in the center telling St. Peter to obtain a coin from the mouth of a fish. Peter is shown in three places. He is standing with the disciples; obtaining the coin on the left; and paying the collector on the right. The men's bodies are shaded on the left with bold strokes of chiaroscuro and illuminated from the right. They appear quite three-dimensional. The space they are in has depth. The building on the right may be the first in art history to have been rendered in one-point perspective. The hills in the background are shrouded in aerial perspective. *The Tribute Money* served as a textbook of pictorial techniques for later Renaissance artists like da Vinci and Michelangelo.

The High Renaissance

At the end of the 1400s, art entered a phase called **High Renaissance,** which lasted about twenty years. This phase brought to perfection the experiments and discoveries of artists like Donatello and Masaccio. A good example of High Renaissance art is Raphael's *School of Athens* (fig. 18–47).

The subject is obviously classical. Famous philosophers from the ancient world, including Socrates, Plato, and Aristotle are assembled. More importantly, the men have idealized bodies and graceful gestures, and a beautiful, spacious environment to move about in.

Raphael's mural, finished in 1511, was not the first successful High Renaissance work. Sixteen years earlier, in 1495, Leonardo da Vinci began *The Last Supper* (fig. 18–48) on the wall of a Milan monastery. Painting was only one of Leonardo's skills. The great artist was also a sculptor, an architect, an engineer, a scientist,

18–46 Masaccio, *The Tribute Money,* fresco, ca. 1427. Branacci Chapel, Santa Maria del Carmine, Florence. Scala/Art Resource, NY.

18-47 Raphael, *The School of Athens*, Stanza della Segnatura, The Vatican, Rome. Fresco in lunette: 25´ 3 ¼˝ at base. ©1985 Scala/Firenze. Scala/Art Resource, NY.

18-48 Leonardo da Vinci, *The Last Supper*, ca. 1494. Oil and tempera on plaster. 14´ 5˝ x 28´ ¼˝ (4.39 x 8.54 m). Santa Maria delle Grazie, Milan.

and an inventor who filled notebooks with descriptions of everything from armored vehicles to parachutes. He was ahead of his time in the fields of astronomy, hydrology, sound, optics, and especially anatomy (fig. 18–49). He is said to have dissected as many as fifty cadavers in his search for knowledge. More than any man in history, Leonardo was a Renaissance Person—an individual skilled and well versed in many fields.

Before Leonardo started painting, artists were unable to show people moving about in a picture without sacrificing stability. In Masaccio's *The Tribute*

Money, for example, the composition is stable, but the men are relatively static. *The Last Supper* is the first major painting to successfully reconcile movement and stability. One reason is that the composition is deceptively simple. The picture is horizontal. The long table is symmetrical and parallel to the picture plane. Jesus is not only located at the middle of the table; his head is at the center of the picture and at the vanishing point. The rectangular space is defined by one-point perspective. These aspects provide stability. Movement is seen in the twelve disciples. They are all reacting to the statement, "One of you will betray me." Despite

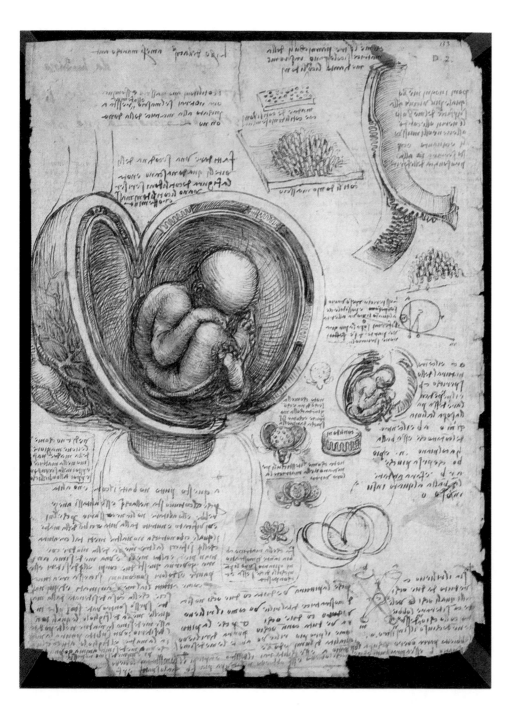

18–49 Leonardo da Vinci, *Embryo in the Womb,* ca. 1510. Pen and ink. Royal Collection Enterprises Limited, Windsor Castle. Copyright reserved. Reproduced by gracious permission of H. M. Queen Elizabeth II.

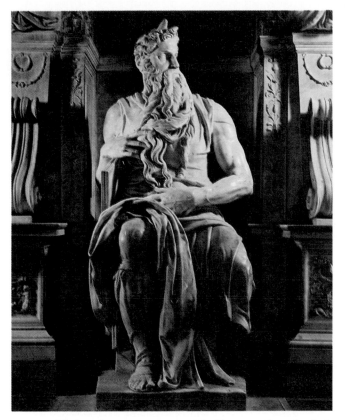

18-50 Michelangelo, *Moses*, 1513–1515. Marble, approximately 8′ 4″ (254 cm) high. San Pietro in Vincoli, Rome.

their agitation, all have idealized bodies and graceful gestures. The one on the left who is leaning back with his face in shadow is Judas. All fit comfortably in the rectangular space. *The Last Supper* was the first painting to successfully integrate active figures in a realistic spatial world. It has been popular from the time it was completed in 1498.

The works of Leonardo's younger contemporary, Michelangelo Buonarroti, have also continued to be popular through time. Like Leonardo, Michelangelo was broadly skilled in the arts: sculpture, painting, architecture, even poetry. However, he was not involved in scientific pursuits. Both artists branched out to other cities: Leonardo to Milan, Michelangelo to Rome.

In the early 1400s, Rome was a collection of old ruins, dirt roads, and cow pastures. When Michelangelo came of age as an artist, Rome was beginning to rival Florence in development and culture. By the time Michelangelo died, Rome had surpassed Florence and went on to become the thriving city and center of culture that it is today.

Michelangelo first began to produce art for the Vatican, a special area in Rome for the headquarters of the Catholic church. The *Pietà* (fig. 8–10), which was

discussed briefly in Chapter 8, was Michelangelo's first work for the Vatican. It is also an excellent example of High Renaissance sculpture. The figures of Jesus and Mary are extremely beautiful and harmoniously related. The *Moses* (fig. 18–50), begun some fifteen years later, falls within the High Renaissance period, and is definitely grand and monumental. But in this case, beauty has given way to righteous anger.

The *Moses* is too awesome to be included in the same category with *School of Athens, The Last Supper,* and the *Pietà.* Michelangelo, a man of strong passions, revered Moses and other heroes of the Old Testament. He aimed to glorify the people of the Bible, often by giving them superhuman proportions. Michelangelo's feelings (which were often disturbed) frequently found their way into his later works. More than anything, it is the psychological power of these works that has fascinated the public for centuries. The *Moses* was originally intended to be part of a grandiose tomb for Pope Julius II. The project was never completed because Julius himself lost interest in it.

One project that Julius did not lose interest in was the ceiling of the Vatican's Sistine Chapel (fig. 18–51).

18-51 Michelangelo, View of the Sistine Chapel, Vatican City. Scala/Art Resource, NY.

18–52 Michelangelo, ceiling of the Sistine Chapel, 1508–1512. The Vatican, Rome. Only five of the nine panels from Genesis are shown. Scala/Art Resource, NY.

He wanted Michelangelo to cover its vast surface with a mural. In 1508, Michelangelo began the fresco on the subject of God's creation. Covering 5,800 square feet (537 square meters), 70 feet (21 meters) above the floor, Michelangelo's creation itself was almost godlike. It took him four years, but in the end, the weary artist had transformed the surface of a vaulted ceiling into a complex pictorial drama (fig. 18–52).

The triangular spaces (called *lunettes*) around the perimeter of the mural are filled with figures representing the ancestors of Jesus, the Jewish people of the Old Testament. Between the lunettes are niches containing the largest figures, who were supposed to have predicted the birth of Jesus. Old Testament prophets alternate with female oracles (fortune tellers) from Greek myth. The nine panels running the length of the ceiling in the center contain episodes from the Old Testament book of Genesis: the Creation, the Fall, and the Flood. (Recall the scene of God separating light and dark in fig. 6–1.)

God is in each of the Creation episodes. In the *Creation of the Sun and the Moon* (fig. 18–53), God is represented by two figures. Clothed in loose-fitting,

billowing gowns, these figures have massive, muscular bodies like that of Moses. Although they resemble Greek gods, the face of the figure on the right is fierce, like *Jehovah*, God of the Old Testament. Throughout the fresco, Michelangelo borrowed from Greek sources as well as Jewish and Christian sources for his ideas. The use of oracles and heroically proportioned bodies is Greek. The Old Testament themes are Jewish. The predictions of the coming of Jesus, which are symbolized throughout the mural, are Christian.

The imagery and subject matter of the Sistine ceiling successfully bring together ideas from different sources. The composition is also successful in reconciling movement and stability. The mural contains more than 300 energetically moving figures. It could have become a teeming confusion of humanity. Not only that, scenes take place on different planes and in different directions, and are drawn to different scales. Worlds being created, prophecy, sin, worlds being destroyed are all scenes that coexist in the same mural. Michelangelo prevented chaos, however, by dividing each scene into its own rectangular or triangular space. The final effect is both energetic and composed. The

Sistine ceiling is considered by some to be the greatest masterwork of the Western world.

Like his sculpture and painting, Michelangelo's architecture came to represent both the High Renaissance and the Catholic church. The west end of St. Peter's basilica (fig. 18-54), the principal church of the Vatican, was designed by Michelangelo and completed after his death. (Although based on Michelangelo's design, the dome itself was modified by Giacomo della Porta.) The use of a pointed dome surmounted by a lantern recalls Brunelleschi and the Cathedral of Florence. But the sense of mass, and the unity of windows, columns, and ribs is Michelangelo's (and High Renaissance). Like the statue of *Moses*, St. Peter's is truly monumental and a fitting symbol for the headquarters of the Catholic church. It is the ancestor of all of the famous domes in the world, including the Capitol dome in Washington, DC.

The High Renaissance represents a peak development in European art. Although the movement itself ended in the mid-1500s, its basic ideals continued as touchstones of Western art. In the late 1800s, most of these ideals were rejected by the modern movement. But that is a story for Chapter 19.

18-53 Michelangelo, *Creation of the Sun and the Moon*, detail from the Sistine Chapel ceiling. 1508–1512. Fresco, approximately 9´ 2 ˝ x 18´ 8 ˝ (3 x 5.5 m). The Vatican, Rome. Scala/Art Resource, NY.

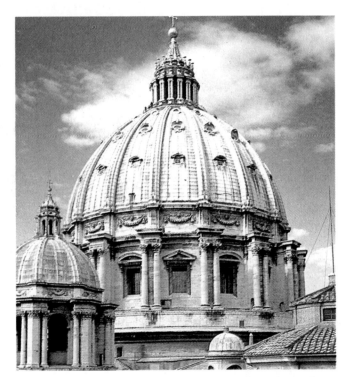

18-54 Michelangelo, *St. Peter's*, 1546–1564 (view from the west). Dome completed by Giacomo della Porta, 1590.

Integration Experience 18.1

Renaissance Influences

Use library resources and contact your history teacher to prepare a report on how the work of Renaissance artists was influenced by the inventions, scientific discoveries, political and religious values of that time period (1400s–1500s).

Studio Experience 18.2

A Renaissance-Style Landscape

Create a landscape painting, using tinting, shading and intensity variations to create the illusion of light, space, movement and depth, that many Renaissance artists tried to perfect in their paintings.

Chapter 19
Islands of Time II

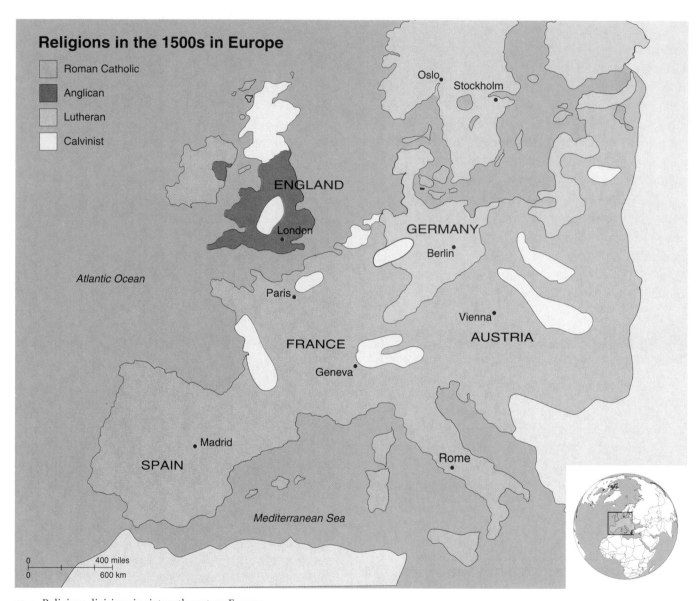

Religions in the 1500s in Europe

- Roman Catholic
- Anglican
- Lutheran
- Calvinist

Oslo

Stockholm

ENGLAND

London

Atlantic Ocean

GERMANY

Berlin

Paris

Vienna

AUSTRIA

FRANCE

Geneva

Madrid

Rome

SPAIN

Mediterranean Sea

0   400 miles
0   600 km

19–1 Religious divisions in sixteenth century Europe.

Chapter 18 ended with a discussion of High Renaissance art in the early 1500s. The 1500s was also the century in which the split in Christianity between Protestant and Catholic began. This development, known as the **Reformation,** affected not only religion but European culture in general. In 1517, just five years after Michelangelo completed the Sistine ceiling,

Martin Luther (fig. 19–2), a German monk, prepared a long list of criticisms of the Catholic church. He nailed the list to the door of a church in Wittenberg. More importantly, the list was printed and circulated throughout Germany. (The printing press had just been developed.) His act eventually led to a revolt against the pope and the Catholic church. New denominations, such as Lutheran, Anabaptist, Mennonite, Calvinist, and Anglican, sprang up in Germany, Scandinavia, Switzerland, the Netherlands, and England.

Meanwhile, Catholics responded with a **Counter-Reformation** led by Ignatius Loyola (fig. 19–3) and his order of monks called the Jesuits. Although Loyola and the Jesuits helped to change many of the practices of the Catholic church, they also helped to harden its doctrines against the Protestants. By the 1600s, the split in Christianity, which had become quite bitter, divided Europe into Catholic and Protestant factions (fig. 19–1). This split is reflected in the art of the 1600s.

The 1600s and the Baroque Style

Italy, as we learned in the previous chapter, was the center of developments in Renaissance art. By 1600 the ideas of this art had spread to other parts of Europe. Gothic styles were abandoned completely. Architects, painters, and sculptors in northern Europe, as well as those in Italy, developed a style called *Baroque*. This new style emphasized complexity, drama, and grandeur. The style was especially popular in Catholic countries. Baroque style was very ornate. To this day, the term baroque is often applied to anything that is excessive or pompous. King Louis XIV's palace at Versailles, France (figures 19–4 and 19–5), is probably the most baroque project ever undertaken. The palace was built by an army of architects, landscape designers, sculptors, stonecutters, and decorators. During the peak of construction, they numbered 36,000 men plus

19–3 St. Ignatius Loyola, engraving.

19–2 Lucas Cranach, *Martin Luther*. Galleria degli Uffizi, Firenze.

19-5 Louis Le Vau and Jules Hardouin-Mansart, Garden façade, Versailles Palace. 1669–1685. Giraudon/Art Resource, NY.

19-4 Versailles Palace (aerial view), 1661–1688. Palace 1935′ (589 m) wide. Scala/Art Resource, NY.

Studio Experience 19.1

A Baroque Pocket Pot

Use clay slabs and various surface decoration techniques to construct a Baroque pocket pot to hang on your wall. Refer to the complex and very ornate style of Baroque metalwork, jewelry, and ceiling frescoes for ideas.

6,000 horses. The palace and its gardens stand as a colossal monument to France's most famous king.

The most popular Catholic painter of the early 1600s was Peter Paul Rubens from Flanders (now Belgium), a small country on the North Sea. Rubens painted for rulers and **aristocrats** (a privileged class with inherited wealth) all over Europe. His subjects included portraits of famous people, classical myths, heroic battles, and scenes from the Bible. His *Massacre*

19-6 Peter Paul Rubens, *Massacre of the Innocents,* ca. 1621. Oil on panel, 6′ 6 ¼″ x 9′ 11″ (199 x 302 cm). Alte Pinakothek, Munich.

19-7 Rembrandt van Rijn, *Adoration of the Shepherds,* ca. 1646. Oil on canvas rounded at the top, 38 ¼″ x 24 ¼″ (97 x 62 cm). Alte Pinakothek, Munich.

of the Innocents (fig. 19-6) is based on the Gospel of Matthew (2:16). It illustrates the killing of all children under the age of two by King Herod's soldiers, after the infant Jesus had been taken to safety in Egypt by Mary and Joseph. It is a vigorously painted commotion of figures charging, fleeing, struggling, and falling. Although true to its subject and full of horror and anguish, *Massacre of the Innocents* is also full of high drama and grandeur. It is set on the steps of a Greek temple, with classical ruins just visible in the distant haze. All of the soldiers, men, women, and children have handsome, robust bodies. Even their costumes, torn or otherwise, are splendid. The painting looks like a scene from an opera. One can imagine hearing a soprano in center stage sing a tragic aria.

Compare Rubens's painting to Rembrandt's *Adoration of the Shepherds* (fig. 19-7), which is based on a different episode of the Christmas story. The Rembrandt is not at all theatrical. Instead of handsome, athletic bodies, all of the people have ordinary bodies. All, including Joseph and Mary, are dressed in peasants' clothes. The setting—as dark, rustic, and dirty as any stable at night—is anything but grand. The newborn child and the intimate group around him are set aglow by the lantern held by Joseph. The faces of the shepherds in the outer circle reflect the radiance of the child. Because *Adoration* is not theatrical, it more successfully captures the mystery of this sacred moment in the Christmas story.

Rembrandt, a Dutchman, made over eight hundred paintings, drawings, and etchings of religious subjects. In this respect, he differed from his fellow Dutch artists. A small country on the North Sea just north of Flanders, the Dutch Republic was predominately Protestant. The Dutch Reformed church, unlike the Catholic church, did not commission artists to make murals or sculptures. Unlike Catholics, Protestants tended to look upon religious art as idol worship, and akin to magic or superstition. Dutch artists turned to other subjects, particularly scenes of everyday life like *Mother and Child* (fig. 19–8) by Pieter de Hooch and still lifes like *Vanitas* (fig. 19–9) by Maria

19–8 Pieter de Hooch, *Mother and Child*, ca. 1660. Oil on canvas, 4′ 8″ x 6′ 2 ¼″ (142 x 189 cm). Rijksmuseum-Stichting, Amsterdam.

19-9 Maria van Oosterwyck, *Vanitas*, 1668. Oil on canvas, 28 ¾″ x 34 ⅞″ (73 x 89 cm). Kunsthistorisches Museum, Vienna.

van Oosterwyck. The clients of Dutch artists were the wealthy middle classes—merchants, bankers, burgomasters, lawyers, doctors.

Rembrandt painted religious and nonreligious works. (Recall *The Mill*, his somber landscape discussed in Chapter 5, fig. 5-31.) His clients bought both kinds, although his art was not appreciated then as much as it is now. Rembrandt was unique in his time. Unlike most Dutch painters, he continued to make religious art; unlike most Baroque painters in Catholic Europe, he filled his pictures with ordinary people in ordinary settings. In other words, Rembrandt illustrated the stories of the Bible in the context of everyday life. He is perhaps the only artist, certainly the greatest, to express Christian content from a Protestant perspective.

Meanwhile, in the century of Rubens and Rembrandt, the field of science was gaining momentum. Francis Bacon, an English philosopher, outlined a method of science based on observation. Galileo Galilei, a Florentine astronomer, constructed a telescope that was able to verify Copernicus's theory that the earth revolves around the sun (Chapter 18). Johannes Kepler, a German mathematician, improved on Copernicus's idea by determining that the planets traveled in elliptical orbits. Isaac Newton, an English mathematician and inventor of calculus, brought together the research and thinking of the century and devised the law of gravity. This principle explains the movements not only of the planets, but of the whole universe.

The Enlightenment, Rococo, and Neoclassicism

The scientific boom of the 1600s led to the **Enlightenment,** a philosophy of life that flourished in the 1700s. Conservative Catholics and Protestants objected to the new science because they felt it challenged the beliefs and doctrines of the Bible. Enlightenment philosophers, however, believed that science not only revealed the secrets of nature, but improved people's lives. These philosophers (fig. 19-10) placed their faith in reason and science more than in religion. They thought of the universe as an intricate machine, like a huge clock. According to them, God started the clock, but then got out of the way. This concept of the universe was known as *Deism.* This religious view influenced America's founding fathers, including Benjamin Franklin and Thomas Jefferson.

Meanwhile, the major art style of the 1700s seemed to be going in a direction all its own. Called *Rococo,* this style did not reflect the views of Catholics, Protestants, or the Enlightenment. Instead, it reflected the views and lifestyles of the pleasure-seeking aristocracy. *The Swing* by Jean-Honore Fragonard (fig. 19–11) is typical of the style. Here is a scene of aristocrats at play

19–10 Voltaire.

19–11 Jean-Honoré Fragonard, *The Swing*, 1766. Approx. 32″ x 35″ (81 x 89 cm). Reproduced by permission of the Trustees of the Wallace Collection, London.

mostly primary. All of its forms, including the people, are starkly defined. They seem to be sculpted in stone.

The Oath of the Horatii was the first painting of a new style. Like Renaissance art (Chapter 18), this style was inspired by the themes and principles of classical art. Indeed, this new art became known as *Neoclassical.* Intellectuals approved of it as a symbol of seriousness and reason. The French middle classes saw it as an allegory of honor and patriotism. It also became a symbol of the French Revolution. David, who was personally active in the French Revolution, eventually became Napoleon's court painter.

Meanwhile, another revolutionary, Thomas Jefferson, was attracted to Neoclassicism when he was ambassador to France (1785–89). Jefferson was an architect as well as a statesman. He admired the Neoclassical buildings that were being erected in Paris (fig. 19–13) as part of Napoleon's grandiose plans to redesign the city. But Jefferson especially admired the Roman temple in Nîmes (fig. 18–19). He used this temple as a model for the Virginia State Capitol (fig. 19–14). Later, he used classical models for the campus of the University of Virginia. Thus Neoclassicism, the art of "noble simplicity and calm grandeur," was brought to America, where it became very popular. Architecturally, Washington, DC is the most Neoclassical city in the world. (Recall the design of the rotunda of the National Gallery, fig. 7–6.)

in a make-believe world. *The Swing* shares with Baroque art fluid brushwork and lively movement. However, its pastel hues, satiny textures, and delicate figures are much lighter in spirit. Its content is also lighter, if not "light-headed."

Later in the century, a reaction set in against Rococo. The **middle classes,** a segment of society that grew dramatically in size and power during the 1700s, felt that Rococo art did not represent their values. Johann Joachim Winckelmann, a German art historian, said that Europe needed an art of "noble simplicity and calm grandeur" to replace Rococo. The hopes of the public and Winckelmann were fulfilled in 1784 when Jacques Louis David unveiled his *The Oath of the Horatii* (fig. 19–12). Painted only eighteen years after *The Swing*, David's picture could not be more different. Rather than fun-loving aristocrats, *The Oath* features Roman warriors swearing an oath to fight a duel to the death. Off to the right their women are slumped in despair. Rather than a beautiful garden, it is set in a severely simple Roman court. It is also very different in style. Its darks and lights are strong. Its colors are

19–13 Pierre–Alexandre Vignon. Façade, La Madeleine, Paris, 1762–1829. 350′ (107 m) long, 47′ (14 m) wide, podium 23′ (7 m) high. Giraudon/Art Resource, NY.

19-12 Jacques Louis David, *The Oath of the Horatii*, 1784. Approximately 14′ x 11′ (4.2 x 3.3 m). Louvre, Paris.

19-14 Thomas Jefferson, State Capitol, Richmond, Virginia, designed 1785–1789. Metropolitan Richmond (VA) Chamber of Commerce.

19–15 Eugène Delacroix, *Arabs Skirmishing in the Mountains*, 1863. Canvas, 36 ⅜″ x 29 ⅜″ (92 x 75 cm). The National Gallery of Art, Washington, DC (Chester Dale Fund).

Romanticism, Realism, Impressionism, and Post Impressionism

As we have seen, cultural styles occur in cycles. The closer we get to the present, the shorter the cycles seem to become. The hopes of the Enlightenment and the artistic and philosophical ideals of Neoclassicism were dashed by the atrocities of the French Revolution and the failure of the Napoleonic Wars. Faith in reason was replaced by renewed faith in God, and especially by faith in emotion. This broad cultural movement was called *Romanticism.* Romanticism peaked in the first half of the 1800s. It could be said that Romantic writers and artists trusted their hearts rather than their heads.

Eugène Delacroix, a colorful man with strong emotions, was the idol of Romantic painters and poets. He loved the outdoors and wild animals. He preferred the simple life of rural peasants, especially the Moslem Arabs of North Africa. Ironically, Delacroix himself was considered a "man-about-town" in Paris. Paris, the capital of French culture, was anything but rural. But to Delacroix, Arabs were not only close to nature, but fierce and courageous warriors. Many of his attitudes are expressed in *Arabs Skirmishing in the Mountains* (fig. 19–15). The painting portrays a fierce battle in the wilderness at the foot of a mountain crowned with an ancient fortress. The colors—shades

19–16 Rosa Bonheur, *Gathering for the Hunt*, 1856. Oil on canvas, 30 ½″ x 58 ⅛″ (77 x 148 cm). Haggin Collection, The Haggin Museum, Stockton, California.

of red and orange set against a bright sky—are vivid. Delacroix's brush strokes, unlike David's, are as lively as the battle.

Marie Rosalle (Rosa) Bonheur's *Gathering for the Hunt* (fig. 19–16) expressed Romanticism and the love of the outdoors in more subdued ways. Instead of Arabs, guns, or falling horses, her picture contains a group of French farmers, horses, and dogs on a hazy autumn morning. The brushwork is calm. The colors are balanced between warm and cool. The composition is horizontal, stressing nature's breadth and continuity. Although *Gathering for the Hunt* is much less dramatic than *Arabs Skirmishing in the Mountains*, it is no less a tribute to nature. It also shows tendencies of another movement of the 1800s: *Realism.*

19–17 Gustave Courbet, *Burial at Ornans*, 1849. Approx. 10″ x 22″ (26 x 56 cm). Courtesy The Louvre, Paris and Réunion des Musées Nationaux.

19–18 Edouard Manet, *Gare Saint-Lazare*, 1873. Oil on canvas, 36 ¾″ x 43 ⅞″ (93 x 111 cm). National Gallery of Art, Washington, DC (Gift of Horace Havemeyer in memory of his mother, Louisine W. Havemeyer).

At mid-century, Gustave Courbet became the leader of the Realist movement. This movement, unlike either the Neoclassical or Romantic movement, portrayed life as it is, without nobility, drama, or condescension. His *Burial at Ornans* (fig. 19–17) is typical of Realism. In this homely scene, townspeople are gathered around a grave. There is no trace of beauty or sentiment. The public at the time thought that such a subject and treatment was too commonplace to be considered art.

Edouard Manet, another Realist, focused on the modern city and its people, especially the well-to-do middle class. Like the woman in *Gare* [Railroad Station] *Saint Lazare* (fig. 19–18), Manet's people often have the offhand look of someone caught in a moment of casual activity. The woman will go back to reading her book. The small girl gazing through the iron bars will lose interest as soon as the cloud of steam fades. Manet not only captured the spirit of everyday city life, he pioneered a fresh approach to painting. The figures, unlike those of David, Bonheur, and even Courbet, appear rather flat. As an American critic said, they look as if they had been clipped out of a sheet of tin. Their sense of flatness is partly due to a lack of shading. It is also due to the brightness of the colors and the bold pattern of the bars directly behind the figures.

19-19   Claude Monet, *La Grenouillère*, 1869. Oil on canvas, 29 ⅜″ x 39 ¼″ (75 x 100 cm). The Metropolitan Museum of Art, H.O. Havemeyer Collection (Bequest of Mrs. H.O. Havemeyer, 1929).

Manet's subject matter and style influenced still another art movement of the 1800s: *Impressionism.* You have already seen examples of Impressionism in this book: *Luncheon of the Boating Party* by Auguste Renoir (fig. 3-1), *The Bath* by Mary Cassatt (fig. 5-25), and *Waterloo Bridge* by Claude Monet (fig. 10-8). Monet's *La Grenouillère* (fig. 19-19), even more than those, illustrates the characteristics of the style. Like Manet's scene at the railroad station, *La Grenouillère* shows an offhand moment in the lives of some city dwellers, in this case at a river marina. But Monet went beyond Manet in his treatment of the subject. He constructed the entire picture out of nothing more than bright daubs of paint, a method known as *broken color.* When viewed at close range, the daubs tend to be more apparent than the forms. But when viewed at a proper distance, the daubs merge into recognizable trees, people, restaurant, and boats. This kind of painting is often more fresh and vibrant than traditional paint-

ings in which the forms are carefully drawn and the colors are carefully blended. The sensation of rippling water is especially effective.

In many ways Monet's real subject matter was light and color, or as he explained, "to reveal no more of reality than the shifting flux of appearances." Some of Monet's fellow painters broke away to become known as *Post Impressionists.* Although they learned about color from the Impressionists, these artists did not accept the idea that art was a "shifting flux of appearances." Paul Cézanne, in particular, desired a more structured art, "something solid and durable, like the art of the museums." The fruit and objects in his *Still Life with Apples and Peaches* (fig. 19-20) seem indeed to be solid and durable. Furthermore, Cézanne took pains to balance the visual weights and directions so that the composition would be as solid and durable as the fruit.

Georges Seurat, another Post Impressionist, admired the Impressionists' broken color. He tried to use it more systematically while composing his pictures with utmost care. (Recall his *Bathing at Asnières,* fig. 10–1.) Still another Post Impressionist, van Gogh, admired the brightness of Impressionists' colors. Unlike Monet, however, van Gogh used color to express emotions rather than just the changing qualities of reflected light. (Recall his paintings, figures 6–32 and 6–33.) Edvard Munch, like van Gogh, often used acrid color and rhythmical lines to express despair, as in his work *The Scream* (fig. 10–7).

The works of the Post Impressionist Paul Gauguin display the flatness of form found in the works of both Manet and Monet. But in Gauguin's paintings, such as his *The Vision After the Sermon* (fig. 19–21), this flatness is much more decorative. Like Cassatt and van Gogh, Gauguin was influenced by Japanese woodcuts (fig. 19–22). Japanese woodcuts had crisp outlines, flat patterns, and bold designs. (These woodcuts were of the ukiyo-e variety discussed in Chapter 16.) Japanese prints, which had been used by the Japanese to wrap their exports, were avidly collected by both Impressionists and Post Impressionists.

Thus by the end of the 1800s, art had reached a turning point. Specifically, it was turning away from the principles of pictorial realism that had been introduced by Donatello and Masaccio (Chapter 18) and that had dominated European art ever since. Instead of

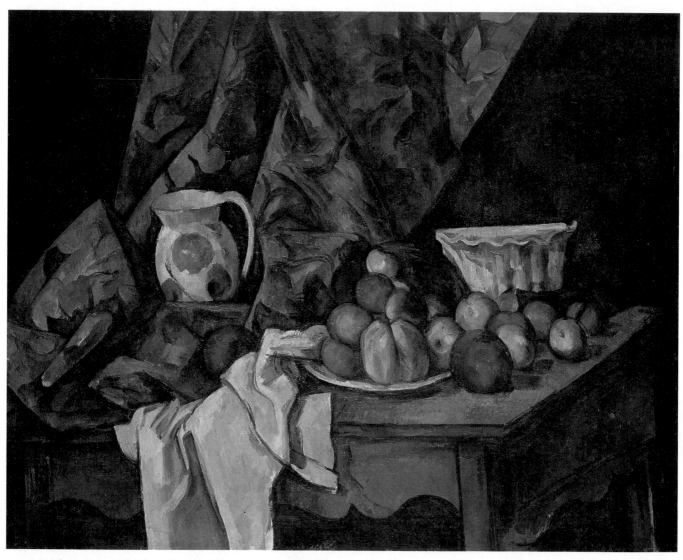

19–20   Paul Cézanne, *Still Life with Apples and Peaches,* ca. 1905. Oil on canvas, 32″ x 39 ⁹⁄₁₆″ (81 x 101 cm). National Gallery of Art, Washington, DC (Gift of Eugene and Agnes Meyer).

19–21 Paul Gauguin, *The Vision After the Sermon (Jacob Wrestling with the Angel)*, 1888. Oil on canvas, 28 ¾″ x 36 ¼″ (73 x 92 cm). National Gallery of Scotland, Edinburgh.

19–22 Katsushika Hokusai, *The Great Wave* from *Thirty-six Views of Mt. Fuji*, Tokugawa period. Woodcut, 10″ x 14 ¾″ (25 x 37 cm). Spaulding Collection, Courtesy, Museum of Fine Arts, Boston.

19–23 Frame construction.

realism, the values of compositional structure, of expressing emotion, and of pattern and color were beginning to take priority. These values were to be asserted with even greater force in the twentieth century.

The Industrial Revolution

In addition to art movements, the 1800s also witnessed the *Industrial Revolution.* Large industries replaced small shops, leading to a rapid changeover from handmade goods to mass production. People had more material things, like clothes, and more leisure time. Post-industrial society also seemed to experience boredom and a sense of rootlessness. All of these side effects of the Industrial Revolution are reflected in Manet's and Monet's people. Note the detached look of the woman at the railroad station and the impersonality of the people at the marina. The impact of the Industrial Revolution, however, was felt more directly in crafts (Chapter 13) and in architecture.

19–24 Joseph Paxton, interior view of the Crystal Palace, Hyde Park, 1851. From a print by R. Cuff after W. G. Brounger.

Architecture: Frame Construction

Up to the 1800s, major public buildings were mainly cathedrals, palaces, theatres, and town halls. All were built according to post-and-lintel and arch methods of construction (Chapter 18). The new industries of the 1800s required new kinds of buildings: factories, massive warehouses, railroad stations, department stores, and office buildings. Masonry architecture was too costly and inefficient for such buildings. Meanwhile, the new industry itself produced such things as standardized nails, rivets, boards, metal beams, and glass panes in huge quantities. This made possible a new method of construction: *wood frame* and *metal frame.*

In masonry methods of construction, walls, columns, buttresses, and so forth are used to support floors and ceilings. By contrast, in frame construction, many thin, relatively lightweight beams are joined to form a rigid framework like a cage. Walls are added to the framework as needed. The walls do not have to support the floors and ceilings. Therefore, these walls may be of any material, even glass. The earliest examples of frame construction were probably wood-frame houses (called "balloon-frame") that sprang up in the boom towns of the American Midwest in the early 1800s (fig. 19–23).

But the most significant early example was the Crystal Palace (fig. 19–24). This vast network of wood and iron beams and panes of glass housed the first World's Fair. Erected in 1851 in less than six months (compared to six decades for some Gothic cathedrals), this enormous glass-enclosed shed covered 800,000 square feet (74,000 square meters). The name Crystal Palace was invented by the fairgoers themselves, who had never seen anything so large or so radiant.

The next stage in the development of frame construction took place not in London or Paris, but in Chicago. During the 1880s, when Post Impressionists were pioneering new styles of painting, Chicago builders were pioneering new kinds of commercial construction. Because of the fire of 1871, new buildings were needed in Chicago's Loop (downtown). However, real estate prices in the Loop were extremely high. So, using the technology of metal-frame construction and the newly invented passenger elevator, Chicago architects developed a new type of building. This new construction took advantage of the inexpensive vertical

19–25   Louis Sullivan, Wainwright Building, St. Louis, Missouri, 1890–1891. Photograph: George Barford.

space of the sky instead of the costly horizontal space of the ground. It was called the skyscraper.

The style of this architecture was called the *Chicago School.* Significantly, it was relatively lacking in columns, arches, arcades, pediments, towers, and domes that people had grown to expect in public buildings. Louis Sullivan, the leader of the Chicago School, coined the motto "Form Follows Function." The design of a building would reflect its function and method of construction. His design for the Wainwright Building in St. Louis (fig. 19–25) became a classic for downtown office buildings. It is a simple cube with a two-story base, a middle section, and an ornate top. Sullivan never intended his motto to mean the complete elimination of ornament, however. He added his own decorative accents to all of his buildings. In the Wainwright, these are visible not only on the ornate top but also beneath each window and around the main entrance.

Art of the First Half of the Twentieth Century

The twentieth century, the century of two world wars, mass genocide, inflations, depressions, and "future shock," has also been a tumultuous one for art, especially during the years before World War I (1914–18). More changes occurred during that period than had occurred collectively in the previous four hundred years.

In 1905 a show in Paris contained such provocative paintings that a critic referred to them as fauves (French for *wild beasts*). They featured brilliant colors and simple shapes, like those in Henri Matisse's *The Red Room* (fig. 19–26). The paintings in that exhibit were truly "modern." In our day, they would not be out of place at all. But they seemed very wild to the 1905 public. Today, *Fauvism* refers to an important breakthrough in the modern movement, and bright colors, like those in *The Red Room*, are considered beautiful. Matisse took red, the most stimulating hue of all, and tempered it with the cool colors in the window, the color of the woman's blouse, and the blue of the many decorative lines. He thus brought the powerful forces of brilliant color under control. Matisse was a master at making balanced paintings with daring color combinations.

At about the time the Fauvists were shocking Paris, artists in Germany were beginning to rebel against traditional art and traditional ways of thinking about art. Some even organized into groups. One group in Dresden was called *Die Brucke* (The Bridge). Another in Munich was called *Der Blaue Reiter* (The Blue Rider). These artists and others active in the modern movement prior to the Nazi takeover (1933) were called *German Expressionists*.

19–26 Henri Matisse, *The Red Room*, 1908–1909. Oil on canvas, 71″ x 97″ (180 x 246 cm). ©1993 Succession H. Matisse/ARS, New York.

German Expressionists tended to use bright color and flat pattern to express personal feelings about life. Sometimes these feelings were sad or disturbing. As its title suggests, *Old Peasant Woman Praying* (fig. 19–27) by Paula Modersohn-Becker expresses melancholy as well as sympathy for peasant life. Its sincerity of expression is reminiscent of the work of van Gogh, who was one of the German Expressionists' heroes. If she had not died at age 31, Modersohn-Becker would probably have become a dominant figure in the Expressionist movement. *Masks* (fig. 19–28) by Emil Nolde, a member of Die Brucke, represents the German interest in primitive art and the grotesque. Serious themes drawn in harsh styles are typical of twentieth-century German art. For example, see Käthe Kollwitz's *Death Seizing a Woman* (fig. 12–24) and Ernst Barlach's *The Vision* (fig. 13–9).

19–27 Paula Modersohn–Becker, *Old Peasant Woman Praying*, ca. 1906. Oil on canvas, 29 ¾˝ x 22 ¾˝ (76 x 58 cm). The Detroit Institute of Arts (Gift of Robert H. Tannahill).

Although Wassily Kandinsky was Russian-born, he was the leader of Der Blaue Reiter and a highly respected member of the German Expressionist movement. Most significantly, Kandinsky was the first artist to pursue total abstraction. As early as 1910, he made a watercolor that was completely without subject matter and recognizable imagery. His *Sketch I for "Composition VII"* (fig. 19–29) is suggestive of turbulent emotion. The painting is typical of the freeform, coloristic abstractions that Kandinsky had developed out of the tradition of German Expressionism.

In 1905, the year of the Fauvists' show in Paris, Pablo Picasso was a struggling young painter in that city. His *The Old Guitarist* (reviewed in Chapter 6, fig. 6–30) is typical of his early work. Inspired by the success of Fauvism, Picasso embarked on a groundbreaking project of his own in 1906. The result of these efforts, *Les Demoiselles d'Avignon* (fig. 19–30), was

unveiled in 1907. In this painting, the human form is savagely distorted. Imagine how radical this painting must have seemed to the 1907 public. Even Matisse was shocked, calling it a mockery of the modern movement. Today, after nearly a century of modern art, it still looks disturbing. But *Les Demoiselles* is not without purpose. The figures and the background are consistently distorted to create a system of shallow peaks and valleys—as if the whole canvas had been wadded and then spread flat. *Les Demoiselles* became the prototype of a significant early twentieth-century style: Cubism.

19–29 Wassily Kandinsky, *Sketch I for "Composition VII"*, 1913. Oil on canvas, 30 ¼″ x 39 ⅜″ (77 x 100 cm). Städtische Galerie im Lenbachhaus, Munich.

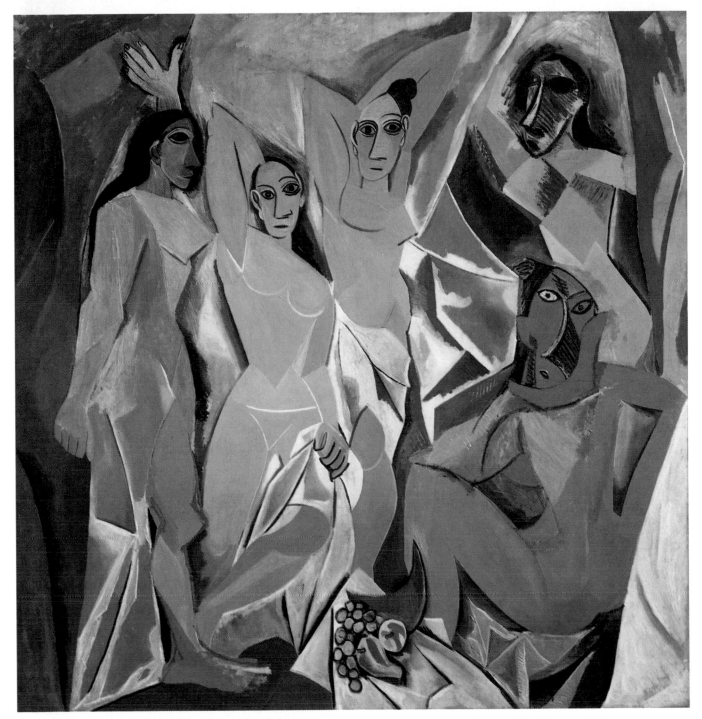

19–30 Pablo Picasso, *Les Demoiselles d'Avignon*, 1907. Oil on canvas, 96″ x 92″ (2.24 x 2.34 m). Collection, The Museum of Modern Art, New York (Acquired through the Lillie P. Bliss Bequest).

Try it Yourself

Can you think of any images on MTV that were inspired by early twentieth century art?

The first variety of Cubism was called *analytical* or *facet* Cubism. Picasso and French artist Georges Braque developed it between 1909 and 1912. A good example is Braque's *Violin and Palette* (fig. 19-31). In this painting, still life objects are broken up and recombined to fashion a network of semitransparent, tilted planes or *facets*—like the surface of a gem. Almost from the time it was introduced, facet Cubism influenced other artists. In *I and the Village* (fig. 19-32), Marc Chagall interspersed images from his memories of rural Russia among the transparent planes of facet Cubism. In *Brooklyn Bridge* (fig. 19-33), Joseph Stella used interlocking facets to express a kaleidoscopic impression of urban America.

In addition to these, we have seen examples in earlier chapters. Piet Mondrian's *Composition in Black, White and Red* (fig. 7-10) is an outgrowth of facet Cubism. Even sculpture was affected by Cubism. Recall Umberto Boccioni's *Unique Forms of Continuity in Space* (fig. 8-15) and David Smith's famous *Cubi* series (fig. 13-32).

Despite their success with facet Cubism, Picasso and Braque continued to experiment. In 1913, the two artists created the first collage (Picasso's *Still Life with Chair Caning*, fig. 12-41). Out of the collage medium, Picasso and Braque developed the second variety of

19-31 Georges Braque, *Violin and Palette*, 1909–1910. Oil on canvas, 36 ¼″ x 16 ⅞″ (92 x 43 cm). Guggenheim Museum, New York. Photograph: David Heald.

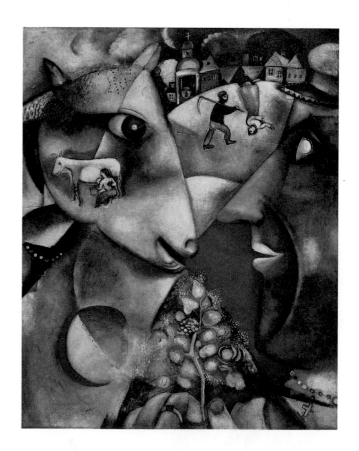

19-32 Marc Chagall, *I and the Village*, 1911. Oil on canvas, 6′ 3″ x 59″ (192 x 151 cm). Collection, The Museum of Modern Art, New York (Mrs. Simon Guggenheim Fund).

19-33 Joseph Stella, *Brooklyn Bridge*, 1917–1918. Oil on canvas, 84″ x 76″ (213 x 193 cm). Yale University Art Gallery (Gift of Collection Societe Anonyme).

Cubism, called synthetic Cubism. Unlike facet Cubism, *synthetic* Cubism features flat shapes and a variety of colors and textures, as in Braque's *The Table* (fig. 19-34). Picasso's whimsical *Three Musicians* (fig. 5-10) is another good example of the style.

About the only things the two varieties of Cubism share are sharp angles and interlocking design. Picasso often returned to Cubism, using a combination of facet and synthetic methods. He also experimented with a variety of styles, including a kind of realism (*A*

Woman in White, fig. 6–8). Meanwhile, Braque spent the rest of his career making still lifes like *The Table*.

Picasso and Braque had experimented with new approaches to style and media in the second decade of the century. At the same time Giorgio de Chirico experimented with a new approach to subject matter. The style of *The Mystery and Melancholy of a Street* (fig. 19–35) is not particularly new, especially for 1914. But the subject matter is new and unusual. There is a peculiar mix of figures and objects. A deserted square contains a child with a hoop, a gypsy wagon, and a long shadow. It is also strange, like a bad dream. Notice how the exaggerated perspective makes the square appear longer, and, therefore, emptier.

The paintings of de Chirico, along with the writings of Sigmund Freud, the father of modern psychology, influenced *Surrealism*. This art movement specialized in unconscious experiences and dreams. *The Persistence of Memory* (fig. 19–36) is a haunting painting by Salvador Dali. It is a good example of an art that often used extremely realistic methods to portray the mysterious and sometimes foreboding world of dreams. Dali's *Mae West* (fig. 10–12) is mysterious, but not necessarily foreboding.

Dada is the final early twentieth-century movement we will review. Dada was born in 1916, when the

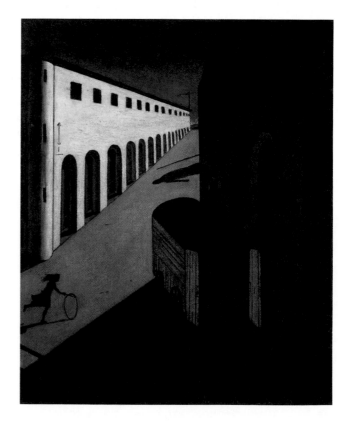

19–34 Georges Braque, *The Table*, 1928. Oil on canvas, 70 ¾″ x 28 ¾″ (180 x 73 cm). Collection, The Museum of Modern Art, New York (Acquired through the Lillie P. Bliss Bequest).

19–35 Giorgio de Chirico, *The Mystery and Melancholy of a Street*, 1914. Oil on canvas, 34 ¼″ x 28 ⅛″ (87 x 71 cm). Private Collection. Photograph courtesy Aquavella Galleries, Inc., New York.

19–36 Salvador Dali, *The Persistence of Memory*, 1931. Oil on canvas, 9 ½″ x 13″ (24 x 33 cm). Collection, The Museum of Modern Art, New York (Given anonymously).

First World War was raging. A small collection of artists, poets, and refugees had gathered in a cafe in neutral Zurich, Switzerland. Relatively sane at first, their activities soon became preposterous. They wrote poetry by cutting words out of seed catalogs, recited two or three poems simultaneously, wore silly costumes, danced to the sounds of a barking dog, and made collages out of random arrangements of garbage. The name Dada (French for *hobbyhorse)* was supposedly discovered by sticking a knife into a French-German dictionary and selecting the first word that appeared. Dadaists tended to thumb their noses at everything.

Dada spread to Paris, Cologne, Barcelona, and New York. The movement died in 1922 and left few lasting works of art. However, it did inject into the art world a taste for the absurd and ironic. (Some would say that Dadaists were simply reflecting the absurdity of modern life, especially the existence of war.) One artwork has become a symbol of the Dada spirit: *Fountain*, a urinal laid on its back and signed "R. Mutt" by Marcel Duchamp (fig. 19–37). Duchamp, a Frenchman who was working in New York at the time, tried to enter *Fountain* in a show, only to have it rejected. Today, however, Duchamp's artwork is part of a distinguished art collection.

19–37 Marcel Duchamp, *Fountain* (photograph by Alfred Steiglitz, reproduced in *The Blind Man, No. 2,* May 1917). Porcelain, 24 ⅝″ (63 cm) high. The Philadelphia Museum of Art (Louise and Walter Arensberg Collection).

19-38 Frank Lloyd Wright, Robie House, Chicago, 1909. Photograph: Thomas A. Heinz.

19-40 Walter Gropius, Shop Block, The Bauhaus, Dessau, Germany, 1925–1926. Photograph: George Barford.

19-39 Tribune Tower, 1925. North Michigan Avenue at the River (north bank). Architects: Hood and Howells. Rosenthal Art Slides, Inc. (Chicago).

Architecture of the First Half of the Twentieth Century

The Chicago School style of commercial building continued into the first decade of the 1900s. However, the most innovative architecture of this period came from a man who specialized in designing homes: Frank Lloyd Wright. His remarkable Robie House (fig. 19–38) has dramatic overhangs and horizontal lines. The house was designed to blend with the prairie landscape of northern Illinois. An apprentice of Louis Sullivan, Wright was the first architect, European or American, to create a distinctive style out of frame construction. The Robie House, like Matisse's *The Red Room* or Kandinsky's *Sketch I for "Composition VII,"* looks modern even today.

By 1910, the Chicago style of architecture was "out of style." The imagination of the American public had been captured by New York architects who were designing skyscrapers in various *eclectic* styles. Eclectic means borrowing from various sources, usually historical. Despite the fact that their buildings were modern metal-frame structures, New York designers decorated them with styles borrowed from Greek, Gothic, or Renaissance sources. The prime example of eclectic architecture is the Chicago Tribune Tower (fig. 19–39), designed by a New York architectural firm. This skyscraper was made to look like a Gothic tower, even including flying buttresses! Ironically, it was completed in 1924, the year of Sullivan's death. That year also marked the end of Sullivan's principle, "Form Follows Function" (at least for the time being).

While architects in America were rejecting Sullivan's principle, those in Europe were discovering

19-42 Le Corbusier, Villa Savoye, Poissy-sur-Seine, France, 1929–1930. Photograph: George Barford.

19-41 Ludwig Mies van der Rohe, *German Pavilion at the International Exhibition, Barcelona, Spain, 1929.* Demolished. Photograph courtesy Mies van der Rohe Archive, The Museum of Modern Art, New York.

it. In 1919, a special German design school called the *Bauhaus* (German for house of building) was established. Walter Gropius designed the school's main building, called The Shop Block (fig. 19-40). This building was the world's first multistoried permanent building to be faced with continuous walls of glass. Gropius was also the school's first director. Some of Europe's most famous modern painters, including Kandinsky and Mondrian, lectured there. Mondrian's style (Chapter 7) was especially influential in the design of modern architecture. The simple geometry of his art is reflected in the sleek lines of the German Pavilion (fig. 19-41). For 1929, this was a very modern-looking building. The architect was Ludwig Mies van der Rohe, a friend of Mondrian who became Bauhaus director after Gropius.

Also in 1929, construction began on Villa Savoye (fig. 19-42), designed by Le Corbusier (born Charles Eduoard Jeanneret). This multilevel house consisted of little more than a box on stilts. The forms of both the German Pavilion and Villa Savoye are simple, unadorned, and *modern*. Thus the legacy of modernism and design honesty, originally championed by Sullivan and Wright, had been passed on to European architects.

Art of the Second Half of the Twentieth Century

The end of the Second World War (1939–1945) marked a turning point in twentieth century history. The war ushered in the nuclear age. America and Russia—the so-called superpowers—took over the world stage. Since then many things have happened: the cold war, baby boom, arms race, space race, Korean and Vietnam wars, détente, budget deficit, the breakup of the Soviet Union, and others that we read and hear about daily.

The end of the Second World War also marked a turning point in the modern movement. Artistic leadership passed from Europe to America. Up to this time, American involvement in modern art was weak and tentative. No American had pioneered a new movement, invented a new medium, or even shocked the world with daring color. Only in the field of architec-ture had Americans demonstrated unusual creativity. Even this creativity, as we saw, was replaced by eclecti-cism. The most popular American art before the war was *Regionalism*. Regionalism was a conservative style that specialized in local themes, particularly the simple lifestyles of rural Americans. A good example is John S. Curry's *Baptism in Kansas* (fig. 10–6). Such a style, however, was inappropriate for the 1940s. Americans had been thrust into world leadership. They needed an art that would match this role.

In the mid-1940s, young American artists like Arshile Gorky began experimenting with abstract styles. His *The Liver Is the Cock's Comb* (fig. 19–43) represents the beginnings of a new American abstract art. However, the real breakthrough came in 1947 when Jackson Pollock began his famous "drip" paintings. Pollock would lay a canvas on the floor and walk across its surface spilling, pouring, and flinging paint as he went along (fig. 19–44). The dancing lines and rhythms

19-43   Arshile Gorky, *The Liver Is the Cock's Comb*, 1944. Oil on canvas, 6′ x 8′ 2″ (1.83 x 2.49 m). Albright-Knox Art Gallery, Buffalo, New York (Gift of Seymour H. Knox, 1956).

19-44 Jackson Pollock painting, 1950. Photograph ©1990 Hans Namuth.

19-45 Jackson Pollock, *Cathedral*, 1947. Oil, 75˝ x 35˝ (191 x 89 cm). Dallas Museum of Art (Gift of Mr. and Mrs. Bernard J. Reis).

in *Cathedral* (fig. 19–45) reflect the rhythms of Pollock's bodily movements as he produced the work.

No artist, European or American, had ever made a painting this way on such a scale and with such energy. Other American painters also began making bold abstract canvases. They did not necessarily use Pollock's methods, however. Their style was called *Abstract Expressionism* or *Action Painting*. An example is Hans Hofmann's *Flowering Swamp* (fig. 7–28). Abstract Expressionism was a new style on the world scene. Even European critics were impressed by this American creativity. Since that time American art has continued to rival, if not dominate, European art.

The spirit of American creativity did not end with Abstract Expressionism. Even as that style flourished, artists continued to experiment. They generated a seemingly endless supply of ideas. By the end of the 1960s, many different styles and kinds of art existed. You may recall the discussion of today's artistic variety in Chapters 1 and 2. You have already encountered many examples of postwar art in previous chapters. We will now summarize that art under a few headings and refer back to some of those examples.

Abstraction

Not all postwar abstract painting contains free forms made with bold gestures. In contrast to Abstract Expressionism, much Abstraction is geometric. It reflects an interest in principles of design, color effects, and even optical effects. See, for example, Josef Albers' *Homage to the Square: Glow* (fig. 1–6), Irene Rice Pereira's *Oblique Progression* (fig. 7–29), Bridget Riley's *Current* (fig. 8–17), and Tadasky's *A-101* (fig. 10–14). Abstraction was also expressed in postwar sculptures: Alexander Calder's mobile (fig. 9–1), Donald Judd's *Untitled* (fig. 9–3), Richard Lippold's *Number 7: Full Moon* (fig. 13–27), and Frank Stella's *Katsūra* (fig. 13–30).

Assemblage

The art of assemblage, invented by Picasso and Braque around the time of the First World War, experienced a revival after the Second World War. See Robert Rauschenberg's *Monogram* (fig. 1–11), Louise Nevelson's *Sky Cathedral* (fig. 13–28), and Joseph Cornell's *Object (Roses des Vents)* (fig. 10–4).

Pop Art

The *Pop Art* movement emerged in the 1960s. It satirized popular culture by borrowing themes from comics, advertising, and ordinary life. Examples are Roy Lichtenstein's *Whaam!* (fig. 1–7), Andy Warhol's *100 Cans* (fig. 10–3), Claes Oldenburg's *Shoestring Potatoes Spilling from a Bag* (fig. 13–52), and Marisol's *Women and Dog* (fig. 13–29).

Related to Pop Art are environment artworks like Red Grooms's *Ruckus Rodeo* (fig. 13–33) and George Segal's *The Diner* (fig. 13–37). Because of their humor

19–47 Le Corbusier, Unité d'Habitation, Marseilles, France, 1952. Art Resource, NY.

and nose-thumbing stance, Pop Art and related styles are sometimes called *neo-Dada* (new-Dada). They recall the spirit of the Dada movement.

Performance, Environment, and Concept

Some untraditional forms of art can also be seen as legacies of Dada: Joseph Beuys's *I Like America and America Likes Me* (Chapter 1), Christo's *Wrapped Coast* (Chapter 1), Mary Miss's *Field Rotation* (Chapter 13), and John Baldessari's *Cremation Piece* (Chapter 12).

Realism

Paradoxically, there has been a significant revival of realistic art (though not the same as the Realistic movement of the 1800s). Examples of this can be seen in Don Nice's *Longhorn Steer, Western Series, American Predella #6* (Chapter 8), Richard Estes's *Nedick's* (Chapter 10), and even in the sculptures of Marilyn Levine (Chapters 1 and 8) and Duane Hansen (Chapter 13).

19–46 Ludwig Mies van der Rohe, Lake Shore Drive Apartment Houses, Chicago, 1950–1952. Photograph: George Barford.

History/Aesthetic Experience 19.2

Art Style Report

Select an art style from this chapter. Research the art style and prepare a short style report. Include information such as where and when the style began, its purposes, possible influences, and characteristics, and world events and artists that helped shape it.

Architecture of the Second Half of the Twentieth Century

Major buildings require large investments of time, materials, and capital. Architects are less free to experiment than artists. Until very recently, postwar architecture has been dominated by Mies van der Rohe and Le Corbusier. These are the two European architects who were so inventive in the 1920s (see earlier discussion).

Fleeing the German Nazis, Mies moved to Chicago in the 1930s, where he taught architecture and received commissions for buildings. Living by his own motto, "Less Is More," he designed starkly simple, glass-enclosed towers, like the Lake Shore Drive Apartment Houses (fig. 19-46). Some praised him for returning the principle "Form Follows Function" to the city of its birth. Others criticized him for carrying it to extremes. Today, the Chicago skyline is dominated by buildings designed by either Mies, his students, or his imitators, like the architects of the Sears Tower (fig. 4-17). Indeed, skylines around the world have been affected by Mies's philosophy of less is more. In downtown Chicago that philosophy has been applied with taste and imagination. But in many other cities, it has resulted in glass-coated monotony and architectural boredom.

Contrast Mies's apartment towers with Le Corbusier's Marseille Apartments (fig. 19-47). Instead of narrow steel columns, the Le Corbusier building is supported on massive concrete buttresses. Rather than being on the same plane as the wall, its windows are deeply recessed. Rather than a smooth envelope of metal and glass, the wall itself is unadorned concrete.

Le Corbusier pioneered the use of *ferroconcrete* (concrete reinforced with metal rods). Like metal-frame, ferroconcrete has tensile strength; but like sculpture, it can be cast into a variety of forms. Notre-Dame-du-Haut Chapel (fig. 19-48), one of Le Corbusier's more dramatic projects, demonstrates the sculptural possibilities of ferroconcrete. Le Corbusier's style provided a postwar alternative to Mies's glass box.

19-48 Le Corbusier, Notre-Dame-du-Haut Chapel, Ronchamp, France, 1955. Photograph: George Barford.

19-49 Alternate view of Notre-Dame-du-Haut Chapel. Photograph: George Barford.

19–50 Eclecticism in art means combining elements of several different styles within one work of art. What is recognizable in this sculpture? How many different kinds of artistic techniques and materials has the artist used? Nancy Graves, *Akroterion,* 1989. Iron, stainless steel, carbon steel, aluminum, bronze, 60 ½″ x 56″ x 47″ (154 x 142 x 119 cm). Courtesy M. Knoedler and Co., New York.

Postscript: The Post-Modern Era

This chapter, starting where Chapter 18 ended, has reviewed the history of art from the 1600s to about 1980. You learned that the period known as Modernism started in the late 1800s. What about the present, though? Many people who study art and culture are saying that Modernism is over, that we live in a **postmodern** period. They believe that modern art, for example, has run out of steam, that it has not produced any significantly new ideas for two decades. The only rules left now are those that Modernism created, and even those are being broken. Look at the satire of Pop Art and other neo-Dada examples, and at the indications of a revival of Realism. In architecture, many young designers are rejecting the modern styles of both Mies van der Rohe and Le Corbusier. Indeed, some architects are even reviving eclecticism—one of Modernism's taboos. Charles Moore's Piazza d'Italia

19–51 Charles Moore, Piazza d'Italia. Perez Architects, New Orleans, Louisiana.

(fig. 19–51), a public square in New Orleans, is a fantastic collection of columns and arches reminiscent of Classical, Renaissance, and Neoclassical architecture.

Now, we are at the end of a century. Maybe this is not the time for new ideas; culture is being put on "hold." Unconsciously, perhaps, people are waiting for the beginning of the twenty-first century, when, like the beginning of the twentieth century, the mood will be right for cultural rebirth. Think how exciting it was for people like Henri Matisse, Paula Modersohn-

Becker, and Pablo Picasso! Weren't they fortunate to be the right age for the beginning of this century? Have you ever stopped to consider that you are the right age for the beginning of the next century? Some people in your generation will be the famous artists of the 2000s. Maybe one of them will be you.

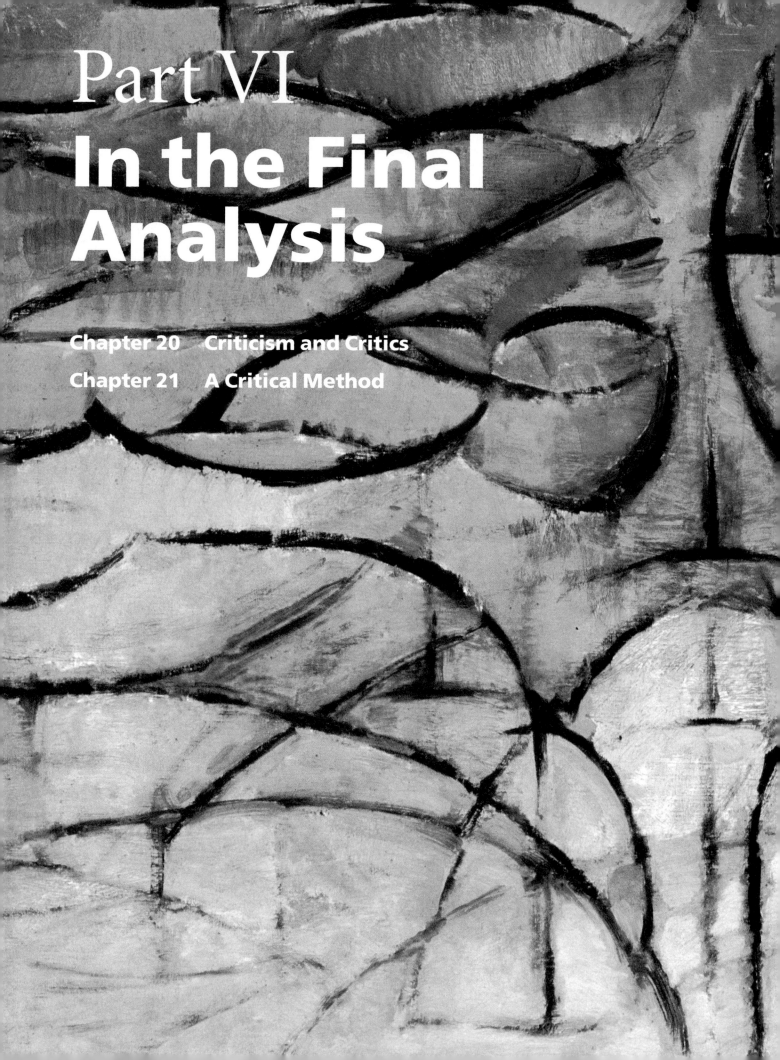

Part VI
In the Final Analysis

Piet Mondrian, *Flowering Apple Tree*, (detail), 1912, 30 ¾" x 41 ¾" (78 x 106 cm), Collection Haags Gemeentemuseum, The Hague.

Chapter 20
Criticism and Critics

20–1 One is a famous sculpture of a biblical hero by Michelangelo; the other is a popular comic by Charles Schulz. Although vastly different in form and content, both have a lot to offer if we take time to examine them critically. (left) Detail of Michelangelo's *The David,* 1501–1504. Marble. Gallery of the Academy, Florence. (right) Charles M. Schulz, *Charlie Brown,* 1973. *Peanuts* reprinted by permission of UFS, Inc.

We tend to think that ***criticism*** means disapproval. For example, if we don't like something, we "criticize" it. This use of the term is very limited, however. Have you ever thought that criticizing something can involve saying positive things about it? For example, when criticizing one of your drawings, your teacher may point out just its good qualities. In one sense, criticism is simply a discussion of the characteristics of something—particularly if that something is a work of art.

For our purposes, we will say that ***art criticism*** *is a systematic discussion of an artwork, usually involving four stages: (1) description, (2) analysis, (3) interpretation, and (4) evaluation.* Sometimes a criticism involves only the first three stages. Recall that in Chapter 3, you described Renoir's *Luncheon of the Boating Party.* In Chapter 10, you analyzed Seurat's *Bathing at Asnières.* In Chapter 15, you interpreted Russell's *The Toll Collectors.*

The next chapter will review evaluation, the fourth stage. Evaluation is something like judgment. Chapter 21 will also explain how to put the stages together to do a criticism.

In this chapter, we will examine several kinds of *professional* criticism, as well as the *critics* who write it. We will also discuss the reasons why we, who are not professional critics, should get involved in criticism.

Professional Criticism

Most of the movies you see were recommended to you by something or somebody. For example, an advertisement may have made a film sound exciting. You may have heard your friends say good things about the film. Usually, when you see the film, you are satisfied, but sometimes you are not. You soon learn that advertisements can be misleading. You also learn that just because other people like a film does not mean that you will.

Yet, to avoid wasting your time and money on every film that comes to town, you need to have some kind of information. One source of information is film criticism. Unlike an advertisement, film criticism does not always try to make you think a movie is exciting. Film critics are not obligated to sell movies, and they say negative things about them as well as positive things. Unlike the opinions of your friends, which are often very limited, professional criticism usually explains a great deal about a particular film. A criticism (sometimes called a *review*) will give you a better basis on which to make up your mind.

Most newspapers have film critics on their staffs who criticize the films playing in the local theatres. Each of the major networks has a film critic who reviews films, usually on the morning show. Even the cable networks and the public networks have such critics. These critics not only discuss the current films, but also show "clips" of those films. No doubt you have seen some of these critics. The interesting thing about all of them is that they often disagree.

Disagreement is especially apparent with two critics—Gene Siskel and Roger Ebert—who appear on camera together (fig. 20-2). Perhaps the most famous of all the national critics, Siskel and Ebert have their own half-hour show in which they criticize (or review) about five or six films. In addition, they write film criticism for two different newspapers. Siskel's column is in the *Chicago Tribune* and Ebert's is in the *Chicago Sun-Times*.

Newspapers like the *Tribune* and *Sun-Times* also contain reviews of art shows, books, musical programs, plays, and even architecture. In fact, every major city newspaper, and many smaller newspapers, review these kinds of things fairly regularly. If your hometown newspaper does not carry such reviews, you can find them in weekly newsmagazines like *Time* and *Newsweek*.

Try it Yourself

Look for criticisms of art, music, and theatre events in newspapers or magazines.

Also look for criticisms of current films. Bring the criticisms to class. Compare two criticisms of the same film by different critics. Do they say similar things? Do they agree in their judgments?

Look through some old magazines for criticisms of movies you have already seen. Did the judgment of the critic agree with your own judgment of the film?

20-2 Roger Ebert (left) and Gene Siskel (right). Scenic design: Michael Loewenstein. Courtesy Public Broadcasting System.

20–4 When you talk about your favorite rock bands, do you ever think that you might be engaged in a form of criticism?

Many publications specialize in just one of the arts. For those interested in the visual arts (painting, sculpture, photography, etc.), there are many magazines to choose from: *Arts, Artforum, Art in America, Art News,* and others (fig. 20–3). Those who want advice about recent books can read the *Saturday Review of Literature* and the *New York Review of Books. Downbeat* and *Rolling Stone* inform readers about the latest in jazz and rock music. *TV Guide* provides information and critical reviews about television programs. There are even publications for criticizing things that are not considered the arts. *Motor Trend* magazine, for example, offers critical reviews of the latest cars.

What is the purpose of all this criticism? We have already suggested a reason for reading film criticism. By providing information and an evaluation, a film criticism helps us decide whether or not we want to spend our own time and money on a film. If we read one of Mr. Ebert's criticisms, we benefit from the time he has taken to see and criticize a particular film. In a sense, a criticism is a *preview* that helps us make a more intelligent decision.

But there are other reasons for criticism besides saving us time and money. Good criticism also educates. It can point out things that we might overlook. It can encourage us to see artworks that are unusual or unfamiliar. In the long run, it can influence our taste. If the influence is good, we may grow to like more difficult things and to dislike childish things.

Professional criticism:

1. informs the public of ongoing artistic events—movies, art shows, musical programs, plays, books, and so forth;

2. provides information and evaluations of particular events so that people have a basis for making selections;

3. points out things in an artwork that might be ignored, thereby helping people to see more and enjoy more about a work;

4. introduces unfamiliar artworks, thereby encouraging people to see and enjoy things that they would ordinarily miss;

5. influences taste so that people may grow in their likes and dislikes.

Criticism Experience 20.1

Critique a Critic

Find a critical review of art, film, music or drama in a local or national publication. Critique the review, and write down what you think about it. Were the reviewer's arguments sound? Discuss your impressions in class.

Nonprofessional Criticism

As long as there are people who are paid to criticize artworks, why should other people—such as you and I —do it also? The rest of this chapter will be devoted to answering that question.

First, criticizing art is good training. Have you ever heard the saying: To learn physics, be a physicist? In this case, it would be: To learn about criticism, *be a critic,* or to learn about the field of art, *be an art critic.*

Second, the reasons for professional criticism that were mentioned earlier also apply to doing your own criticism. In this case, however, you would be making selections, discovering new things in familiar works of art, exploring unfamiliar works of art, and developing your taste without the help of professionals.

Third, criticism enables you not only to discover new things about artworks. It also helps you to organize this knowledge so that you can share it with others. Have you ever written about a popular song or talked about it with a friend? Did writing or talking about it increase your understanding of it?

Fourth, artworks, like good films, often deal with attitudes or ideas about life. Have you and your friends ever analyzed a good film? If so, you probably came up with a lot of interesting things to discuss. Analyzing an artwork can also generate ideas for sharing and discussion.

Finally, the more you learn about art and the ideas it expresses, the more you learn about yourself and your own ideas and feelings.

Summary

Art criticism, as defined here, is a systematic description, analysis, interpretation, and evaluation of an artwork. Sometimes criticism includes just the first three stages. A specific method of criticism will be explained in the next chapter.

Professional criticism of the arts can be found in newspapers, magazines, radio, and television. Basically, professional critics inform and educate the public through studying and writing about works of art.

People who are not professional critics can benefit from criticizing art in many ways: learning more about art and criticism, developing their own taste, and sharing experiences with others.

Chapter 21
A Critical Method

Chapter 20 explained the purposes of art criticism. Developing your own critical skills will contribute to your enjoyment and understanding of art.

In earlier chapters, you learned about the three stages in the critical analysis of artworks: *description* (Chapter 3), *analysis* (Chapters 9 and 10), and *interpretation* (Chapter 15). Criticism may include a fourth stage, *evaluation.* This process is explained at the end of this chapter.

The four stages of criticism are outlined here. The outline can help you understand and talk about art.

21–1 Honoré Daumier, *Connoisseurs,* ca. 1862–64. Crayon, charcoal, wash and watercolor. © The Cleveland Museum of Art, Dudley P. Allen Fund.

Description

Identify things about the work that you can see, name, and describe with certainty. Be sure your statements do not include opinions, evaluations or interpretations. Just record what is there.

Label Information

1. Title of work and artist's name.

2. When and where the work was created.

3. The medium (or media) used.

Subject Matter

1. Recognizable images such as people, buildings, trees, and other things.

   a) Describe what living forms are doing

   b) What is large/small, near/far, in front/behind

2. If the work consists of geometric shapes or free forms, indicate that and then go on to Art Elements.

Art Elements (Chapters 4–8)

1. **Line**

   Straight, curved, dotted, broken, wavy, swirling, jagged, textured, horizontal, vertical, diagonal, continuous, heavy, thin, etc. Are there lines that direct your attention from place to place?

   Contour lines or outlines.

   Implied by abrupt color, value, or texture changes.

2. **Color** and **Value**

   Are colors warm, cold, bright, dull, dark, light, opaque, transparent? Are they like or unlike real world colors? Is there a dominant color?

   Do values result from combinations of black and white, or shades and tints of color? Are value contrasts strong, soft, or both?

3. **Shapes** (two-dimensional) and **Forms** (three-dimensional)

   Are shapes representational, abstract, non-objective, organic, geometrical, open, closed.

4. **Textures**

   Are they visible in the work? Where? Are they rough, smooth, coarse, soft, bumpy, hairy, sandy?

   Are they *simulated* (you can see, but not feel it) or *real* (an actual part of the work you can feel)?

   Don't confuse texture with *pattern*, which is the repetition of some design in a recognizable order, such as polka dots or a checkerboard. Identify patterns.

5. **Space**

   Two-dimensional art (implied depth): Does space appear shallow or deep? Due to shading, colors that seem to advance/recede, foreshortening, linear perspective, aerial perspective, overlap, high-low placement?

   Three-dimensional art (real depth): Due to voids, concaves, convexes, volumes?

Analysis

How have the things listed under Subject Matter and Art Elements been organized or inter-related? How do they work together?

Similarities

1. Are some things similar in shape, color, texture, form, or size?

2. Are some lines similar in direction or kind?

Contrasts

1. Are there contrasts in color such as dull/bright, cool/warm, dark/light?

2. Are there contrasts of shape, form, texture, movement, size, complexity, simplicity?

Movement and Continuation

1. If movement is suggested in the work, which of the following devices is it due to: Repetition of something, alternating elements, progression from large to small, dark to light, etc., living forms doing something?

2. Are there elements that lead your eye through the composition—edges, rows of things, continuous lines, directional shapes, figures painting, or eyes looking in a particular direction?

Dominance

1. Is there some area, element, or arrangement that seems most important?

Balance

1. What contributes to balance in the composition?

2. Is balance symmetrical, asymmetrical, or radial?

Relationships

1. What are the relationships between the subject of the artwork and the art elements?

2. What are the relationships between the subject of the artwork and the medium or procedure used to produce it?

Interpretation

Use the information from your description and analysis to help you identify the *meaning* of the work (what it expresses about human experience).

Describe the expressive mood of the work: sad, happy, serious, lighthearted, calm, chaotic, depressing, ominous, sensual, somber, joyful, angry, aggressive, passive, tense, relaxed, etc.

Metaphor may help to get at meaning: In a metaphor, one thing is spoken of as if it is another, different thing, e.g., "He is a bull in a china shop." "Her voice is music." "Colors roll across the canvas in thunderous waves." "The red shape is a loose cannon among misty greens."

Hypothesis (an assumption or informed guess, about the meaning of the work)

Defense

1. Defend your hypothesis with evidence from your description and analysis.

2. Defend your hypothesis with evidence from other sources such as art history, past experiences the work reminds you of, or presumed purposes: to praise, criticize, predict, record an event, make a political or social statement, ridicule, and so on.

Evaluation

Based on your analysis in the first three stages, how would you judge the quality or success of the work? Judgment may be affected by the following criteria.

Craftsmanship—the degree of skill in use of media and procedures, and how well the medium relates to the subject matter and purpose of the artwork.

Design Quality—the degree of visual organization of the materials and elements that make up the work. Consider unity, variety, proximity, balance, dominance, and rhythm.

Expressiveness—how well the work expresses its subject, idea, or theme.

Personal Response—the extent to which the artwork provokes a personal response, one that could be shared with others.

Originality—the degree of uniqueness, imagination, and freshness in the artwork.

Comparison—how the work compares with other artworks of similar kind.

Using the First Three Stages of the Critical Analysis Model

The following examples will provide you with some guided practice in art criticism. This guided practice will help you learn how to gather facts about a work of art before you draw conclusions. Once you have learned the process, you will feel more confident in your ability to discuss and enjoy artworks.

An adequate analysis can be based on completion of the first three stages of the model. Because the last stage, evaluation, is difficult even for art professionals, it will be discussed separately.

Hemlock in November

Description. You will find it easy to describe this work by Charles Burchfield, a well-known Regionalist painter. It is a watercolor of a wooded grove. It includes an evergreen tree identified as a hemlock in the title (fig. 21–2). The hemlock is surrounded by trees that are losing their leaves. The forms of the tree and stump in the foreground appear three-dimensional. These forms are emphasized by warm, dark colors and strong textures. The clearing in the background contains some different varieties of evergreens. It is flooded with white light that filters down through the trees. The painting includes a mixture of warm and cold, transparent and opaque colors. Colors have been tinted and shaded. The space in this painting appears deep because of overlapping, the diminishing sizes of the trees, and aerial perspective.

Analysis. The first thing you see in this painting is the hemlock. The hemlock contrasts with the surrounding trees because of its size, textures, green needles, and dark colors. The entire tree is silhouetted against a cool, silvery light. The rhythm of the branches and needles causes a lively upward movement. Due to these factors and its slightly off-center placement, the hemlock is the dominant form in the composition.

Light is everywhere, filtering down through the branches and giving the tree trunks a silvery glow. Clusters of the evergreen's needles reflect the light. The light becomes a background haze into which distant trees disappear. The brown, gold, yellow, and white foreground colors are repeated in the fallen leaves, the leaves on the trees at each side of the picture, and in the top branches of the hemlock. These colors produce a framing effect around the painting.

The bases of the trees on each side of the hemlock are progressively higher on the picture plane as they go back in the distance. This progression causes a directional flow from the foreground to the background. The triangular shape of the leaf-covered foreground reinforces this flow and leads to a small evergreen shimmering with light.

Relationships between subject and elements can be seen in the artist's use of predominantly cool colors and the transparent gray washes to suggest a cold fall day. Relationships between subject and procedure are seen in the heavy lines, warm colors, and rhythmical brushstrokes applied to the hemlock.

Interpretation. Our description and analysis suggest several meanings for *Hemlock in November.*

1. It is about the effects of seasonal change upon the natural environment.

2. It is about the mood of a cold fall day in a wooded grove.

3. It is about the hemlock's defiance of approaching winter.

We will defend the first hypothesis for our example of interpretation. The picture is filled with a cool, hazy kind of light that we associate with cold fall days and the feeling that winter is in the air. The trees have lost or are losing their leaves, which have been transformed from green to the colors of fall. Even the trunks of the bare trees and some of the hemlock's needles have been transformed to a silver-white color by the light. However, the green of the hemlock and the lively upward movement of its branches are a promise of continuing life. These are all effects that we associate with seasonal change.

What description and analysis information would you use to support either of the other hypotheses?

21-2 Charles Burchfield, *Hemlock in November*, 1947–66. Watercolor, 42˝ x 32 ½˝ (107 x 83 cm). Private Collection. Kennedy Galleries.

21–3 Robert Stefl, *Illinois Landscape #14*, 1988. Color photograph cibachrome, 11″ x 14″ (28 x 36 cm). Courtesy of the artist.

Burchfield's painting expresses the effects of fall and a seasonal change upon the environment. *Illinois Landscape #14* (fig. 21–3) by Robert Stefl, a contemporary photographer, refers to the effects of winter on the land. Like a painting, a photograph can express ideas and feelings that may be teased out in the process of critical analysis.

Illinois Landscape #14

Description. This photograph by Robert Stefl depicts a gently rolling field lined with rows of corn stubble that pokes through and casts shadows on wind-packed snow. On the horizon are three leafless black trees and several clumps of grass. Warm browns appear in the rows of stubble that extend in rough lines across the field, and in the clumps of grass on the horizon. The distant trees support angular branches that end in a maze of feathery lines. The sky and the snow-covered field are filled with light values of gray-blue and white. There is an illusion of deep space.

Analysis. When you first look at *Illinois Landscape #14*, your eyes follow the converging lines of corn stubble. These lines direct your attention to the tree on the right. The branches of the lone tree seem to point toward the two trees on the left. The spaces between the rows of stubble become progressively wider from the left to right. They cause a wave-like flow across the foreground to the widest rows on the right. These rows then direct your eyes back to the lone tree.

The warm browns of the corn stubble and grass contrast with the cold colors in the field and sky. However, the cold colors dominate the warm colors. The linear movement of the rows and one-point perspective direct our attention to the trees and the empty space between them. The silhouetted trunks of the trees and the fragile lines of their branches contrast with the cold gray-blue of the sky. The texture of the snow looks crisp and crunchy to the step.

Interpretation. We will hypothesize that *Illinois Landscape #14* expresses the wonder of the trees' survival under very threatening conditions.

The composition of this photograph directs our attention to the trees. The most obvious hardship they must endure is the cold grip of winter, which is evident in the bleakness of the land and the isolation of the trees. A second threat comes from man, who continually clears the land for farming. The rows and furrows extend up to and beyond the trees. The trees are the last sentinels of a grove that existed before the field was cleared. They too may feel the axe.

Before you read the title of figure 21–4, can you guess what the subject matter is? Abstract works of art may change the form of the object to emphasize qualities that you normally might not see. Even though a work is not representational, you can respond to its visual forms. The critical analysis process can help you explain the organization of abstract works and propose meanings for them.

Flowering Apple Tree

Description. This oil painting by Mondrian, a major figure in the Modern movement, consists of lines and primarily geometric shapes, rather than recognizable objects. The lines vary in thickness and intensity. They are mostly curved or arched. Some are horizontal and vertical. The colors are dull grays, blue-greens, and brownish hues with black line. The outlined shapes are flat, and some are leaflike. There is a minimal sense of spatial depth and no perspective depth, which you can see in *Hemlock* and in *Illinois Landscape #14*.

Analysis. You can identify similarities and contrasts in this work. The orderly, repeated lines create rhythmical movements up, down, left, and right on the surface of the painting. The vertical lines in the lower central area direct your attention to the enclosed leaflike shapes. An area in the center, with lines radiating from it, tends to be a focal point, creating a feeling of formal balance. The two-dimensional shapes and the colors are all at about the same value level, making the composition appear relatively flat. One-half of the painting is approximately the same as the other, so the work is basically symmetrical.

21–4 Piet Mondrian, *Flowering Apple Tree*, 1912. 30 ¾ ˝ x 41 ¾ ˝ (78 x 106 cm). Collection Haags Gemeentemuseum, The Hague.

Interpretation. *Flowering Apple Tree* is about the rhythm, movement, and balance that can be found in the structure of a tree. The title indicates that the painting is based on a tree. Knowing that, we can relate the central vertical and upward curving lines to a tree trunk and branches, and the outlined shapes to leaves. Since there is no definite tree form in the work, we can concentrate on the rhythmical movements caused by the lines and shapes.

Evaluation

So far, our examples of critical analysis have covered the first three stages of the critical analysis outline. Often, these stages are enough to allow you to explain and understand a work of art. However, evaluation is a step that can let you estimate the quality or lasting importance of an artwork. We will use *Hemlock in November* to illustrate the process of evaluation.

Craftsmanship. Craftsmanship is demonstrated by the artist's skillful control of washes. The washes effectively suggest the changing light in a heavy growth of trees. To suggest deep space, Burchfield used contrasts of opaque and transparent colors and aerial perspective. The forms are crisp and the colors are fresh—a favorable characteristic of watercolor.

Design quality. Our analysis of *Hemlock* indicated that all of the parts are effectively organized around the dominant evergreen tree. The stronger the design of an artwork is, the less aware we are of individual parts, and the more we can focus on the meaning of the work.

Expressiveness. This area of evaluation involves a judgment about the strength of human feelings aroused by the work of art. Sometimes our reactions to an artwork are based on what it reminds us of. Our feelings are related more to that experience or event than to the art form. A successful work should arouse feelings that come from the work itself. The artist organizes symbols and forms to express human feelings that are connected to some experience. For example, assume that *Hemlock in November* is about the effects of seasonal change upon the natural environment. How successful do you feel the painting is not only in arousing your feelings about seasonal change, but in providing you with fresh insights about this theme?

Originality. Originality is closely associated with expressiveness, and involves a judgment about the uniqueness or freshness of an artwork. Is the hemlock tree in Burchfield's painting an unusual interpretation? Or is it what you would expect to see in a calendar or greeting card picture of the same subject? Have you seen similar approaches to lighting, color, and form in other pictures representing late fall? Are there unique qualities here?

Comparison. Comparing an artwork with historical examples is more a task for art professionals such as museum directors and art critics than it is for nonprofessionals. Well-known works that have stood the test of time provide touchstones for judging the quality of other works with similar subjects in similar styles.

Pine Trees with Setting Sun (fig. 21–5) by Vincent van Gogh is a work that has many similarities to *Hemlock in November*. Although the paintings were done with different media (the van Gogh is oil, the Burchfield is watercolor), they are similar in subject and style. Both are landscapes with trees as a principal subject. Both emphasize the vertical. Both emphasize the effects of light, and both employ lively brushwork and exaggeration— seen particularly in the trees—to make the picture vivid.

Art professionals would probably prefer the van Gogh for a number of reasons. The brushwork is more animated. It seems to come from within the forms and to enliven the whole picture. The painting also contains more variety. Notice the asymmetrical composition and the different directions of the branches. Note especially the way in which the diagonal and horizontal branches of the near tree provide a counterpoint to the vertical emphasis. Despite its variety, the van Gogh is at least as well organized as the Burchfield.

Still, on the grounds of craftsmanship, design quality, and expressiveness, you might prefer the Burchfield. This is your right. However, imagine you are a museum director with a large budget to spend on art, and can afford the best. You no doubt would select the van Gogh over the Burchfield for a number of reasons not seen in the works themselves. Some things that professionals consider before purchasing an artwork are:

1. how well-known the artist is;

2. the importance of the artist's achievements;

3. the importance of the artwork in the history of art;

4. the recognizability of the artist's style;

5. the demand for the artist's work;

6. the probable lasting value of the work;

7. the opinions of other curators, art dealers, collectors, and investors; and

8. the freshness of treatment of an idea, a medium, a style, or a technique.

Given these reasons, the van Gogh wins easily. Consider reason 8, for example. Van Gogh pioneered an expressionistic style in the late 1880s when such a style was not popular. For all of his efforts, he received almost no recognition during his lifetime. His style was too fresh for the times. But in the early part of this century, his work became celebrated. Van Gogh influenced and paved the way for artists like Burchfield in this century. Reasons 1, 2, and 3 also weigh heavily in the choice of the van Gogh over the Burchfield.

21–6 *Hall of Bulls,* left wall, Lascaux, ca. 15,000–13,000 BC. Dordogne, France. Courtesy of Scala/Art Resource, NY.

Conclusion

We have reached the end of our text, but we have not concluded the story of art. That story begins with the images made on cave walls by prehistoric people, and continues through the cultures of the world, past, present and future. We began with questions about what art is, how and why it is created. In the process of answering these questions, you learned about the elements and principles of design and how the artist uses these elements to create art. You have learned about the wide variety of art forms and art media, and seen how artists use them in their work.

As an art student, you have learned how to use the elements and principles and some art media in your own artwork. You have been introduced to the art history of both Western and non-Western cultures to help you learn about works of art: where, when and why they were created, the style of art, and cultural influences upon artists. Throughout the text, you have used information obtained from all of these experiences to practice art criticism. As you have learned, art criticism is concerned with questions such as: What should I look for in the work? How is it organized? What does it mean? How successful is the work? Most importantly, you have discovered how to learn from the nonverbal language of art. Art provides all civilizations of the world with a means of communication.

Now that you have completed the book, we are certain that you not only know more about art, but also are better prepared to continue learning from it. No one can predict just what forms art will take in the future, or what social functions it will serve. However, art has been important in human affairs over the past 3,000 years. The diversity of forms it has taken suggest that the art of your future will be both exciting and important. We hope that you'll continue to look for ways art can help you learn about and enjoy the world around you.

Criticism Experience 21.1

Analyzing an Artwork

Write a critical analysis of an artwork that has not been discussed in class. Use the four-stage model provided in your text.

Try it Yourself

Continue your role as a museum director. How would you choose between the Burchfield and the Stefl? Between the Burchfield and the Mondrian? You may have to do a little research.

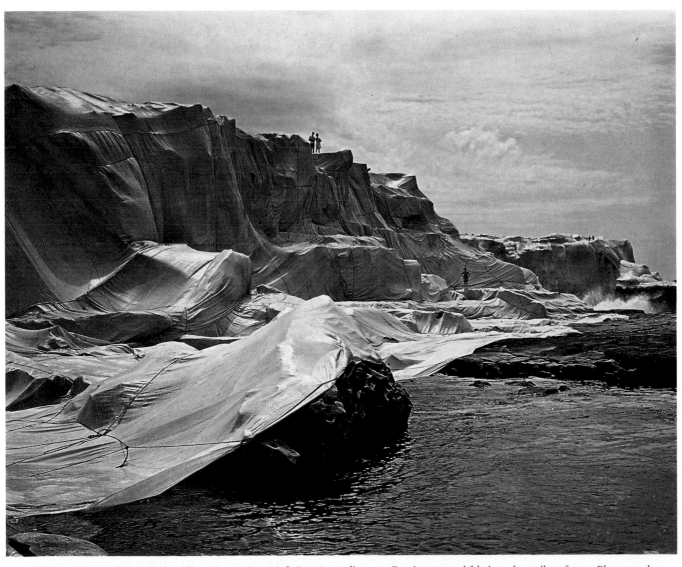

21-7 Christo, *Wrapped Coast, One Million Square Feet, Little Bay, Australia*, 1969. Erosion control fabric and 35 miles of rope. Photograph: Harry Shunk. ©Christo 1969.

Glossary with Pronunciation Guide

abstract art Art stressing the form of its subject rather than its actual appearance. The subject is broken down into elements: line, shape, etc., not necessarily resembling the subject itself.

Abstract Expressionism A twentieth century style in which feelings and emotions are emphasized. Accident and chance are stressed rather than accurate representation of subject matter.

abstract line Lines found in very abstract and nonobjective artworks which do not describe anything. They are meant to be seen only as line.

acrylic paint A synthetic painting medium in which pigments are mixed with acrylic, a plastic emulsion that acts as a vehicle and a binder.

aerial perspective The diminishing of color intensity to lighter and duller hues to give the illusion of distance.

aesthetic (es-*thet*-ik) The theory of perceiving and enjoying something for its beauty and pleasurable qualities. This theory tries to explain and categorize our responses to art forms.

aesthetic response A response that occurs when something is seen and enjoyed for its own sake, or for its beauty and pleasurable qualities.

analogous colors Colors that are next to each other on the color wheel and are closely related, such as yellow, yellow-orange, yellow-green and green.

approximate symmetry The use of forms which are simillar yet different, on either side of a vertical axis.

aquatint A form of intaglio printmaking in which resin is melted on the metal plate to resist the biting action of acid so that tonal areas can be produced when the plate is printed. May be combined with engraving and etching on the same plate.

arabesque (*air*-uh-besk) A flowing, intricate pattern of stylized organic motifs arranged in symmetrical designs.

arcade A series of repeated arches, in some cases supported by columns.

arch A masonry construction in which a number of wedge-shaped stones, held in place by pressing against one another, form a semi-circular curve.

architect A person who designs and directs construction of buildings and environmental areas.

architecture The art and science of designing and constructing buildings.

aristocracy A privileged class whose wealth and privileges are inherited from previous generations.

armature A framework used to support material being modeled in sculpture.

art criticism A systematic discussion of the characteristics of an artwork, usually involving four stages: description, analysis, interpretation and judgment.

art education An area of education which provides programs in art production, art history, aesthetics and art criticism for students in the public schools.

art elements The sensory elements including line, shape, form, color, value, texture and space that are used to create artworks.

artist A person who makes artworks and is skilled in composing subject matter and the art elements with a variety of art materials and procedures.

artwork An object or performance that satisfies conditions or requirements recognized by the art world as necessary for an artwork.

assemblage An artwork composed of objects, parts of objects or materials originally intended for purposes other than art.

asymmetrical balance A feeling of balance attained when the visual units on either side of a vertical axis are actually different but are placed in the composition to create a "felt" balance of the total artwork.

aqueduct A Roman masonry structure supporting a trough for carrying water.

balance A principle of design referring to the arrangement of visual elements to create stability in an artwork. There are three kinds of balance: symmetrical, asymmetrical and radial.

Baroque (bar-*oak*) A period and style in seventeenth century European art in which painters, sculptors and architects used dramatic movement, light, soaring spatial illusions and ornate detail to encourage emotional involvement.

barrel vault A semicircular masonry ceiling.

bas relief (*bah* ree-*leef*) See *low relief.*

batik (ba-*teek*) A method of dyeing cloth using removable wax to repel the dye on parts of the design where dye is not wanted.

Blaue Reiter, Der (*blah*-way *right*-er, dehr) (The Blue Rider) A group of Munich artists including expatriates such as the Russian Wassily Kandinsky, and the Swiss born Paul Klee. Concerns were with presentation of subjective feelings toward reality, and imagination. This group greatly influenced the development of Modern art.

Brücke, Die (*broock*-eh, dee) (The Bridge) A small group of German artists led by Ernst L. Kirchner who emphasized violent color and distortion of features in their paintings and woodcuts in protest of the economic and social conditions in Germany prior to World War I. Emil Nolde was also a member.

Buddha (*boo*-dah) Any Buddha sage who has achieved enlightenment in accordance with the teachings of Gautama Siddhartha, founder of Buddhism.

Buddhism (*boo*-dizm) A religious belief based on the teachings of Gautama Siddhartha, who held that suffering is a part of life but that mental and moral self-purification can bring about a state of illumination carrying the believer beyond suffering and material existence.

calligraphy Handwriting or letters formed by hand. Elegant penmanship usually featuring a flowery, precise line.

came Channeled lead strips, either H or U shaped, used in stained glass windows to join the pieces of glass together. The U shape is used on outer edges of the design and the H for all other purposes.

caricature A likeness of a person, distorted by exaggerated features or mannerisms.

cartoon A comic strip or caricature showing some action, situation or person. May be single or multiple frame. In painting, a full-size preliminary drawing from which a painting is made.

carving The process of producing a sculpture by cutting, chipping or hewing wood or stone.

casein (*kay*-seen) A type of paint made from milk or cheese protein used to achieve a transparent or opaque effect.

casting The process of making forms by pouring a fluid substance such as molten metal, liquid plaster or plastic into a mold.

ceramics Objects made of clay and fired in a kiln to a permanent form. Ceramics are often decorated with glazes and fired again to fuse the glazes to the clay body.

chalk A stick of color including a binder, preservative, chalk and pigment, mixed with water, formed into sticks and dried.

chiaroscuro (key-ah-ross-*kyoo*-roh) From the Italian meaning "light-dark." The use of value contrasts to represent the effects of light and shadow.

cire perdue (sear per-*dew*) See *lost-wax process*.

Classical The art of ancient Greece produced in the 400s and 300s BC. Any art form influenced by ancient Greek or Roman examples.

cloisonné (kloy-soh-*nay*) A decorative enameling technique in which thin metal strips are attached to a metal base to outline design areas, or cloisons, which are then filled with enamels and fired.

close-up In the graphic arts (including comic strips) figures and objects are made large to appear close to the viewer. Also a film shot.

closed form Forms in painting and sculpture that have few or no openings, or negative shapes.

closure The tendency to complete partial forms or shapes by seeing lines that do not exist.

collage A two-dimensional composition made by gluing various materials such as paper, fabric, etc., on a flat, firm surface. Introduced by the Cubist artists Picasso and Braque.

color An element of design with three properties, hue, value and intensity. Also the character of surfaces created by the response of vision to wavelengths of reflected light.

commemorative art Art that is produced in remembrance of something or someone.

complementary colors Two colors which are directly opposite each other on the color wheel, meaning they are in extreme contrast with each other.

composition The act of organizing the elements of an artwork into a harmoniously unified whole.

concave Surfaces that are hollow or curved inward.

concept art A style of the 1970s emphasizing the idea behind the work of art rather than the work itself. Artists tried to deemphasize the artwork in favor of the concept to demonstrate that the conception of the work is more important than the product.

conditions Requirements that philosophers and critics of art generally agree something must fulfill to be an artwork.

construction A sculpture built by connecting several or many parts to one another. The parts may be made of a single material or of a variety of materials. *Number 7: Full Moon* by Richard Lippold (p. 168) is an example.

contemporary art Artworks created in our own time.

content The essential meaning of an artwork interpreted by an individual or critic.

continuation An element or series of elements that passes through a composition that may direct the viewer's attention, and contribute to unity.

contour line Lines that define the outer edges of forms and surfaces within a form such as shapes or wrinkles and folds. Used in contour drawings to suggest depth in addition to height and width.

contrast A principle of design that refers to differences between elements such as color, texture, value and shape. A painting might have bright colors contrasted with dull or angular shapes contrasted with round ones.

converging lines In perspective, lines that represent the parallel edges of an object are drawn to converge to a vanishing point.

convex Surfaces that curve outward.

cool colors Those colors in which blue is dominant found on the right side of the color wheel.

corbeled arch An arch constructed from an overlapping arrangement of stones, each layer projecting a bit beyond the row beneath it, and held in place by the pressure of the stones against one another.

Corinthian One of the classical styles of ancient Greek architecture featuring tall, slender columns topped with ornate capitals.

Counter Reformation The reform movement in the Catholic Church following the Reformation.

crafts Works of art that may be expressive, but generally have utilitarian purposes. This includes fiber arts, ceramics, metalsmithing, fabrics, furniture, basketry, etc.

crosshatching Shading created by crossed parallel lines.

cross vault A masonry ceiling consisting of two barrel vaults intersecting at right angles.

crusade A military expedition of Christian knights against the Moslems in Palestine and/or other parts of the Near East from the eleventh through the thirteenth century.

Cubism A twentieth century art movement developed mainly by Picasso and Braque in which the subject matter is broken up, analyzed and reassembled in an abstract form, emphasizing geometric shapes.

culture The attitudes, values, beliefs, patterns of behavior, social organization and concepts of reality of a given people which persists through time.

descriptive lines Lines created with a variety of tools; can be outlines, contour lines, single lines or hatching.

design The plan the artist uses to organize the art elements (line, shape, form, space, etc.) in a work of art to achieve a unified composition.

dome A hemispherical vault or ceiling over a circular opening.

dominance A concept of design which suggests that one element, or a combination of elements, attracts more attention than anything else in a composition. The dominant element(s) is usually a focal point in a composition and contributes to unity by suggesting that other elements are subordinate to it.

Doric The earliest of the classical styles of ancient Greek architecture.

dynasty The period of time when a certain family ruled.

earthenware Ceramic ware that is made from natural clay. It is soft, porous and fired at low temperatures.

eclectic Borrowing from many sources, particularly of architecture, which imitates styles of the past.

edge Where one shape ends and another begins, resulting in implied line.

elements of design Space, line, shape, form, color, value and texture. The tools the artist works with to create an artwork according to the principles of design.

ellipse An oval shape produced by drawing an elongated circle so that it appears to be viewed from an angle. A foreshortened circle that is longer in one dimension than it is in the other.

emulsion A liquid in which droplets of a second liquid are suspended until painted on a surface where they dry and bond together.

engraving A technique in which a design is incised in a plate of metal, wood or plastic. A print is then made from the plate.

Enlightenment A philosophical movement of the eighteenth century marked by faith in science and reason.

environmental art An artwork which is part of the environment surrounding it, or which provides an enclosed environment that viewers can enter; or an arrangement which the viewer can walk around or through.

etching A technique in which a metal plate covered with an acid-resistant coating is incised by needle scratches. The plate is then immersed in acid and a print is made from the plate.

Expressionism An art movement developed at the end of the nineteenth and the beginning of the twentieth century in Germany. This style emphasized the expression of the artist's emotions through the use of strong color, exploitation of media and the use of suggestive and symbolic imagery.

expressive lines Lines that are produced to express an idea, mood or quality (e.g., graceful, nervous, delicate, aggressive, etc.).

eye level A horizontally drawn line that is even with the viewer's eye. In landscape scenes it can be the actual horizon line, but can also be drawn in still life.

façade (fah-*sahd*) The front of a building. The façade accents the entrance and usually prepares the viewer for the architectural style inside.

fashion design Creating and producing apparel for every occasion.

Fauvism (*foe*-vizm) An early twentieth century style of painting developed in France. The artists, led by Matisse, used brilliant and explosive color to express the inner quality of their subjects rather than how they appeared in nature. They were called Fauves, or "Wild Beasts" because critics thought they used colors in a violent uncontrolled way.

ferroconcrete A principle of construction employing concrete reinforced with steel rods.

figure-ground The perceptual tendency to divide visual patterns into two kinds of shapes with the figure(s) appearing to be on top of, and surrounded by, the ground. In the pictorial arts, the relationship between images and the background. Figure and ground are often referred to as positive shape and negative shape.

film and television graphics The design and production of films and tapes.

fine artist Person skilled in the making of symbols, the use of media and techniques, and one who creates compositional arrangements that demonstrate uniqueness of interpretation and individuality of technique.

flat wash An area of thin paint that is uniform throughout.

flying buttress An external support for the wall of a Gothic cathedral consisting of a half arch connected to a narrow masonry pier outside the building.

foreground The area of a picture that appears to be closest to the viewer.

foreshortening A method of applying perspective to an object or figure so that it seems to recede in space by shortening the depth dimension, making the form appear three-dimensional.

form An element of design that appears three-dimensional and encloses volume such as a cube, sphere, pyramid or cylinder. The term may also refer to the characteristics of an artwork's visual elements (lines, color, textures, etc.) as distinguished from its subject matter.

forum In a Roman city, a center of civic, legal and commercial activity.

frame Each individual drawing in a sequence such as a comic strip or a storyboard.

frame construction A method of construction in which a skeleton of studs and joists is erected as in a new house. An exterior of wood, brick, metal or plaster is added.

framing Once the artist decides on the horizontal and vertical borders of a picture, framing determines the space and point of view for a picture.

fresco A method of mural painting in which pigments are applied to a thin layer of wet plaster so that they will be absorbed.

Futurism A style of art originating in Italy during the early twentieth century that emphasized representation of a dynamic, machine-powered world.

genre (*jsahn*-ra) A type of localized art that depicts realistic scenes or events from everyday life.

genre subjects Subject matter of ordinary people in ordinary settings.

geometric shapes (rectilinear) Mechanical, humanmade shapes such as squares, triangles, circles, etc. Geometric shapes have regular edges as opposed to the irregular edges of organic shapes.

glaze A thin coating of minerals which gives the surface a glass-like quality. Used in painting and ceramics.

good design A condition that is fulfilled when a logical and harmonious relationship exists among all the parts of an object.

Gothic A style in European art and architecture that prevailed from the twelfth through the fifteenth century. Gothic architecture, specifically in cathedrals, was characterized by pointed arches, ribbed vaults, flying buttresses.

gouache (gwash) A form of water-soluble paint used to create opacity.

graded wash An area of thin or transparent paint that increases or decreases in intensity from dark to light, light to dark, or both.

graphic art The art of printmaking in any form. In commercial art, advertising, book and magazine illustration, cartoons and signs, etc., for commercial purposes.

graphic design Creating visual communications with two-dimensional media and images.

ground The treated surface on which a painting or drawing is made. A coating such as priming or sizing is used to prepare a support (e.g., bare canvas or wood) for a painting.

harmony A condition in which the elements of an artwork appear to fit well together.

hatching Shading using closely spaced, parallel lines used to suggest light and shadow.

hieroglyph (high-row-*gliff*) A form of ancient writing in which pictures or symbols are used to represent sounds, words or ideas.

High Renaissance In art and architecture, the flowering of the Renaissance (c. 1495–1525).

Hinduism (*hin*-doo-izm) The world's most ancient religion. It is polytheistic (worshipers believe in many gods). Hindus believe in reincarnation, that life is an endless cycle of birth and death.

historical context The historical circumstances of an artwork, periods of history and style prevalent when the work was created.

hue The property of color that distinguishes one gradation from another and gives it its name.

humanism Devotion to human concerns; the study of humanity.

hypothesis An informed assumption proposed for the purpose of argument.

idealism A concept of perfection, particularly in the treatment of the human figure.

idolatry The worship of an image.

illustration A drawing with any medium used to clarify ideas.

implied line Lines that are indicated indirectly in artworks at edges where two shapes meet, where a form ends and the space around it begins, or by positioning several objects or figures in a row.

implied movement The appearance of movement in a static artwork resulting from an artist's use of elements such as: subject matter, line, shape, progression, repetition and alternation, running or pointing figures, etc.

impressing Figures and shapes made by stamping or pushing patterns and symbols into soft surfaces such as clay, leather or copper foil.

Impressionism The first of the Modern art movements developed in France during the second half of the nineteenth century which emphasized the momentary effects of light on color in nature.

incising Making lines and figures by cutting into a surface with a sharp tool.

industrial design Conceiving of, and designing objects which meet the needs of people.

Industrial Revolution A significant change in the economies of Western Europe and the United States during the nineteenth century marked by the introduction of power-driven machinery and mass production.

intaglio (in-*tahl*-ee-oh) A technique of printmaking where lines and areas are etched, engraved or scratched beneath the surface of a metal or plastic plate. Ink is then transferred from the plate onto paper.

intensity The degree or purity, saturation or strength of a color. High intensity colors are bight; low intensity colors are dull.

interior design Planning space inside a house or building, including furnishings.

intermediate colors Colors produced by mixing a primary color and the adjacent secondary color on the color wheel. (For example, yellow and green for yellow-green.) They are also made by mixing unequal amounts of two primaries. (For example, adding more yellow to a combination of yellow and blue produces yellow-green.)

Ionic (eye-*ahn*-ik) Classical Greek architecture characterized by slender, elegant columns with spiral device capitals and fluted shafts.

Islam (is-*lahm*) The Moslem religion and all the nations in which that religion dominates.

isometric perspective A method of applying perspective by drawing the height, width and depth of an object or figure on the same scale at equal angles of 120° with one another. Planes recede on the diagonal, but the parallel lines along edges remain parallel rather than converging as in linear perspective.

kiln (kill) A furnace capable of controlled high temperatures used to fire ceramic ware and sculpture.

kinetic art Any art construction that contains moving elements which can be set in motion by the action of gravity, air currents, motors, springs or magnets.

line An element of art which is used to define space, contours and outlines, or suggest mass and volume. It may be a continuous mark made on a surface with a pointed tool or implied by the edges of shapes and forms.

line of sight Implied lines suggested by the direction in which figures in a picture are looking, or from the observer's eye to the object being looked at.

linear perspective A technique of creating the illusion of depth on a flat surface. All parallel lines receding into the distance are drawn to converge at one or more vanishing points on the horizon line. In one point linear perspective receding lines converge to one vanishing point. In two point perspective receding lines converge to two vanishing points.

lithography A method of printing from a flat stone or metal plate. A drawing is made on the stone or plate with a greasy crayon and chemically treated so that only the greasy drawing will hold ink while the remaining surface resists it. A print is then made from the plate.

load carrying Pertaining to a wall or post that supports a ceiling, as distinguished from a nonload-carrying wall or post.

lost-wax process (cire purdue) A method of casting metal in which a mold is lined with wax, filled with a solid core of heat resistant materials (vestment) and heated to melt the wax leaving a thin cavity between mold and core into which metal is poured.

low relief (bas relief) Sculpture that projects slightly from the surface.

Mannerism A sixteenth century European art style that rejected the calm balance of High Renaissance art in favor of emotion, distortion of the figure, exaggerated perspective views and crisp treatment of light and shadow.

masonry A medium of architecture consisting of stone or brick.

mastaba (mah-*stah*-bah) A low, rectangular Egyptian tomb made of mud brick with sloping sides and a flat top.

medieval (mee-*dee*-vuhl) Pertaining to the Middle Ages.

medium (pl. media) The materials used to create an artwork such as oil, watercolor, etc., or a category of art such as drawing, painting or sculpture.

metal frame A principle of construction in which narrow light-weight members of iron or steel are joined to form a framework to which walls and ceiling can be attached.

Middle Ages The period of Western European history from the decline of the Roman Empire to the beginning of the Renaissance (476 AD to 1400 AD).

middle classes The class of society between the upper class and the lower class. In pre-industrial Europe, the class of merchants, traders and professionals that were beneath the aristocracy and above the peasant class.

minaret (min-ar-*et*) A high, slender tower attached to or near a mosque with balconies from which a crier calls the people to prayer.

minimal art A twentieth century style that stressed reducing an artwork to minimal colors, simple geometric forms, lines and textures.

mixed wash Transparent colors are placed on a damp paper and allowed to flow together, resulting in mixed colors.

mobile A kinetic sculpture, invented by Alexander Calder in 1932, constructed of shapes that are balanced and arranged on wire arms and suspended from above so as to move freely in air currents.

mold A hollow container that produces a cast by giving its form to a substance (molten metal, plastic or plaster) placed within it and allowed to harden.

monochromatic One color which is modified by changing the values and saturation of the hue by additions of black or white.

monotheism Belief in one God.

mosaic A mural technique formed by placing colored pieces of marble or glass (tesserae), small stones or ceramic tiles in a layer of adhesive material.

mosque (mahsk) A Moslem house of worship.

movement A principle of design associated with rhythm, referring to the arrangement of parts in an artwork to create a sense of motion to the viewer's eye through the work. (See *implied movement, optical movement.*)

mural A large design or picture created directly on the wall or ceiling.

negative space The space not occupied by an object or figure but circulating in and around it, contributing to the total effect of the composition.

Neoclassicism ("New Classicism") A style of art in the nineteenth century in which artists and critics sought inspiration from the classical art of ancient Greece and Rome and imitated its themes, simplicity, order and balance.

neutral colors Colors not associated with any hue such as black, white and gray and are neither warm nor cool. Also colors which have been "grayed" or reduced in saturation by mixing them with a neutral or complementary color.

nonload carrying Pertaining to a wall attached to a frame structure. A wall that does not support a roof.

nonobjective art Artworks that have no recognizable subject matter such as figures, flowers, buildings, etc.

Nonwestern Civilization Any culture that is not related to Western Civilization (the people of North America and Western Europe).

one-point perspective A way to show three-dimensional objects on a two-dimensional surface, using one vanishing point. One object faces the viewer; the lines defining other objects in the artwork recede at an angle to a single vanishing point on the horizon line. (See *perspective.*)

Op art A twentieth century style in which artists sought to create an impression of movement by means of optical illusion.

opaque (oh-*payk*) In the two-dimensional arts, an area that light does not pass through. The opposite of transparent.

open form Forms in paintings and sculpture which emphasize openings.

opinion Personal belief or impression which may be true for the individual but not for other people.

optical mixing Colors or black and white laid side by side seem to blend together; mixing takes place in the eye.

optical movement An illusion of movement, or implied movement caused by the response of the eye to lines, shapes and colors arranged in artworks. (See *Op art.*)

organic shapes (bimorphic) Free forms, or shapes and forms that represent living things having irregular edges, as distinguished from the regular edges of geometric shapes.

outline Lines with little variation that describe the outer edges of shapes which appear flat.

pan Moving a camera from side to side in a stationary position.

papier-mâché (*pay*-per ma-*shay*) A technique of creating three-dimensional or relief sculpture by molding strips of paper soaked in glue or paste.

pastel A chalky, colored crayon consisting of pigment and adhesive gum. Also paintings done with such crayons.

patina (pah-*tee*-nah) The surface coloration on metal caused by natural oxidation. This effect can also be produced by the application of heat, chemicals and polishing agents.

pattern The repetition of elements or combinations of elements in a recognizable organization.

performance art Works of a theatrical nature performed by the artist before an audience. A performance may involve props, lights, sound, dialogue, etc.

perspective The representation of three-dimensional objects on a flat surface to produce the same impression of distance and relative size as that received by the human eye.

photography The art of making photographs for fine art or commercial purposes.

picture plane The flat surface or plane that the artist organizes the picture in.

piece mold A mold with sections completely free of undercuts. It may consist of two or more pieces and is generally made from plaster.

pigment A powdered coloring material for paint, crayons, chalks and ink.

pilgrimage The journey of a pilgrim to a shrine; in the Middle Ages, the journey to a cathedral to see and be in the presence of a relic.

plane A flat, two-dimensional surface.

planographic print Prints made from a flat surface area on which ink is placed. The lithograph is planographic as are monoprints made from ink spread on a flat, nonporous surface.

pluralism A condition of art or culture in which many styles and doctrines of taste coexist.

pointed arch A masonry construction in which a number of wedge-shaped stones form curves that come to a point.

polytheism The belief in many gods.

Pop art An art style, also known as neo-Dada, developed in the 1950s. Pop artists depicted and satirized popular culture such as mass media symbols, comic strips, fast foods, billboards and brand name products.

porcelain Ceramic ware made from a specially prepared, fine white clay that fires at the highest temperatures. Porcelain is hard, translucent, thin walled and rings when struck.

positive and negative shapes In pictures, positive shapes are the figures and negative shapes make up the ground.

positive space The enclosed areas or objects in an artwork. They may suggest recognizable objects or nonrepresentational shapes.

post and lintel A method of construction in which two vertical members (posts) support a horizontal member (lintel) to create a covered space.

Post Impressionism A style developed in the 1880s in France in reaction to Impressionism. It included artists such as Cezanne, Seurat, Gauguin and van Gogh. The first two artists explored the formal structure of art while the other two championed the expression of personal feelings.

Post Modernism A loosely defined term referring to a new cycle in art history and culture in general.

pottery Ceramic ware made of clay and hardened by firing at low temperatures.

Pre-Columbian The history of the peoples living in Central and South America before the time of Columbus.

primary colors The three basic colors, red, yellow and blue, from which it is possible to mix all other colors. The primaries cannot be produced by mixing pigments.

principles of design Balance, emphasis, rhythm, movement, repetition, contrast and unity. The methods or techniques that artists use to organize or design artworks by controlling and ordering the elements of design.

proximity The placement of objects very near to each other to make them look related.

radial balance A composition based on a circle with the design radiating from a central point.

Realism A mid-nineteenth century style in which artists turned to painting familiar scenes and events as they actually appeared in nature in the belief that subject matter should be shown true to life, without stylization or idealization as in Neoclassicism and Romanticism.

Reformation A sixteenth century religious movement marked by the establishment of the Prostestant Church.

relic An object that is worshiped because it is believed to be associated with, or part of the remains of, a Christian saint or martyr.

relief A type of sculpture in which forms project from a background. It is classified according to the degree in which it is raised from the surface: high relief, low relief, etc.

relief print A print produced when raised surfaces are inked and applied to paper or other materials. Woodcuts, linocuts and collographs are examples of relief prints.

Renaissance (ren-eh-*sahnss*) A period in Western history (ca. 1400–1600) marking a "rebirth" of cultural awareness and learning, founded largely on a revival of Classical art and writing.

repoussé (ree-*pooh*-say) A metalworking process of hammering or pressing sheet metal into relief on one side to create shapes or patterns on the other side.

rhythm A principle of design that refers to ways of combining elements to produce the appearance of movement in an artwork. It may be achieved through repetition, alternation or progression of an element.

ribbed vault A cross vault reinforced at the intersections with ribs.

Rococo (roh-*koh*-koh) An eighteenth century style of art and interior decoration which emphasized portraying the carefree life of the aristocracy. Love and romance were portrayed rather than historical or religious subjects.

Romanticism A style of art that flourished in the early nineteenth century. Romanticism emphasized personal emotions, dramatic action and exotic settings using literary and historical subject matter.

saturation The purity, vividness or intensity of a color.

screen print Stencils are attached to porous fabrics such as nylon and polyester. Ink is squeezed through openings in the stencil to produce a print. Originally called silkscreen because that was the fabric first used for the process.

sculpture Three-dimensional forms (sculpture in the round) or forms in relief created by carving, assembly or modeling.

secco (*se*-koe) A mural technique created by painting on a dried lime-plaster wall with pigment ground in casein.

secondary colors Colors that result from a mixture of two primary colors. On the twelve-color wheel, orange, green and violet.

sequence In the popular arts of comics and movies, the following of one event or image after another in logical ordering.

serigraph (sehr-*ig*-raff) A term originated to refer to the screen process when done by an artist rather than commercially. It means "drawing on silk."

sgraffito (skrah-*fee*-toe) Decorating a surface such as clay, plaster or glass, by scratching through a surface layer to expose a different color underneath.

shade Variations in the dark and light of color made by adding black to the color.

shape An element of art. An enclosed space defined by other art elements such as line, color and texture.

shape constancy The tendency to see the shape of a three-dimensional object as unchanging regardless of any change in position or angle from which it is viewed.

Shintoism (*shin*-toe-izm) A Japanese religion which emphasizes reverence for family, race and above all, the ruling family as direct descendants of the gods.

shot and sequence An unbroken segment of a scene or action in a film or videotape; a series of shots.

similarity Making components of an artwork alike in one or more ways such as color, shape, texture, size or form.

simulated texture An artist may use color and value contrast to give a painting or drawing the appearance of texture as distinguished from the texture of the artwork itself.

size constancy The tendency to see the size of an object as unchanging regardless of the distance between the viewer and the object.

social context The environment in which the artwork was created, and how it was experienced by people of that time and place; their aesthetic preferences.

space An element of art that indicates areas between, around, above, below or within something.

split complementary On the color wheel, a hue which is combined with hues on either side of its complement.

stabile A term adopted by Alexander Calder to identify standing constructions that emphasize space, similar to the mobile, but do not have moving parts.

stoneware Ceramic ware made from clay that is fired at a relatively high temperature (2200°F). It is hard and nonporous.

storyboard In filmmaking, a series of pictures that resemble comic strips, corresponding to a sequence. Each illustration represents a shot.

stupa (*stew*-pah) A large, mound-shaped Buddhist shrine.

style The identifying characteristics of the artwork of an individual, a group of artists, a period of time or an entire society.

subculture A group of people who share in part the culture of a larger group to which they belong nationally or ethnically, but who have identifiable differences as a group.

subject matter Things that are represented in an artwork such as people, buildings, trees, etc.

symmetrical balance The organization of the parts of a composition so that one side duplicates or mirrors the other.

tactile The sensation of touch. Some surfaces may be perceived through touch.

Taoism (*dow*-izm) A philosophy based on the belief that to achieve lasting happiness one must follow a life of simplicity, modesty, patience and obedience to the laws of nature.

tempera A technique of painting in which the waterbase paint is mixed or tempered with egg yolk.

tesserae (*tess*-ah-ree) The small cubes, usually pieces of glass or clay, used in making mosaics.

texture The surface quality of an artwork usually perceived through the sense of touch. However, texture can also be implied; perceived visually though not felt through touch. (See *simulated texture*.)

three-dimensional Having height, width and depth.

tilt A movie camera can tilt, or move up and down in a stationary position.

tint A lighter value of a hue made by adding a small amount of another color to it.

totem (*toe*-tem) An object, such as an animal or a plant, that serves as an emblem of a family or clan.

track In filmmaking, to move or follow an action.

traditional art Works that have form, style and subject matter that are familiar to the public as art.

trapezoid A shape with four angles and four sides only two of which are parallel.

triadic color scheme Any three colors equidistant on the color wheel.

two-dimensional Having height and width.

two-point perspective A way to show three-dimensional objects on a two-dimensional surface, using two vanishing points and two sets of converging lines to represent forms. These forms are seen from an angle and have two receding sides. Two dimensions appear to recede: width and depth. (See *perspective*.)

ukiyo-e (oo-key-oh-eh) ("the art of the floating world") Japanese art that centered around the district of Edo and popular culture. Commonly produced in woodcuts.

unity A principle of design related to the sense of wholeness which results from the successful combination of the component elements of an artwork.

value An element of design concerned with the degree of lightness of colors. Darker colors are lower in value.

vanishing point A point on the eye-level line, toward which parallel lines are made to recede and meet in perspective drawing.

variety A principle of design concerned with the inclusion of differences in the elements of a composition to offset unity and make the work more interesting.

vault An arched roof or covering made of brick, stone or concrete. (See *barrel vault* and *cross vault*.)

vehicle A liquid binding agent in paint such as water, oil, or egg yolk that allows the paint to adhere to the painting surface.

viewers For purposes of this program, people who look at and analyze artworks.

warm colors Those hues in which yellow and red are dominant and are located on the left side of the color wheel.

wash A transparent layer of color applied to a surface allowing underlying lines, shapes and colors to show through. Watercolor or ink that is diluted with water to make it lighter in value and more transparent.

waste mold A plaster mold from which one cast is taken. The mold is formed around a clay model in two or three removable parts which are reassembled and filled with liquid plaster that is allowed to harden. The mold is broken away (wasted) to reveal the cast.

wood engraving A technique of relief printmaking in which a design is cut into the end grain of a wooden block with gravers like those used for metal plates. Wood engravings contain more detail than woodcuts.

wood frame A principle of construction in which narrow lightweight members of wood are joined to form a framework to which walls and ceiling can be attached.

woodcut A technique of relief printmaking in which a design is cut into a block of plank wood with knives and gouges leaving raised shapes to receive ink. A print is then made from the block.

zoom In filmmaking, to make an image appear nearer or farther by means of a zoom lens.

Index with Pronunciation Guide